The DNA Code

The Forensics of Purpose, Passion and Performance

Mark R. Demos, M.A.

Library of Congress information for this title is available.

ISBN 978-0-9885604-0-6

Printed in USA
Lightning Source—Ingram House

Mark has taken forensics, the scientifically comprehensive evidence discovery process, to help you discover Evidence that applies to the important matters of life. From how to navigate through the toughest situations to decisions about profession, education and parenting, and ultimately defining your course in life, you will be directed and encouraged to discover Evidence of your Strengths and apply them to creating a life filled with the three important P's: Purpose, Passion and Performance. —**Dr. Elizabeth Loftus, PhD, Distinguished Professor, University of California–Irvine and author of *Memory* and *Eyewitness Testimony*, Past President of the American Psychology-Law Society**

It is said that the examined life is the one most worth living. But how are we to examine life? The DNA Code: The Forensics of Purpose, Passion and Performance *uses the metaphor of forensic science to provide a wealth of practical and provocative tips for examining ourselves and living better. I recommend this book most highly.* —**Dr. Christopher Peterson, PhD, Professor of Psychology, University of Michigan–Ann Arbor and author of *A Primer in Positive Psychology***

Times are tough! The value of human capital is rising. Companies need innovative approaches for building human capital to maximize organizational effectiveness. The best approach I know is Life Scene Investigation. The DNA Code *is a system for discovering strengths that is based on the best and most effective research.* The DNA Code *is engaging and will have your people coming alive as they discover who they are, where they best fit, and how to produce maximum output. Corporations and individuals who know their DNA-Strengths will be the ones to thrive, not just survive this economy! You and your company need* The DNA Code. —**Dr. JoyLynn Haily Reed, PhD, University of Texas at Dallas Graduate School of Management**

I found The DNA Code: The Forensics of Purpose, Passion and Performance *to be positive, up-tempo, insightful in reference to the life we live in, and powerful in the realm of providing new opportunities and avenues which will result in positive rewards, concrete direction and so forth. I believe this book should be read by as many individuals as possible, but more importantly by those who are trying to find themselves, business people who need a different direction in their lives and individuals who need new direction to get moving in their lives. The use of forensics is a powerful and contemporary analogy. Your application of the forensic process to discover human strengths is thorough and delivers what you intend for it to do. This book will change lives!* —**Lawrence W. Daly, MSc, forensic investigator and Department Chair in Criminal Justice, University of Phoenix, Western Washington Campus.**

Acknowledgments

To begin to thank everyone who needs to be thanked would probably require another book of this length. I am grateful for the countless people who have been part of my Life and experience:

My mother and father, who always provided, encouraged and sacrificed so I could discover and develop my Talents. They were always there.

Penny, my sister, whose incredible intellect has challenged me to think about the Design and Talents philosophy this book seeks to explain; who came to my rescue and supported me often; and whose example of positive and sustained giving in the face of Life-threatening illness has allowed me to finish this book and have it published.

My boys, André and Adam, and my daughter, Amy. This book is because of them. I learned about forensics because of their experiences and discovered how to apply and integrate my beliefs about human potential and Talents. Their lives are models of known and developing Talents. I see the same in Abi, my daughter-in-law. They have all been involved in the development of this book through their working with me in touching young lives that were lost and seeking. I could not be more proud of this next generation.

Dr. Elizabeth Loftus, who taught me to think in a new and exciting way and to understand forensics. She is one of the world's greatest minds and hearts, whose intersection in my Life at the darkest time taught me a new way to discover and seek truth.

Philip Dunlap, without whose help I may have never seen my children again. A man whose professional ethics, deep caring, and clear mind in the biggest battle of my Life resulted in the truth ultimately being seen.

The countless people who have believed in me, even when they had good reasons not to, who supported the ideas in this book, and who have seen how they make for a clear path to discovering Purpose, Passion, and Performance. Thank you for sticking with me as I discovered and have attempted to grow.

Susan Reinfeldt, Rhonda Addison, Cynthia Tobias, Mark Fallis, Maryann Wyatt, Bill Terry, Harry Everett, Randy Hiller, Deborah Shircore, and countless others, for the encouragement to write this book.

Lucien Nanton and Krisandra Parsons, whose amazing clarity of mind and encouragement have assisted in refining and presenting a better product in an understandable form. Thank you for your guidance. Michele Tomiak, who helped me finalize the book. There were many changes to be made that just seemed to overwhelm me, and I struggled to finish. Michele brought a breath of fresh air and her amazing editing talents to help me finally complete this book and relieve me of that burden.

Without those who sought to harm me for whatever motives, I would never have learned about the incredible discovery process called *forensics* without you. Thank you.

Last, but most important, the Designer of Life and Giver of Gifts and Strengths. My belief is that what I possess has been given as a gift from a giver I call God. I possess nothing by virtue of my own doing, creating, merit, choice, or creation. My Purpose in Life is to discover what I have been endowed with by my creator. It is then my responsibility to develop it and use by giving it to the world in which I live. This book is my attempt to fulfill that Purpose.

Contents

Part 4 Where to Discover Evidence: The Five Fields of Evidence

Part 5 How to Interpret Evidence

Preface

I was reminded every day this week why I wrote this book. It is relevant. It touches the lives of real people and directs them to a new way of discovering their Purpose in Life, living with greater Passion, and experiencing sustained high Performance.

I encourage you to read this book from your experience and perspective. If you are looking for answers about who you are and where you fit in this world, read it to discover the answers.

If you are a CEO or in leadership, this book will address how you can change the mission and culture of your corporation to one focused on *Talent*. You will learn how to hire the right people and position them in the right places to have the greatest return on investment. You will learn that the best way to lead and motivate is to know the Talents and DNA Code of your employees. You will discover that in the toughest of economic times, Talents are the way to navigate through those times to profitability.

Maybe you are looking to try and build a relationship or to parent with greater effectiveness. Knowing and encouraging the Talents of those you are in relationships with is the best pathway to build strong bonds, experience gratitude, and enjoy a partnership that is positive and more satisfying than you ever imagined.

I talked to a software engineer who is extremely bright. He is probably in his late twenties and is miserable doing his well-paying but Passion-sucking job. He lives in the country of his dreams. He is living the dreams of his peers and the countless millions of people from his country of origin. He has a family to support. His greatest desire is to work with cars, do mechanics, and maybe engineer, but anything to do with cars and as little to do with software as he can. He wonders whether the next forty years of his Life will be chained to everything except what he loves.

A news channel in Dallas interviewed me about bullying in local schools. I told the interviewer that the best approach to dealing with bullies, regardless of where they reared their heads, was to focus on those being bullied. Parents, school administrators, and police can't protect everyone all the time. Change the equation and teach the kids how to stand up and deal with bullies using their Talents. Kids who know their own Talents and are living them are not the focus of bullies. They don't need their mommies and daddies protecting them, but rather helping them learn to be strong and prepared for Life, where they will encounter bullies in college, in corporate Life, and possibly even in their families. The primary task of parenting is helping our children discover and build their own unique Talents. Bullies don't prey on the strong.

I was in a counseling session with my sister, a licensed professional counselor (LCP). I had been invited to share some of my insights into positive psychology with a vivacious mother of three. She had recently gone through a divorce and some other major Life issues and was determined to change the direction of her Life. She was adamant that she didn't want to continue the data management job she was currently dragging herself through daily and wanted no more long days of Passionless pushing, doing work that held no Purpose for her. She had dreams of living her Passion: working with people facing terminal illnesses, where she had demonstrated real effectiveness and had profoundly touched lives. She was unsure how to change direction and make a huge midstream correction in her Life toward living her Talents.

Recently I was online looking at Facebook and received a chat message from a young man in his early twenties who had grown up with my son Adam. He was desperate and lost. He wanted direction in his Life and to feel alive and have some sense of Purpose and meaning. He had always loved working with animals, but after years of destructive addictions and choices, he didn't believe his family would support him or his direction. He needed courage to follow his Talents and direction to help him make a new Life.

I was speaking to a group of managers of luxury car dealerships in Florida. One-third of U.S. dealerships have closed up shop in the past five years. These managers were determined to find ways to make their jobs and futures secure and not wind up as grocery store managers, the fate of many of their competitors. They saw the necessity of defining and living their strengths and Talents because, as the old saying goes, "When the going gets tough, the tough (strong) get going."

There is Joe, who in his sixties so much wants to finish his Life and leave a legacy of significance and be able to share with others his experiences and successes. He talks big but probably lives out of his car. He wants to know what he can do at this last stage of his Life. Brenda is worried about being a mom and doing what is best for her children and hoping they will make the right choices and find their path in Life. Josh is coming to the end of his senior year of high school worried, uncertain, and with many choices ahead: military, college, travel—many possibilities with a world wide open, but just not sure.

I have had at least five other significant conversations, all dealing with the same basic question, *"Who am I?"* The answer to that question delivers direction. It tells me where I fit in a planet of seven billion people. It determines my Purpose and my future. It reveals what my Passions are. It tells me where I can expect to perform with excellence.

The United States is mired in one of the toughest economic downturns in its history. Millions of people are out of work. Many countries around the globe are in worse situations where unrest, political turmoil, and worse rule the everyday lives of individuals.

This book delivers hope. Simple or even fanatical belief only gets us so far. We desire deeply, determine hard, set goals, and believe we can make it, even when confronted with an economy that changes, a marriage that ends, a future that like a mirage never seems to quite solidify long enough to grasp, the deep and gnawing belief that we were made for so much more than we are living. Belief or hope that is not founded and directed by reality—or as this book will designate, Evidence—will be short-lived and end in more frustration and even despair.

That is what this book will deliver to you: your DNA Code, the answer to the question *"?RU—Who are you?"*

I know as you begin to read it you will see the light start breaking through. You will be given not only a new direction but also an entirely new and powerful way of looking at and approaching Life, your Talents. The focus is Talents to a Life of Purpose, Passion, and Performance. The method of discovery is the powerful, cutting-edge twentieth-century process of *forensics*.

Part 1

Introduction

Chapter 1
Introduction

Who Are You?

Who are you? The theme song of the fantastically popular TV show *CSI: Crime Scene Investigation* blasts out to confront us with the most important question of Life.

Without answers to this question, you will never have a sense of Purpose to guide you through Life.

Without the ability to clearly articulate who you are, you cannot experience the Passion we all desperately seek.

Without that Passion you will never have the motivation or fuel to demonstrate and sustain exceptional Performance.

CSI is about the discovery of Evidence, the process of forensics. This book will show you how to discover the Evidence that is essential to answer the question *?RU*.

Forensics is all about answers to questions about Evidence: where, when, what, why, who, how, and so on. These questions are as old as mankind. Philosopher Søren Kierkegaard asked these forensic questions about the meaning and Purpose of Life:

> *Where am I? Who am I?*
> *How did I come to be here?*
> *What is this thing called the world?*
> *How did I come into the world?*
> *Why was I not consulted?*
> *And if I am compelled to take part in it,*
> *Where is the director?*
> *I want to see him.*

He wanted answers! He needed answers! He demanded answers! He *really* wanted to know! That is what this book will give you—Evidence to help you answer the most important question of all, *Who am I? ?RU*

Forensic Concept—Trial Theory

Prosecutors and defense attorneys come up with a line of thinking that they believe makes sense of the Evidence. A story line needs to be told that clearly and logically reflects the Evidence. The idea is then to tell that story and be as convincing as possible to the jury. Juries need to be able to connect the dots.

All the Evidence must be consistent with the *trial theory*. As you come to answer the big question, *?RU*, all the Evidence you have needs to be consistent with and fit the *Life Theory* or *Design* that has begun to develop.

This book will show you step by step how to develop your own Life Theory. It will give you the positive forensics tools that will result in affirmative verdict for a Life of Purpose, filled with Passion and sustained Performance!

What is the DNA Code? The DNA Code uses the process of forensics to help you discover the Markers that identify what your Talents are. Talents are those things that define what you do best, that result in your experiencing happiness, and that you have the ability to perform regularly at a high level.

DNA, or *D*eoxyribo*N*ucleic *A*cid, is the basic substance of Life. Nearly every cell in a person's body has the same DNA. It is the unique differences in an individual's code that distinguishes each person who has ever lived. Those differences are codes, or Markers, which when discovered tell us what we can become great at. They determine not only the color of your eyes or hair but also parts of your emotional makeup, your leadership capacity, your intellectual capacities, how fast you can run, and an entire design comprising amazing hard-wired Talents.

If you want to know what you were born to be or to do, you must know your DNA Code. Your DNA Code determines what your Purpose in life is, unless you want to be aimless, unfulfilled, and never more than average.

For most of us discovering our Purpose is also what we would call Success. To be successful means we have discovered our Purpose and we are living it. Living that Purpose brings with it a sense of positive emotion we call Passion. When we are Passionate, it propels us to sustained high performances. We love to do what we are excellent at or have mastery doing.

The reason you are reading *The DNA Code* is to discover answers about your Purpose and the most fundamental question of all: "Who am I?" I know that as you begin to gather Evidence you will notice a greater sense of clarity. Be patient; it takes time; the answers will come.

You will begin to feel the stirrings of Passion developing as you anticipate living your DNA Code! Piece by piece, the Evidence will give a clearer picture of that Design. Like early morning mists lifting to reveal wondrous beauty and scenery, so too your Life and Purpose will be revealed.

You will begin to picture yourself doing and living out what the Evidence reveals; you will envision Performances that are going to make a significant difference in this world. You will see your Talents touching lives and doing great things.

What an exciting place to be in Life. The Life Theory you have been working to develop is more than you could imagine!

Forensic Effervescence

I have often observed a process I call *effervescence* begin when people attend a Life Scene Investigation class/seminar/retreat or are working with me in a coaching relationship. Everything is being seen in a new way. Their mind starts moving; bubbles start floating to the surface; the cogs engage and there is a definite change in the way they look at Life. Ideas, experiences, people, great plays, past relationships, their Life—all start pushing to the front of their mind Evidence that has been waiting to be discovered for years. It naturally seeks expression in the forum of Life; it needs to fit a Life Theory.

I received this email from a client I was working with; it illustrates this effervescence process so well.

> *Mark,*
> *Been thinking about all of this today. Have this overall sense of transformation. I can't explain it well but when people start to really get what they are good at, how they should operate, is there a sense of excitement, confidence that takes over? I have been operating for so long trying to be good at the jobs I*

have had, etc. that I think I really had a sense that I had no strengths or talents that could be used in the workplace. Felt very inadequate for a very long time . . . no flow. It's all still new and I am just starting to form a plan. There is a general sense of well-being that is happening, even though I have barely started. It was fun to look at my Strengths report and go "Oh, that's why people are drawn to me and have been my whole life." It's not bragging, just a fact. Feels good to see it in writing! Anyway, just wanted you to know what was occurring with me. I am excited and nervous at the same time.
Michelle

I have every expectation you will experience the same sense of transformation. Expect it. Embrace it. It will probably make you both excited and a little nervous at the same time, like Michelle. Those feelings are normal. Life is bubbling up in you. Unless you screw the top back on and run, you have every reason to expect that a Life of Purpose, Passion, and Performance is yours to experience!

?RU—My Life

As you read this book you will notice that I use many illustrations from my Life, my family, and my personal experiences. I hope you will indulge me. I want you to see how positive forensics is lived and integrated into real Life and experience. I share stories and observations about my experiences, my relationships, and my children. I share about the substance of my Life; my hope is that you will look at your Life through your experience. This is not some academic exercise; the Evidence is you.

I have written and used these illustrations this way because I want you to look at your Life and integrate this Life-defining material into your experience. I could have limited my illustrations to well-known and exceptional individuals such as Mother Theresa, Albert Einstein, and Michael Jordan.

These illustrations or Life stories are called *Life Scenes*, and they describe the lives of real people and highlight their strengths and unique capacities. Each Life Scene is identified with Life Scene tape:

MYLIFESCENE.COM—CROSS NOW—MYLIFESCENE.COM

Just as any crime scene is roped off and the crime scene investigators begin their task of collecting Evidence in that specific area, I have attempted to share with you the Evidence I have observed and collected in the lives of these people.

As you read these Life Scenes, I hope you will see people in your Life who in their Life Scenes are no less exceptional in displaying Evidence of their unique Purpose, Passion, and Performance!

This is not a book about dry research and theory; it is about Life. It relies on the best and most current research while bringing that research into where we live, breathe and carry out our lives.

I emphasize various words by capitalizing them because I think they are important—words like **Design, Strengths, Talents, Evidence, Purpose, Passion, Performance,** and **Life**. They are used to talk about superlatives—the very best—and to define concepts. They are not used in a general but a specific sense. I also use the words *Design* and *Purpose* somewhat interchangeably. Most of the time you can simply switch them, but take care in reading them as sometimes they are determinative.

I have made enough mistakes in my Life to fill this book and many others. I struggle with Life as you do. I continue to seek more answers and Evidence to engage and live with greater Purpose, Passion, and Performance every day.

I have taken roads I should have known better than to travel down again after repeated failures. I have made decisions that were wrong and that affected the lives of others deeply, which I regret. I wish I could change many things I have done and find all those whom I have or might have harmed and ask their forgiveness. That is not what this book is about. Those things are about a nature and a part of our humanity that is best avoided and marginalized. These things need the application of grace, forgiveness, redemption, and a new determination to live our God-given Talents.

Though this book will not focus directly on deficits or our failings, I believe that *The DNA Code* will address how we deal with those stipulated facts in our lives and those elements that need to be changed. There are parts of us which, because we have not answered the question *?RU*, will only be changed when we get a clearer sense of who we are and why we are here. When we live a Life based on the belief that our path to a better Life can only be attained through the avoidance of those weaknesses, we never will discover a Life of Purpose, nor will we ever experience real Passion or greater Performance. Those things are not and cannot be found by *avoidance*.

I have traveled to more than thirty countries and all fifty U.S. states. I have observed the very best and worst of human government and political systems. I believe that the United States is the greatest country in the history of the world because it, more than any other, has allowed for the freedom of each human being to pursue his or her unique Purpose. That is Liberty. Freedom to define their lives and discover who they are is seen as the right of individuals, not the domain of government. You, however, are ultimately responsible to *discover, develop,* and *live* your *DNA Code.*

Why Am I?

I assume that many people who read this will have different beliefs from mine. What I believe and you believe is vital to this process of discovery. The process of positive forensics will enable you to answer the question *Who am I?* You need to answer the questions *Why am I? Why am I here? Is there a Purpose bigger than my knowing what I am and possess in terms of human potential and capacity?*

MYLIFESCENE.COM—CROSS NOW—MYLIFESCENE.COM
Life Scene—Dr. Elizabeth Loftus, PhD

Dr Elizabeth Loftus is one of the greatest scientific minds of our time. She was recognized as the most influential female psychologist of the twentieth century. Beyond her PhD from Stanford University, she has received numerous honorary doctorates, awards, and honors from the greatest academic and scientific institutions in the world.

Dr. Loftus became a friend of mine in 1992 when I went to live in Seattle. She helped me in one of the greatest challenges of my Life. I spent some time helping her catalog over twenty years of forensic legal files from cases she had been involved in, including Ted Bundy, O. J. Simpson, the Hillside Strangler, Michael Jackson, Nazi war criminals, and many more.

Dr. Loftus is a remarkable woman and someone I admire greatly. She uses her Talents magnificently. When it comes to beliefs about where Design originates, we are at the opposite ends of the spectrum. She belongs to the Skeptics Society, which essentially seeks to dispel myths such as a belief in the supernatural—any belief that cannot be subjected to scientific scrutiny. I don't believe Dr. Loftus holds to any belief that includes the supernatural or God.

Her beliefs and work have resulted in the exonerations of many falsely accused, wrongly convicted and condemned people. These were often people condemned to death or lengthy prison sentences but ultimately were freed because of the research, science, and commitment of this incredible woman. I have never saved a Life or helped a falsely accused person gain freedom, but Dr. Elizabeth Loftus has.

So though we may differ greatly in our beliefs about the origin of Design, what is important is that you have a point of origin. You need to know where you start and be consistent with that belief. You cannot have any direction in your Life without a point of origin. If you try to get directions on Google or Yahoo Maps, they will always ask for a place of origin. To go anywhere you need to start from somewhere, so where do you start?

MYLIFESCENE.COM—CROSS NOW—MYLIFESCENE.COM

Where do you believe your DNA Code and Design or abilities come from? If they are not *God-given* or did not originate with God's fingerprint evident, where do you believe they come from?

The other popular option for who we are and what we have in terms of unique capacity essentially says that what I possess is based on the process of *natural selection*, which basically is the luck of the draw. If I have certain Talents it is because I got lucky and my gene pool randomly produced a combination that had positive outcomes. There are not too many other choices that I am aware of, so state your belief as a possible starting point and let's begin to discover what you have.

You need to have this question answered as a fundamental starting point of your Life Scene Investigation. Point of origin is a necessity for any sense of direction in Life. If you don't know where you are starting from, you cannot accurately chart a course anywhere.

Either way you look at your point of origin, one thing is absolutely sure: you had nothing to do with it.

Those are my beliefs. What are yours? We all start at the same place. We are unique, and if we are to discover who we are, why we matter, and what our Purpose is, we need the information, the Evidence.

Let the Evidence speak. What does the Evidence say about you?

My greatest hope for this book is that through discovering your DNA Code, you *discover your Purpose, live with great Passion, and produce exceptional Performance!* That will come when you answer the question *?RU*.

Forensic Evidence Development Workbooks

Collecting Evidence requires asking lots of questions. You will constantly be asked to evaluate, think about, analyze, compare, and come up with Markers from your DNA Code that will lead you to a more complete picture of your Life Theory. There are probably hundreds of questions to answer and pieces of Evidence to collect.

You will be encouraged to go further in your discovery by going to www.mylifescene.com to read, answer questions, and do various exercises that will enable you to discover even more. Many chapters have Forensic Evidence Development exercises.

We have developed a series of companion questionnaires for the following applications and interest groups:

- General Workbook for book clubs or personal growth
- Teen Discovery for teens in high school
- Professional Development and career
- Leadership Development in organizations and also for personal development
- Women in transition
- Others in development

You may want to use this book in a group, for personal enrichment, for professional development, in corporate trainings, as a book club discussion, or for another purpose. The workbooks have activities for you and others to participate in to help you discover more while doing the activities within your own Life Scene, where you live and with those people who participate in Life with you.

You will be given access and linked to a wide variety of tests and profiles. Most of these are *free*. There are some that require a fee.

You will find links to online courses and videos, which you will be encouraged to watch. They will inspire and educate you. They will expand your Evidence search.

The website also contains a number of great *free* downloads.

There are other resources, such as books, that embrace the philosophy described here. I refer to many of these resources throughout this book. They are carefully selected and highly recommended.

There are also *Life Scene Journals* for you to record what you discover in a very personal way.

Faith Integration

Another great resource is a workbook called *Faith Follow On*. I would encourage you to look at it even if you don't embrace the same beliefs as I do. Many of the books on discovering Purpose have a faith basis, so one of the ways I wanted to address and integrate that was to include this workbook, which can be used in Bible studies, youth groups, and Sunday School classes, or just for your personal study. I have approached this workbook from a Judeo-Christian perspective, which is my own belief.

Your faith may be different from mine, but I encourage you to seek authentic integration of these concepts within your belief system. Make your faith relevant to your Life.

Chapter 2
Life Scene Investigation Forensics

CSI: Crime Scene Investigation is the most watched television program in history, according to Eurodata TV Worldwide. The original *CSI* spun off two other exceptionally popular shows: *CSI: NY* and *CSI: Miami*. It is estimated that one in three people on the planet have seen a *CSI* episode. All the *CSI* programs have huge followings. Each show has its faithful supporters. Grissom, Mac, Nick, Catherine, Horatio, Dr. Raymond Langston, Dr. Tara Price, Yelina, and many more cast characters are household names. Fan clubs and online communities follow every move and discuss every episode in minute detail. Video games, DVD series, forensic kits, posters, t-shirts, mugs, even colleges offering forensics degrees and other programs all give Evidence to their popularity.

Not only has the original show spawned other *CSI* programs, but scores of other similar programs feature the application of forensics to medicine, history, common myths, metaphysics, and much more.

- *House* is a popular prime-time medical show about a doctor who is confronted with a medical mystery each week. Doctor House consults with a team of specially trained doctors to diagnose and cure the "mystery" illness. The show is forensics through and through.

- I regularly hear an advertisement on local Seattle radio for a forensic accountant who specializes in recovering money investors have lost to shady investment schemes.

- The July 8, 2009, edition of the online *Forensic Magazine* has a short article on the new field of *animal forensics*.

- New terms such as *battlefield forensics* and *forensics of the pharaohs* are now commonplace when describing history and archaeology.

Forensics dominates television along with reality shows. To say there is a *forensic frenzy* would not be an overstatement.

Evidence of the Forensic Frenzy on TV

The following provides a sample of legal- and forensics-based shows currently on television: *CSI: Miami, CSI, CSI: NY, NCIS, NCIS: Los Angeles, Without a Trace, Law & Order, Law & Order: Special Victims Unit, Law & Order: Criminal Intent, House, M.D., Castle, The Mentalist, Lie to Me, The Closer, Crime Time, Fringe, Mental, Justice, Criminal Minds, The Forgotten, Kidnapped, Medium, America's Most Wanted, Boston Legal, The New Detectives, Medical Detectives, Forensic Files, The FBI Files, Crossing Jordan, Unsolved Mysteries, Suspect: True Crime Stories, Profiler, Video Justice, The D.A., The Agency, Homicide: Life on the Street, Silent Witness, The Exonerated, Cold Case Files, Investigative Reports, American Justice, The Prosecutors: In Pursuit of Justice, Justice Files, Autopsy, History's Crimes and Trials, Exhibit A: Secrets of Forensic Science, Secrets of the Dead, Cops, Masterminds, Celebrity Justice, Without Motive, Prime Suspect, Major Crimes, Sherlock Holmes, Young Sherlock Holmes, Monk, The First 48, Da Vinci's Inquest, DNA, Unusual Suspects, Forensics: You Decide, Secrets of the Dead, Forensic Firsts, Treasure Quest, Hardcover Mysteries, Solved: Extreme Forensics, Battlefield Detectives, Cold Blood, The Glades, North Mission Road, Nancy Grace: Closing Arguments, Missing Persons Unit, Parco P.I., Jami Floyd: Best Defense, LA Forensics, Catherine Crier Live, Banfield & Ford: Courtside, Bloom & Politan: Open Court, Judge Judy, The People's Court, Judge Mathis, Judge Alex, Judge Hatchett,* and *Judge Joe Brown.* There is even an entire network channel, Discovery ID, dedicated to legal and forensics shows.

Even many of the reality shows have forensic elements as their basis. *American Idol* is one of those. *American Idol* asks the question, "Who believes they have the exceptional talent to become the next American Idol?" If people believe, they have the Evidence they need to demonstrate it. They are "judged" by experts who, if they believe the contestants have enough talent, send them to the next round of competition. Contestants must have witnesses who will be a part of the ultimate "conviction," texting in their verdicts by the millions. The person who becomes the American Idol has had to demonstrate the Evidence in many ways over a lengthy period of time to get the verdict: "guilty" of being the American Idol.

Forensics is the new process of scientific discovery. It is seen and applied not only in television but also in education and how we learn. Many high schools teach science using a forensic application and framework. Redmond High School, where my sons attended, offers the courses "Forensics" and "Forensics and the Law" in addition to biology and chemistry.

Life Scene Investigation (LSI) has taken the forensic discovery process as popularized in the current media and developed a scientific process for discovering the most important information in Life: human potential. *?RU*

Forensics is a process. It has specific steps and order to help the investigator discover what happened or "Who done it?" It is a scientific process in that it follows specific steps that have been tested and verified. It looks at all the angles and tests for reliability. The process then places the Evidence in context to answer the question, *?RU*.

Crime Scene versus Life Scene

LSI uses forensics as the process of discovery. We don't call it simply "forensics" but "Positive Forensics." The focus of that discovery is the polar opposite of what CSI looks for. The contrasts are distinct and stand in sharp contrast.

CSI	LSI
Crime	Design
Death	Life
Weakness	Strengths
Deficit	Asset
Terrible	Exceptional
Evil	Goodness
Lose freedom	Gain freedom

Destruction	Construction
Loss	Gain
Pain	Pleasure
Negative emotions	Positive emotions
Wrong	Right
Disconnect	Connect
Break	Build

Positive Forensics is just that, positive. What we profile is what builds Life. On our Facebook page (Positive Forensics) our headline is "Profiling |4| Success' – The Process of Discovering Positive Evidence to Enhance and Grow Human/God-Given Potential." When you read the word *Forensics* in the context of discovering your DNA Code, think Positive Forensics and not criminal forensics.

This is a book about *discovery*. It is the beginning of the process. It is Life Scene *Investigation*. You have to know what you bring to Life before you develop it and apply or deploy it in Life. This is forensics, the scientific process of discovery.

Steve Jobs was one of the great minds of our generation. He is often looked at as the main competitor of Bill Gates. At a commencement address at Stanford University he made this well-quoted statement:

> *The only way to do great work is to love what you do.*
> *If you haven't found it yet, keep looking. As with all*
> *matters of the heart, you'll know it when you find it.*
> *So keep looking until you find it. Don't settle.*
> —Steve Jobs, founder of Apple

The question to be asked is this: *How do you discover what you love to do?* As this LSI formula will show you, there is a pathway to discovering what you love. It is not some random process of hit and miss or endless searching for Shangri-La. The process is not one that is simply left for our hearts to discover, though our hearts will certainly know it when we discover it. Understand the LSI formula and follow the LSI Positive Forensic Process, and you will find what Steve Jobs encouraged the Stanford graduates to search for.

Life Scene Investigation is the first step in the discovery of your Life Design and discovering what you love. Dr Martin Seligman, one of the founders of Positive Psychology, believes that the pathway to high Performance and happiness is discovering and living your Talents and not simply fixing your weaknesses. Those who are stuck in the "fix" mode as a pathway to happiness and performing better will find it is a road that never gets them to their desired destination.

Before you can achieve a Life of Purpose, experience Passion, and demonstrate exceptional and sustained Performance, you need to have the Evidence. Evidence is the starting point.

The development of Design and Talents is secondary and comes after discovery. You cannot develop what you don't know. Development is a focused process. When ability is observed in a person, it should be pushed and given the opportunity to develop into a full-fledged Talent. Development is the designed growth, discipline, refinement, and application of Talents.

When we don't know the Evidence, development and engagement in Life is a long, random, and often failed process. It is a shotgun approach to Life: just shoot and hope you hit something. When you have the Evidence, you can then direct it toward a target, a focus, and the energy to develop is not wasted.

Thousands of books are all written with the idea of helping you discover your Passion, your Purpose, and your path in Life. The most popular book in recent years was *The Purpose Driven Life. The DNA Code* is one of those books, too, but it takes a different approach. It is unique and unlike anything you have read.

1. LSI is based on a *philosophy* or *formula.*
    a. *Design DNA determines Purpose*
    b. *Purpose DNA creates Passion*
    c. *Passion DNA fuels Performance*
2. LSI uses a *process of discovery* that is recognized as the most thorough and cutting-edge discovery process used in contemporary culture and the scientific community—positive forensics.
3. LSI focuses on *Talents* and human Design, not weakness.

Locard's Exchange Principle

Paul L. Kirk, in his 1953 book *Crime Investigation: Physical Evidence and the Police Laboratory,* described the teachings of Edmond Locard, one of the fathers of forensics, and what is now called Locard's exchange principle:

> *Wherever he steps, whatever he touches, whatever he leaves, even unconsciously, will serve as a silent witness against him. Not only his fingerprints or his footprints, but his hair, the fibers from his clothes, the glass he breaks, the tool mark he leaves, the paint he scratches, the blood or semen he deposits or collects. All of these and more bear mute witness against him. This is Evidence that does not forget. It is not confused by the excitement of the moment. It is not absent because human witnesses are. It is factual Evidence. Physical Evidence cannot be wrong, it cannot perjure itself, it cannot be wholly absent. Only human failure to find it, study and understand it, can diminish its value.*

This forensic principle states that you leave Evidence everywhere you go. The Purpose of positive forensics as we apply it to *Life Scene Investigation* is to collect that Evidence and see what that Evidence tells us about your Purpose in Life.

Locard's Exchange Principle—*Revised*

One of the ways you need to think as you apply the forensic CSI model/process to LSI is to focus on what we look for. Here is the LSI version of the Locard principle:

> *Wherever you step, whatever you touch, whatever you leave, even unconsciously, will serve as an open witness for you. Not only your fingerprints or your footprints, the calm your presence brings, the songs you sing, the baseballs you throw, people you motivate, the good grades you get, the piano you play, the truth you hold in the face of pressure, the photographs you take, the patient you heal, the endurance you demonstrate, the part you act in a play. All of these, and more, bear loud witness of your*

Unique Design DNA. This is Evidence that does not forget. It is not confused by the excitement of the moment. It is not absent because human witnesses are. It is factual Evidence. The Physical, intellectual, social, emotional, spiritual/motive Evidence cannot be wrong, it cannot perjure itself, and it cannot be wholly absent. Only your failure to find, study, and understand it can diminish its value to discovering your Purpose in Life.
—Mark R. Demos, LSI creator

Life Scene Investigation (LSI) is about Life, *your* Life. It is not theoretical. It is a process about discovering your Life. You leave Evidence of who you are all around you every day. You leave Evidence of your presence, your actions, your connections, your relationships, your motives, your thinking, your decisions, your attitudes, your accomplishments, your Unique Design and Talents.

Everything you do leaves DNA (physical DNA, intellectual DNA, social DNA, emotional DNA, and spiritual/motive DNA) that defines and describes you. LSI will help you discover that Evidence, not just any Evidence, but Evidence that is based on your Design DNA and the Talents displayed by it.

What Never Lies? The Evidence!
Not Knowing the Evidence Will Hurt You

I have a brilliant sister whose name is Penny. It is a great British name. I call her *Nelope*. Nelope attended the same undergraduate college as I did in Virginia. Both of us had attended summer school so that we could finish our degrees in the shortest time possible. The result was that we both completed our degrees in the middle of the school year in December. Nelope then left to go to Dallas and begin her doctoral work in psychology.

Penny chose to return to Virginia to walk in the graduation ceremony in May of that year. She decided she would drive a car she had recently bought that purportedly got great mileage and would make the trip much more economical than when she drove to Dallas in a huge gas guzzler that got eight to ten miles to the gallon. The car she bought was a small foreign car that had a great reputation and was supposed to get at least thirty-five miles to the gallon on the highway.

When Penny arrived she talked about how the car was really nice but certainly didn't deliver what she had been told it would. She said that when she got on the highway and was going sixty-five, the car not only didn't have the cruising ability she anticipated but basically got around twenty-five miles to the gallon, and on top of that the car had a high whine.

A few days later we were going down Highway 29 in central Virginia, and I was driving. Penny looked over at me and asked what I had just done. I didn't know what she meant. She asked what I had just done with the gearshift (the car had a stick shift). What had gone awry in her earlier trip was that Penny had driven stick shifts her entire driving career but had never driven a stick shift with five gears. The fifth gear was engineered to maximize highway driving, but Penny had never driven a car with a fifth gear. She had been driving in fourth gear.

This story is simple but profound in terms of what it tells us about Design and Life. The essential lesson is this: what happens when we don't know our Design and those Talents that define that Design?

1. What we don't know can *hurt us*. We end up spending more for gas because we end up using more gas. Trying to do and live what we are not uniquely Designed to do always requires more effort. We put out more effort and we always get fewer results. It is more than that, though. When we know what our Purpose is and engage our Talents, we are more productive. When we are more productive, it is more likely we will earn more or get better grades.

2. We are left feeling *disappointed* with Life because it doesn't deliver what it promised. We feel we were sold something second-rate.

3. There is a *distraction* or high whine always in the background. We often get used to it, but we know that something is wrong and just can't figure out what it is.

4. We tend to *break down* because the stress of using so much energy to produce the speed expected of us wears on us. There are times when we just plain overheat and break down.

Penny didn't experience the very Design property the car was known for and for which she purchased it. She could have saved herself a lot of frustration, disappointment, money, wasted time, and more if she knew the Design of this car. Before you drive, make sure you read the instruction manual. The manual tells you the car's capacities, what it was built to do. We don't attempt to use what we don't know or are not convinced of.

Some people just keep trying and trying and never really discover their Passion. The truth is, you don't discover your Passion. Passion is not what we should seek. The same goes for happiness. Happiness is as elusive as a cloud, as the Holy Grail. Passion is the result of knowing your Design and then living that Design. It is discovering what your Talents are—those unique capacities that when utilized give you a sense of control and connection and a feeling of Passion!

There are others who just work harder, faster, and longer. The belief is that the busier you are, the bigger difference you are making. Lots of energy and action do not equate with Purpose and meaningful change. Spinning one's wheels just makes a deeper hole and sends lots of dirt flying around. Does that sound like you? Are you busy, doing many good things, active and moving? Sometimes the noise of doing makes us deaf to our lack of Purpose, but when the noise fades and we are quiet, we have a deep sense of needing to ask the question *?RU,* and the answer is *I don't know!* There is no Passion, just an exhaustion that leaves us wondering whether we really want to start up and move faster this next time, because the last whirlwind didn't leave us knowing any more about who we are and why we are here.

Not Knowing Will Make You Mad

Some of the angriest people I know are teens who have not been allowed to discover or had the opportunity to live their Talents. Their parents have hovered over and watched them so closely they seldom, if ever, have the opportunity to do anything but what their parents allow. These types of parents even have a name: "helicopter parents." The problem is that not only are these teens denied the opportunity to discover their Talents, but they are not even allowed to fail. Every problem is covered or litigated. These teens have no demonstrated successes of their own to be proud of. They have no demonstrated pathway to succeed.

One of the greatest books on parenting and culture is called *A Nation of Wimps* by Hara Estroff Marano. Marano talks about how we have protected and coddled the strength and growth out of so many young people and how it has resulted in their becoming aimless and weak.

Parents hover over their children and never let them fall and build the strengths that come from picking themselves up. Children are seldom challenged to find their own ways to solve problems. They are stopped from exploring. When they do something wrong, parents protect them from "bad teachers" or others who don't see how fragile and precious they are. These children never learn right from wrong. Their parents exempt them from natural consequences, so they experience no pain.

Even when teens go to college, these parents follow them. They hire lawyers to file lawsuits if their lazy progeny get grades that accurately reflect their efforts and objective scores on tests. These parents even spend weeks living in dormitories or hotels that are in close proximity so as to help with the anxieties that they have produced in their weak and fragile children. They smother the very Life out of them!

I have seen rage that is extreme: teens who carve up brand new kitchen cabinets with a hunting knife; one who took a baseball bat to things he knew his parents greatly valued; the violence and attempts to embarrass have no bounds. When I talk to these teens, I see in them a desperation about Life. They fear almost everything because they are unsure of their own abilities and Talents. They don't know what they can do; they are human jellyfish.

I also see many of these teens run to alcohol and drugs as the only way they can relate and connect. They have never been allowed to connect based on their own competency and demonstration of Talents.

For many teens and college students, the way to connect and feel part of a group is drinking and drugs. Their social connections and gatherings are centered on substances that allow them to be less inhibited and anxious, and ultimately they can become part of a group without demonstrating any social skills whatsoever. They will do almost anything to belong.

I see their rage and desperation, and my job then begins as I attempt to help them discover their Design DNA and do whatever I can to have their parents pull back on one hand and on the other provide opportunities for them. I have likened the problem to holding someone's head under the water in a pool. He may submit at first, thinking it is a game and you are just playing. After a few seconds, he starts pushing up and against what is holding him down. Eventually, fear and desperation kick in, and his arms and legs begin to fight and flail around. Purpose is powerful and must find expression. It has a power that if not channeled will leave one disappointed and angry at Life!

And this anger is not limited to teens. It is also felt by adults who are in careers and jobs they know do not reflect their Design DNA; college students who are in majors that their parents demanded they enroll in; and successful people who are controlled by mortgages, families, and futures and who are held captive to visions of money and status, but not Design. *PRU*

I have met so many people and seen so many lives demonstrating a low-grade anger at and depression about Life. They live "lives of quiet desperation," and all those around them—their spouses, children, friends, work associates—know and experience their misery. *PRU*

Courage Is Necessary to Live Your Evidence and Design

I was given the book *A Bold Fresh Piece of Humanity* for Christmas one year. The book, written by Fox News commentator Bill O'Reilly, is a biography that describes his Life, philosophy, and political thought.

In the book, Bill talks about his father with a sense of great sadness and regret as he describes one of the elements that drove him to perform as one of the most popular radio and television hosts on air today.

Bill talked about how his father gave the most important years of his Life for a major corporation and slaved day after day, held captive by his sense of duty to his family and other social and economic conditions. Bill watched how his father died a slow death and ultimately was rewarded with only a cheap watch and a meager pension after thirty-five years of faithful service.

Got Courage?

Got courage? Many people don't. Maybe you need to put this book down. I advise you to do just that if you are not willing to take what you are about to discover and live it. If you discover and then don't have the courage to live the Evidence, you will be more miserable than you are now—that is a promise!

The courage I am talking about is the courage Bill's father never exercised: the courage to live what you discover and to embrace the changes you need to make. It will never work just to know *?RU* and then not be willing to live *?UR*.

Courage might mean changing your major at college, finding another job or profession, closing a relationship that does not encourage and promote your being true to who you discover, and maybe even more.

Courage is required, but the benefits are more than worth it. The *Return on Courage* (ROC) is a Life of *Purpose, Passion,* and *Performance.* If you are ready and have the necessary courage to discover and live the answers to *?RU,* read on and discover what you were *meant to Live!*

F O R E N S I C S	Forensics is the application of various sciences to answer questions relating to examination and comparison of biological, trace impressions (such as fingerprints, shoeprints, and tire tracks), controlled substances, firearms, and other Evidence in criminal investigations. Many tools are useful in gathering Evidence, and most require a meticulous approach to collection so that the Evidence is not compromised.
	Forensic anthropology—Discovery from bones and skeletal remains
	Forensic pathology—Finding causes of death using medical knowledge
	Forensic psychiatry—Discovery from psychological and psychiatric conditions and profiles
	Forensic biology—Discovery from DNA, blood, hair, semen, skin, and so on
	Computer forensics—Discovery from websites visited, documents created, and so on from computers and the Internet
	Forensic accounting—Discovery from financial records
	Forensic photography—Identifying and authenticating from photographs
	Forensic entomology—Use of insects and bugs to help determine time and place of death
	Forensic toxicology—Discovery from poisons and substances that cause harm and death

	Digital forensics—Discovery from cell phones and other digital devices
	Forensic document examination—Authenticating documents
	Forensic geology—Discovery of trace evidence in soils, minerals, and petroleum
	Forensic odontology—Use of dentistry and teeth to determine identity
E **V** **I** **D** **E** **N** **C** **E**	Evidence is information presented to judges or juries in an effort to convince them of the truth or falsity of key facts. Typically this includes testimony of witnesses, documents, photographs, items of damaged property, government records, videos, and laboratory reports. *Prima facie*: Latin for "on its face." A *prima facie* case is one that at first glance presents sufficient Evidence for the plaintiff to win. Weight of Evidence: In a criminal trial, the weight of Evidence must be beyond a reasonable doubt or "to a moral certainty." In effect, there is little to no probability that the Evidence could point in any direction other than at the guilt of the charged person. In a civil trial, the weight of Evidence must be a *preponderance* of the Evidence. Essentially, the scale must tilt 50 percent or more in favor of one party in order for the verdict to be made on that party's behalf.

Part 2

What Is LSI Evidence?

Chapter 3
Discovering Evidence of Design

To be what we are, and to become what we are
capable of becoming, is the only end of Life.
—Baruch Spinoza

I was drafted into the military of what was then Rhodesia immediately after high school in 1978. Every eighteen-year-old male was required to perform at least eighteen months of military service before he could go on into Life, college, whatever was next.

After basic training and a couple of brief assignments, I was posted to the Chaplain Corps, the division of the military that focused on the spiritual and religious needs of servicemen and their families. The chaplains performed weddings, funerals, and services; visited the wounded in hospital; and notified families when a soldier was wounded or killed.

Much of what I did in the Chaplain Corps was to ride with chaplains when they went to areas of the country where there was military conflict. The chaplains would drive, and I would ride shotgun.

One of the more frequent destinations I was required to accompany chaplains to was Tsanga Lodge. Tsanga was a rehabilitation center situated over seven thousand feet high in the Inyanga Mountains. The area looked and felt very much like the highlands of Scotland and had foliage, small dams, and rivers with names like Connemara, named after places in Ireland and Scotland.

Tsanga was run by Lt. Dick Paget, who owned the facility prior to the Rhodesian Bush War and ran an Outward Bound wilderness program. Dick had no psychological or psychiatric training but was able to inspire and find ways to motivate the toughest and most terribly wounded cases to seek a new and better Life. Dick wrote a book about his Life experiences, *Paget's Progress: A Tale of High Adventure and Low Salaries.*

Dick Paget and his wife, Anne, a nurse, had developed a great reputation for working miracles with some of the toughest and often most hopeless situations. He would take on severely wounded soldiers who essentially were dropouts from other rehabilitation facilities. These were soldiers who had for the most part healed physically but were severely depressed and had given up on Life.

On reporting for duty one morning I was advised I would be taking a chaplain to Tsanga Lodge to hold services and minister to the patients. I was told we would first be going to St. Giles, a rehabilitation facility in the capital city, where soldiers who had suffered serious injuries were sent to recover after being released from the hospital.

I went with the chaplain to St. Giles, and we picked up three young soldiers. One was a paraplegic, so we had to load his stretcher and wheelchair into the back of the Land Rover. He had been blown up when his vehicle went over a land mine, and he was paralyzed from the waist down. He lay propped up in the back. The next young soldier had a white phosphorus grenade explode in his hand. Most of one hand was blown off, but even worse, he was completely blind. The last soldier had both his legs blown off below the knee after standing on an anti-personnel mine.

After loading everyone into the Land Rover we began the trip up to the mountains. The trip was about three hours on paved roads and then the last two hours on dirt roads through some beautiful mountain scenery. All three soldiers were quiet and sullen for most of the trip. We passed Troutbeck Inn, a beautiful mountain lodge with a golf course and lakes with swans. Since the war had started, the hotel was virtually empty. It was not far up the road from there to Tsanga Lodge.

On arriving at Tsanga we were met by Lt. Paget. He asked us not to unload but said he wanted to spend some time with his new patients and asked if we would head on back with him to Troutbeck Inn, where we would have a drink and socialize.

We drove back down and spent some time in the pub, where Lt. Paget talked to the soldiers about what he expected and what they should expect at Tsanga. After about an hour we went out to the Land Rover, and I was about to help the paraplegic soldier into the back, but Lt. Paget told me to close the door and wait. He then advised the three soldiers that they already knew their way to Tsanga Lodge and would need to make their way back by themselves. It wasn't far, but to make them walk back was just not fair.

The chaplain wasn't sure what to do and tried to complain. Lt. Paget was the commanding officer, so even though he was lower in rank than the chaplain, he had to be obeyed. There was a bit of a commotion but because I had no rank, I had no right to say anything and simply drove back with Lt. Paget and the chaplain.

It was hard to imagine these three soldiers—one blind, another in a wheelchair, and one with two prosthetics—walking up the rocky road during the late afternoon.

I heard from the chaplain the next morning, and he was still incensed and was talking about what he intended to do when he returned to our headquarters. I assisted the chaplain in gathering the patients for a service that day and also while he did rounds, talking with the various soldiers who were in the facility.

The following day I was having breakfast when I was asked to accompany the chaplain and Lt. Paget to look in on two of the soldiers we had brought to Tsanga. The soldier who had lost his legs was integrating well, but the other two had not been seen since going to their rooms after arriving the first evening. I wasn't sure what my role was, but I had to follow as I was told. I believed we would be looking in on the soldiers and offering some encouragement to get them participating in the Life of the facility.

I was wrong. The first room we went into was that of the paraplegic. Lt. Paget started civilly but soon began a verbal barrage that I found hard to comprehend. The soldier had soiled himself in his bed and was very sullen, lying there in his mess. Lt. Paget told him that he was stinking up the room and that it resulted in his roommate not wanting to sleep in the stench. He advised the young soldier to either clean his mess up, clean himself up, get out of his room, and start participating in the program or take the road he had walked on from Troutbeck Inn and lose himself in the wilderness. So much for words of consolation and solace.

The chaplain was dumbfounded and attempted to interject. He was asked by Lt. Paget to keep his words to himself and told if he wished to pray with the soldier he could do so at a later time. We had another patient to see.

We moved on to the next soldier's room. He was crouched in the corner of his room on the floor. He received the same treatment. He was told if he didn't stop crouching in the corner, he would be asked to join the paraplegic for a trip down the road. Either get up and get moving or get the hell out of Tsanga Lodge.

The chaplain made his objections and anger known. He told Lt. Paget that he would be reporting his abuse and treatment of the soldiers when we returned to army headquarters. The chaplain promised there would be changes and apologies from Lt. Paget. He also promised never to bring any other soldiers to Tsanga Lodge. We left within a day or so and returned to the chaplains' HQ.

I returned to Tsanga about six months later with another chaplain who was going to perform Christmas services. December is the middle of summer in the southern hemisphere, and so it was very warm.

The same day I arrived, I went down to the swimming pool to cool off after the long, dusty drive. As I arrived there I saw a number of soldiers in and around the pool. In the pool was the paraplegic soldier we had brought up on the previous trip. He had an inner tube around his waist, and he was splashing water in a playful fight with some other soldiers. I was amazed at the difference.

Later that day I saw the blind solder. He was seated on a horse being pulled in tow by another soldier. They had been out for a ride. He was laughing, talking away and having a great time.

I never saw the other soldier we transported up but understood he had returned to his military unit and was doing well.

One evening I was in the dinner area with the chaplain. He was sitting with Lt. Paget and talking about the dramatic changes that took place in the lives of the soldiers who came to Tsanga. He recounted to Lt. Paget how he had been told horror stories about the treatment of soldiers, by Lt. Paget in particular, and how he was asked to check up on the soldiers who had been brought up earlier in the year.

Lt. Paget began talking about his approach with these soldiers and rehab dropouts. He began by saying that when they arrived, he was open and honest with each one of them. He told them that reality was just that, reality. There was nothing he could change about what had happened to them. He would also no longer entertain any further talk of rehabilitation, nor would he commiserate about their losses and seek to understand their plights. Did he feel sorry for them? Without a doubt! What was, was. What they had lost, they had lost, and neither he nor the doctors nor God was going to give them new legs, arms, eyes, or anything else.

He then said that what he did was to focus on what they did possess. What they had, they had. It was his job to help them know what capacities they had and then to find ways for them to engage and live Life using what they had the capacity to do. His job was to analyze *asset* and not *deficit*. That concept stuck with me. The *Analysis of Asset!* What a concept.

With his simple philosophy, Lt. Paget had worked miracles, or what many doctors and mental health professionals called miracles. Each of these soldiers had his deficits (what he had lost, what he would never do again, and so on) that had been identified, analyzed, and confirmed with medical language: blind, paraplegic, amputee, deaf, emasculated, and so on.

Lt. Paget's miracle working is basically the same as what is taught and promoted by Marcus Buckingham and Donald Clifton in their groundbreaking book, *Now Discover Your Strengths*. Their mission is to change the way corporate America and the world of business do business. The philosophy practiced in the rural mountains of Africa to rebuild shattered lives is the same that is used to build greater productivity and strong, vibrant businesses in the concrete jungles of the world's cities.

There is a pervasive belief that the pathway to success is guided by determining what is wrong or weak and then *fixing* those weaknesses. "Mental health" begins with a diagnosis of "mental illness" and then "therapy" to treat people. Therapists say they want to know why people are depressed in order to help them become happy. The human resources departments in corporations are primarily focused on rehabilitation, or helping employees' deficiencies. The process has been inverted.

This focus on finding faults and fixing them as the pathway to success is misguided. The way to find success is to study success, health, optimal functioning, and what works. It is to ask why people excel. Happiness, health, and success have their own patterns, elements, and DNA. If we want to learn or discover why a corporation or system is performing, we don't do that by studying failing businesses. If we want to discover how to help students graduate, we need to study those students who are graduating and succeeding. We look for Evidence of Talent!

Life Scene Investigation is *the Science of Human Talents*. Positive forensics is the scientific process we use to discover or diagnose those Talents.

Though this analogy has its limitations when applied to Life in general, the reality is that we all have deficits. When we compare ourselves with others, we can always find something they can do that we can't or are very limited in ability to perform at any acceptable level.

That is the reality. The pathway to Purpose, Passion, and Performance is in discovering Evidence of your Talents. That is the *greater* reality.

MYLIFESCENE.COM—CROSS NOW—MYLIFESCENE.COM
Life Scene—Ellie Moore

Ellie Moore weighed over six hundred pounds in 2000. She had been overweight for more than thirty years. She grew up in a very abusive home, being sexually, physically, and verbally abused by many of those who were closest to her.

After having graduated high school as valedictorian, she was told by her parents that she could not go to college because she was a woman, and she was married soon afterward. Ellie had three children and lived in a very unhappy marriage for many years.

Ellie started to gain excessive weight and then began many attempts to control and lose that weight. She had surgery, tried every diet that was on the market, and went through various weight-loss programs. Ellie's weight and Life continued to go through many ups and downs. She went for counseling for many of her past abuse issues as well as those related to her marriage, until she eventually decided to get divorced.

In 2000, Ellie attended the first LSI program. (The program was called the *Dynamics of Strong Living*.) Ellie's perspective in dealing with her past and current struggles was dramatically changed. Instead of constantly looking backward and attempting to deal with the issues from her past, she began assessing her Talents. Ellie's Life changed dramatically; instead of looking to repair her past, she performed an *Analysis of Asset* and began to live her Life focusing on her Talents. In her own words, she was trying to gain by looking backward all the time and never got anywhere. When she started focusing on what she had the capacity to do and give to others, what she was good at, she began to heal and, most of all, lose weight.

Over the next five years Ellie lost an amazing four hundred pounds. She traveled all over the United States, Canada, and the United Kingdom challenging other women to focus on what they possessed in terms of Talent and unique ability as a way to grow and develop their lives. She developed a weight-loss program that did not focus primarily on losing weight but on the discovery of personal Talents as the foundation of a Life that can be taken back and lived with emotional strength and control. Ellie's belief was that many of the issues related to weight gain are emotional, and when we discover and focus on living our Talents, we *feel* better. We are then able to use those positive emotions to feed ourselves and our ability to perform positive actions.

In 2006 Ellie fought breast cancer and again was forced to look at what resources she possessed to deal with this Life-threatening giant. She had to deal with weight gain due to the treatment, which included steroids and other medications. In early 2008 Ellie was cleared of her cancer threat and began anew helping others, including starting to develop a program for obese teens using the new LSI Discovery materials.

Ellie died in the early part of 2009, but she never stopped encouraging people everywhere she went. One of the last times I saw Ellie, she had just undergone major surgery, and all she could do was tell me about a nurse who was in the room with her. She talked about all she knew that was good and strong in what this nurse did for her and how exceptional the nurse was. Even in her extreme pain and discomfort, Ellie kept focused on the most important information of Life. She was my great friend, and I will miss her because of how she looked at the world and people, always through their Talents.

MYLIFESCENE.COM—CROSS NOW—MYLIFESCENE.COM

You cannot build by knowing what to avoid. You gain no direction by doing a thorough inventory of what you lack, are not endowed with, are missing, don't possess when compared to others, and so on.

Educators Karen Reivich and Andrew Shatter, in their book, *The Resiliance Factor*, stress over and over that if we believe we can minimize issues such as depression and other negative factors and are constantly stuck doing damage control, we lose. The only way to achieve high Performance is to maximize our Talents as opposed to attempting to minimize our weaknesses.

The message of this book is right along the same lines of thinking. The focus is on discovering the Evidence that will make you flourish. That Evidence is what we call Talents, and those Talents make up your Individual Design.

Dr. Martin Seligman, past president of the American Psychological Association, has a similar philosophy to Dick Paget's, all the while sitting in the offices of the Ivy League University of Pennsylvania's School of Psychology. Dr. Seligman talks about avoidance and the Analysis of Deficit in his book *Authentic Happiness* and in other books and articles. His theme is consistent. You cannot build Life by avoiding! There is no Evidence, research, or support for the belief that we can grow or become happy or productive human beings by avoiding or following the pathway of "don't"!

It is important to know where you have been and where you don't want to go again. Failure needs to teach us. When we look at Evidence in context and the *Forensic Evidence Timeline,* we will discuss failure and negative issues we need to avoid.

Let me restate what I said: You cannot live by avoiding. You cannot reach your destination by identifying what you are determined to avoid. You might reach it by chance and years of wasted searching, aimless attempts and elimination of wrong routes taken, wasted energy and regular disappointments. This is not a good plan.

The Purpose of each Life is to discover what you possess. We all have commonalities of Design, but for each of us, our Purpose in Life is to discover our uniqueness, our Talents. It is in discovering and applying those unique Talents that we engage and make our greatest contribution to Life.

The prime objective of *The DNA Code* is the discovery of your unique Human Talents.

Chapter 4
LSI Evidence Defined

I love the song by Nikka Costa, "Everybody Got Their Something." Everybody, and that includes you, has their "something." That something is what we call *Evidence*. So what is your "something?"

Evidence is any item or information gathered at a Life Scene, or at related locations, which is found to be relevant to a Life Scene Investigation. There are many different types of Evidence, from DNA and report cards, an act of caring, leadership, or selling a car, to solving an algebra problem and physical fingerprints.

U Leave Evidence Everywhere

We are going to look at how to discover your "fingerprints" or DNA Markers in every area of your Life. Everywhere you go and everything you do leave Evidence of your presence. In crime scene investigation, identifying latent fingerprints, the Evidence of a person's presence, is the most common method of linking suspects to the scenes of their crimes. Everywhere you go and everything you do will leave Evidence of your presence.

These latents can be made visible by using various chemicals, iodine fuming, and laser technology. The most popular method of identifying and preserving fingerprints, particularly on hard surfaces, involves using fingerprint powder and special lifting tape.

In CSI, these latents are fed into a massive computer system called AFIS, or the Automated Fingerprint Identification System. They are then matched with a single impression in the computer. Identifying unknown crime scene latents in this way is one of the few instances where forensic science can solve and prove a case.

Combined DNA Index System (CODIS)

The development and expansion of DNA profiles and databases at the local, state, and national levels have greatly enhanced law enforcement's ability to solve cases with DNA. Convicted offender databases now store hundreds of thousands of potential suspect DNA profiles against which DNA profiles developed from crime scene Evidence can be compared.

Given the repeat nature of many crimes, the likelihood exists that the individual who committed the crime being investigated was convicted of a similar crime and already has his or her DNA profile in a database that can be searched by the *Combined DNA Index System* (CODIS) software. CODIS also permits the cross-comparison of DNA profiles developed from biological Evidence found at crime scenes. Even if a perpetrator is not identified through the database, crimes may be linked to one another, thereby aiding an investigation, which may eventually lead to the identification of a suspect.

Recently the Detroit Police Department announced it was going to run more than nine hundred unsolved rape DNA kits against CODIS. Justice will be coming to criminals who thought they got away.

Different kinds of Evidence will require different types of expertise in interpretation. Analyzing DNA Evidence is a completely different discipline from understanding gratitude or happiness, analytical thinking or memory, hand-eye coordination or sensory capacity, serving orphans or prayer.

Evidence has many roles in the investigation of human Design. It can link a suspect to a Life Scene if, for instance, a footprint matching the shoe of the suspect is found. Evidence can also eliminate a suspect. And in CSI, if the shoe size of the suspect does not match that of footprint Evidence, then those footprints cannot tie the suspect to the crime scene.

At the start of every *CSI* episode, a crime scene is identified and roped off with yellow crime scene tape. This is where the work of discovery begins. This is a *Field of Evidence*. The investigation of your Life Scene will look at the essential Five Fields of Evidence: physical, intellectual, social, emotional, and spiritual. You need to look at each of these *crime scenes* or *Life Scenes* to construct a complete and convincing case that will hold up and allow you to engage in Life with *Purpose, Passion,* and *Performance.*

In other words, you need to look at the totality of your Life and look carefully for Evidence of your Talents and unique capacities. You will perform a 360-degree analysis of your Life. This is what you will build your *Life Theory* on. Your future depends upon your knowing, developing, and living these Talents and capacities.

In CSI, Evidence is collected, processed, and then presented at trial to aid in convicting alleged criminals and depriving them of their freedom. LSI goes through the same process, but its aim is the opposite. We look to convict you of *Individual Design Talents,* which you can then use to give your Life direction and Purpose. LSI's goal is helping you discover Evidence that will give you the most incredible *freedom* to navigate with confidence a future that is guided by great information, your Talents.

You have a future to live and a Purpose to pursue, Passion to experience, and Performance to demonstrate.

You have the possibility of college, military service, vocational school, starting a job, making a major change in direction.

- What are you going to do?

- How will you build a business?

- Where are you going to go?

- Who are you going to marry?

- How will you manage your employees?

- How will you make great decisions?

- Where are you going to live?

- What are you going to do when you are not working to help you relax and rejuvenate?

- Who are your friends going to be?

- What will guide the way you parent your children?

- What associations or clubs are you going to belong to?

- Are you going to change careers?

- Will you begin a new Life that honors your values and reflects your motives?

LSI is about answering these questions. The Big Question we all want to have answered is ?RU. Do you have a good answer? Can you articulate what is significant about you? Can you tell other people about your uniqueness? Can you clearly frame your Talents and capacities? If you were to be interviewed for the job of your dreams, how would you convince the person who is interviewing you that you are the person for the job? ?RU

Learning the art of Evidence identification and collection is not difficult. You first need to know where to look. Then you need to know what you are looking for. That is what you will be taught to do. You are going to learn the most important skills in Life not just for yourself, but for looking at the lives of others. You will start wanting to find the best in them. You will discover talent by knowing where to look.

CSI teams begin the meticulous task of carefully looking for any Evidence they can find within the roped/taped-off scene. A *Field of Evidence* is the place where we look for and collect Evidence. There are five Fields of Evidence at which we will look. You are encouraged to *cross the line* to discover *?RU*. This is not a crime scene but your Life Scene!

The Five Fields of Evidence

Intellectual Capacity	My capacity for knowledge or knowing How I think, learn, and understand or process information	Education Pedagogy Cognition
Physical Capacity	What I look like; my physical characteristics and abilities How I perceive and receive information, especially through the senses (sight, smell, touch, hearing, taste) and subject to the laws of nature	Kinesiology Physiology Medicine

Emotional Capacity	How I feel and express emotions, both internally and externally How conscious I am of inward impressions, states of mind, or physical conditions	Psychology Psychiatry
Social Capacity	My process of relating, associating, connecting, and giving to others How I interact with other individuals and groups	Sociology Social Anthropology
Spiritual/ Meaning and Purpose Capacity	My motivations for Life My ability to transcend the physical How I understand Life and afterlife in terms of meaning and Design How I know and relate to God, serve God, etc.	Theology Philosophy Ontology Teleology

?RU—The Mix

You have all the following capacities in varying measures or percentages. When you put them all together and mix them up, the result is *you!*

Intellectual Memory Gratitude Analytical Giving Social Bravery Global IQ Leadership Emotional Emotional Intelligence Optimism Tactile Meaning/Purpose Close Friends Eyesight Physical Learning Styles Crisis Management Physical Strength Sensory Bravery Musical Hand-Eye Coordination Math Social Intelligence Singing Volunteerism Serving Relator Scientific Artistic Auditory Intuitive Anger Motivation Gratitude Strategic Thinking Spiritual Intelligence Empathy Futuristic Balance Networking Executive Decision Making Perspective Activator

My Unique and Magnificent Design

My uniqueness is a combination of these Design components, my essential being, the real me! There are approximately seven billion (7,000,000,000) people on the earth today.

Throughout human history there have been possibly twenty billion people who have walked this earth—a big number. You are 1 in 20,000,000,000. There has never been anyone exactly like you, nor will there ever be anyone exactly like you. From your retina to your fingerprints to your DNA, they all uniquely define you.

A *retina scan* is a biometric tool used for identification. Retinas are complex structures made of neural cells, and because of this complexity the retina of each person is unique. The actual phenomenon that creates this uniqueness is the pattern of blood vessels in the retinas. This is so complex that even identical twins will have a different retinal structure. Another factor that backs the retinal scan as an identification tool is that the retina usually maintains the same structure from birth until death. These factors make the scan a good choice of identification procedure. It is used currently by the FBI, NASA, and the CIA. Various Scandinavian airports are using a retinal scan as a means of allowing people who are in their database to move quickly through immigration.

There Is No One Like You!
?RU—1 in 20,000,000,000

LSI Evidence—Defined

Evidence needs to be understood. We need to know what we are looking for. LSI is based on a Design and Talents philosophy. In the previous chapter I talked about Assets and Talents. I will now begin the process of defining exactly what I mean. I need you to be clear as to what you are looking to discover as you *cross the line* in each field of Evidence.

ev·i·dence:

- An external sign of something that furnishes proof of what is true
- Something submitted in a legal forum to a judge or jury to determine the truth
- One or more reasons for believing that something is true

- LSI Evidence definition: Anything collected in a Life Scene that could possibly link a person to his or her DNA Code

Capacity	The ability to perform or produce
	The inherent potential of a Talent or ability
	The maximum production possible
Talent	Any pattern of feeling, thought, or behavior that can be positively applied and repeated with ease
	A special natural ability or aptitude
	An ability that can be significantly maximized and developed through instruction and practice
	An exceptional strength that defines an individual's Unique Design, creates Passion, and fuels exceptional Performance
	The ability to repeat exceptional Performances

The question you must ask is: *Can I see myself doing this repeatedly and successfully, and will it make me happy?* Keep that definition in mind because it is simple and easy to use as a *forensic discovery test.*

How do we better understand what Evidence is? The next chapter will help describe it for you using some common, everyday vehicles.

Forensic Definition—Trace Evidence

Trace (transfer) Evidence: This is the category of Evidence that includes materials that are often microscopic in nature and easily exchanged between people, objects, and places upon contact. A few examples of this type of Evidence include hair, paint, fiber, glass, and plastic. Examination of questioned and known materials can determine whether samples could (or could not) have the same source of origin. *Every contact leaves trace Evidence.*

Chapter 5
LSI Evidence Described

This above all: To thine own self be true.
—Shakespeare, Hamlet

Forensic Evidence

By competent Evidence, is meant such as the nature of the thing to be proved requires; and by satisfactory Evidence, is meant that amount of proof, which ordinarily satisfies an unprejudiced mind, beyond any reasonable doubt.

—Simon Greenleaf

So how do we best understand what Evidence is? I have used the following illustrations, and they seem to translate well. I will also illustrate Evidence in other ways and in other chapters, such as in chapter 6, "'Potential' Evidence." The Animal Story will give you another way to look at and evaluate your Talents.

The Two Types of Design Evidence

Design is classified in two levels: Common and Individual.

Common Design (CD)—What I have in common with almost everyone else. Physical, intellectual, psychological, social, spiritual capacity.

Individual Design (ID)—What is specific to me? What defines me as me? What is the unique outcome and combination of all my common Design capacities in their different measures? My ID. (It is your personal ID or identification, what you carry in your wallet or purse that has your photo, date of birth, eye color, weight, and other information. Keep that simple concept in mind.)

Question—What Makes a Car a Car?

One of the best ways I have found to help understand the differences between Common Design (CD) and Individual Design (ID) is to use cars as an example. Certain basic components or Design capacities are common to what we define as a "car."

1. Chassis—A body, shell, or outer representation.
2. Size or interior space—Cars have internal space that depends on what they are Designed for.
3. Wheels—Usually four, which enable the car to move smoothly.
4. Engine—Cars are also called *motor vehicles*. A motorized engine powers the car.
5. Accelerator—The mechanism that controls the speed of the engine and therefore how fast the car goes.
6. Special features—Some cars have great stereo systems; vans often have special audiovisual systems; sports cars might have extra reinforcement for protection; sedans have extra comfort for regular and long-distance travel; and trucks have extra external space for carrying and hauling.
7. Other basics—Brakes to stop or slow the car's movement; extra features.

Common Design—CD	Individual Design—ID
Chassis	Sedan—Regular travel and transport for everyday Life
Engine	Sports car,coupe—Fast, fun travel for two
Internal Space	Van—Transport for groups of people and/or materials
Wheels	SUV—Multifunction; travel, transport, and fun
Accelerator	Truck—Regular travel and transport

Assess and Rate the Importance of Each of These Individual Design Capacities

As you observe and look for Evidence in these cars, ask and answer the follow questions:

1. How are the ID features described in the name of the car (i.e., Subaru Forrester, Ford Mustang, Geo Metro, etc.)?
2. What is obvious—*prima facie*—Evidence? What can you see by casual observation?
3. What are the primary ID features? What is obvious?
4. What two or three ID features make it unique?

Why don't you rate these cars from your perspective in terms of the level of importance/capacity from 1 to 10? 1 = Not Very Important and 10 = Very Important.

Car Type	Sedan	Sports	Van	SUV	Truck
Chassis	5	8	8	8	8
Engine	5	9	6	8	8
Internal Space	5	2	8	4	3
Accelerator	5	8	3	3	4
Wheels	5	8	4	8	8
Special Features	5	8	7	8	8

Why Is Understanding My Design Essential?

Keep the car analogy in mind as I continue to help you see the importance of understanding your ID.

Understanding Design, that is, a fundamental, personal, individual architecture, is the starting point of Life. Life is not a random set of choices with no foundation or direction. An analysis of your Individual Design is the starting point that gives you direction for your future.

Forensic Question

What happens when you drive your car/vehicle on a road it was never designed to drive on?

A friend of mine went on vacation to San Diego and found a great Porsche Boxster while she was there. She ended up buying it and driving it back to Seattle, where she lived. The drive from San Diego to Seattle along the I-5 Interstate Highway was fun, especially when she was able to accelerate and go a decent speed.

What we know about a Porsche is that it is a German car Designed for a German road called the Autobahn, where there are no speed limits. (Well, there are no *upper* limits, only minimum speeds.) You can and are required to drive fast on the Autobahn. The Boxster can go at speeds of 228 to 280 mph, depending on the model. This fact alone makes me wonder why these cars and others like it are so popular when the speed limit in the United States is sixty-five and in some places seventy-five. These cars are Designed to go up to three times faster than they are legally allowed to go in the United States.

The biggest problem was that when my friend returned to Seattle, she returned to her rural home with its winding roads and speed limits that average thirty-five mph, and the fun was very limited. On a few occasions when she did drive to work, she had mishaps—a stone hit a headlight once, and another time one hit her windshield. The repairs were very costly. Another time, she had her car keyed by some jealous fool.

So here is a question: *What happened to her enjoyment of this great car when she returned to Seattle and her rural home?* She had a car that was not Designed for where she lived. The result was that even though it still had all the Design capacities, she could not use them. She became anxious when she drove her car because of the many stones that could easily fly up and damage her car and cost her. She was frustrated because she had to drive slowly and couldn't drive it the way in was meant to be driven.

Another big problem was that the Boxster was a convertible yet she lived in the Seattle area, where it rains almost nine months a year. One of the best additional features was marginalized. Imagine living in Seattle and having a Porsche convertible!

Another perspective: *What would happen if you drove an SUV or truck over a long distance?* I did. I drove from Seattle to Los Angeles in a two-door Ford Explorer Sport. It worked fine but was a little cramped. We had four people in the car, plus their luggage. The luggage fit well; the people didn't. I am tall but could not push my seat back all the way even though I was the driver for most of the two-day trip. It was cramped. The passengers were not comfortable, and with one being a teen, a fair number of verbal moans and complaints were endured.

The Explorer had large wheels because it had four-wheel drive. That ability meant it got only around ten to fifteen miles to the gallon. That is a lot of gas on a long trip, and so the drive almost cost, with hotels, the same amount as the airfare for four people would have cost. It seemed that we filled up with gas every few hours. Every time I filled up I was thinking about how the trip would have been different driving a roomier, gas-efficient sedan.

In both examples, the cars were more than able to do what the owners and drivers wanted them to do. This was a part of their Common Design. They could perform, but they were not specifically Designed to do what they were used to do.

I have collected lots of other questions from seminars I have taught, such as:

- What would happen if you put three or four people in a sports car that was meant to hold only two people? Answer: Dangerous, uncomfortable, lose the feeling of how fun it is to ride fast in a great car, and so on.

- What would happen if you used a van to transport building materials? Answer: It would damage the interior, harm the suspension, and so on.

Take some time and think of other examples that make you think and apply this analogy. Using analogies in this way is a great way to discuss these concepts with children and teens.

Many people's lives mirror the examples of these cars. Their lives and jobs work fine and move along. They also know that what they are doing is not what they were Designed for:

1. They have a family, mortgage, and kids who are headed for or are already in college. They believe they have to wait it out and hold their breath until they retire.

2. They look forward to when they will no longer be doing what they are doing. All they can think of is retirement or a vacation

that will take them away from what they are doing in drudgery each day.

3. They are in college pursuing a major that makes no sense other than they will be able to earn well when they graduate, but they have no desire to go to class or study.

The Great Forensic Question

DO YOU HAVE THE OPPORTUNITY TO DO WHAT YOU DO BEST EVERY DAY?

That question cuts to the chase. It is a laser that cuts deeply and exposes reality. Don't run from the question; answer it honestly. If the person closest to you in your Life were to answer it for you, what would that person say?

People who cannot answer that question with a positive and resounding "Yes!" are likely to observe the following:

1. They dread going to work—do you?
2. They have more negative than positive interactions with their colleagues—do you?
3. They treat customers poorly—do you?
4. They share with their friends what a miserable company they work for—do you?
5. They achieve less on a daily basis—do you?
6. They have fewer positive and creative moments—do you?

Let's apply this question to our car analogy: *"Do you get to drive your car in the way it was Designed to be driven every day?"*

What if . . . ? That question is one that haunts the minds of almost all of us at one time or another. We want to know what if:

1. I really knew what I was meant to do in this Life?
2. I wasn't doing what I am doing now and hating almost every moment of every waking day?
3. I had the courage to make some changes and do something, anything different?
4. I were able to go to school or work and love what I did?
5. I not only knew my Design but also determined to live it where I know I could make the greatest difference?

Porsche—Could you imagine how my friend would have felt if she had been able to drive and enjoy her Porsche Boxster:

- On long, open roads?
- In a different country with high speed limits or no speed limits?
- On a racetrack?
- With the top down in the warm sunshine?

Ford Explorer—I can just see others driving that Explorer into the mountains during winter to go skiing. They know that regardless of the weather, they don't have to worry because of the four-wheel drive, big tires, and ski rack on the roof, plus other options like:

- Short trips
- Camping, hiking, outdoor sports trips
- Skiing
- Pulling a boat
- Off-road driving

Forensic Question

What would you be doing if you had the opportunity to live your Life based on your DNA Code?

Evidence of Not Knowing and Living Your Design

Have you ever heard of the phrase *crime of passion*? It essentially means doing or acting out of pure emotion and, in the CSI scenario, an emotion totally out of control. In LSI we also talk about *lives of DISpassion*, where little or no Life or positive emotions are present.

Look around you and observe the many lives devoid of any sense of real Passion! How terribly sad! What are the Passion killers in your Life? Those actions, choices, involvements, careers, relationships, or planned futures that just rob you of any positive emotion?

There are many sad results of not knowing and living your Design. Which of these do you regularly experience? Which of these do you see in your spouse or children? Which of these do you see in your world every day? Check those that apply.

- Dissatisfied with Life
- Anxiety

- Lack of motivation
- General depression
- Angry at God
- Angry at other people for not making Life work for you
- Angry at others who you believe didn't help you or didn't provide the opportunity for you to be happy
- Sense of missing out on Life
- Needing distractions and substances to substitute for your lack of Purpose and Passion
- Constant questioning about the meaning of Life and why you are even here
- Giving up on Life and accepting what is because you just can't seem to find any traction
- Anger or jealousy at others who are living to their potentials
- Need to find unhealthy distractions from Life (contamination)
- Not earning what you could because you are not allowed to do what you are great at
- Allowing past issues and people to dictate your present lack of Purpose and Passion
- Not finding the satisfaction you hoped for
- Blaming others for your lack of Purpose and Passion
- Breaking down because of long-term stress when you have to go against your Design and play without being able to engage and use your Talents

What we know about teens when they are not connected to their Design:

- Need for excitement in whatever form it comes.
- Abuse drugs and alcohol because they need something to make them feel different and something to make Life exciting, even in the short term.
- Commit crimes because they are bored and really have nothing of value in their Life: "What do I have to lose?"
- Failure to engage or dropping out of school because it doesn't matter. They can't see how school will help in their Life.

- Promiscuity and teen pregnancy because they want someone who will love them and whom they can love, who gives them a sense of Purpose.

- Anger and defiance because they feel stupid and can't do anything that people respect. There are no open doors that make sense.

Dr Martin Seligman asserts that this focus on *Analysis of Asset* is preventative. It helps stop problems before they start. In many ways it is like taking your vitamins, eating healthfully, and exercising. If you focus on health, you are less likely to get sick.

Seligman believes that through his research and that of others in the Positive Psychology movement, there is a set of human talents or strengths that when discovered and lived provide protection against mental illness. He lists in this set attitudes and perspectives such as optimism, honesty, interpersonal skills, a strong work ethic, and the ability to keep going in the face of adversity. His stated mission is to create a science of human Talents to change the course of Life for many young people by encouraging these attributes.

When individuals don't have something to fill and guide their lives, they find substitutes to create temporary emotional highs. Even teen pregnancy is so often a situation where young women want something to live for and someone to love them, and the baby becomes a substitute for a Life Design. How sad.

At-risk has become a code phrase to describe teens likely to do things that will result in their taking drugs, participating in criminal behavior, dropping out of school, and doing anything that will harm their lives. I believe that the concept of *at-risk* needs to be defined in a new way to mean that teens are "at risk" of not discovering their Purpose and not living their Design. That is the greatest "risk." If they discover their Design, it becomes less likely they will be *at risk* of doing those behaviors that will rob them of Life. Real prevention means discovering their Talents and living their Individual Design.

Preserving Trace Evidence

Trace Evidence is not always visible to the naked eye. Special care must be taken to preserve it and prevent its loss or contamination.

All trace Evidence, or items suspected of bearing trace Evidence, must be submitted to the laboratory. This evidence must be sealed, labeled, and otherwise protected from loss of sample or contamination.

Adhesive tape that forms a tamper-evident seal or heat-seals should always be used. A seal is defined as a complete closure that will ensure against the loss or contamination of microscopic Evidence. A proper tape seal must extend across the entire opening of the container.

Evidence—you now know what we are looking to discover. It is time to *cross the line* into your *Fields of Evidence* and look for Evidence of Talents that define your Design and will launch you into a Life of *Purpose, Passion,* and *Performance.*

Chapter 6
"Potential" Evidence

Your Potential. Our Passion.
— Microsoft Corporation

Be All You Can Be
— U.S. Army slogan

Motivational speakers, preachers, coaches, schoolteachers, and speakers at graduations all have an often singular message: *You can become anything you set your mind to! If you just believe in yourself, you can do anything!* What a lot of nonsense. It sounds great and optimistic, and it challenges the hopes of each listener who is on the verge of a new and exciting Life, but it's not true!

That got you up and jumping mad at me. *"Of course I can!"* I hear that almost every time I speak about Potential, and I get emails telling me I am full of it.

I am told again, *"We all can become anything we want to become if we work hard enough and believe sincerely enough."* My answer is still the same: *"No, you can't!"* Life Scene Investigation is not based on that flawed philosophy.

Potential is *discovered* and *developed* but never created. You cannot create potential; you already possess it; it is inherent in your DNA Code. You are not God, a little god, an apprentice god, or a potential god.

Please keep an open mind while I attempt to explain what I mean. Humans don't have the ability to create simply because they believe hard enough. The only person capable of that is God, and I am not God, nor are you. Belief is a vital part of Life, but belief in what?

Here are some myths and beliefs about human potential:

1. I can do anything if I set my mind to it!
2. If I believe hard enough, I can achieve anything!
3. I have unlimited potential!
4. If you believe in someone hard enough, they will perform miracles!

Many motivational speakers, preachers, and self-help gurus keep people captive for years believing there is something wrong with them because they don't achieve a certain status, have the yacht, drive the sports car, or go on the dream vacations they are promised they can achieve by believing. These sincere and often desperate followers are made to accept that they just didn't believe hard enough or follow the formula closely enough.

They are told to *"fake it until they make it,"* to pretend until one day when they wake up and find they have created the reality they visualized and affirmed. There are small elements of truth in much of what they are taught, but fundamentally these systems are based on nothing but wishful thinking.

Take some of these beliefs and test them in the world of reality (some of you might have these realities, but not many):

1. I can be the fastest runner in my school.
2. I can do my taxes without help.
3. I could pass the medical school MCATS.
4. I could get through the first round of American Idol.
5. If I practiced hard enough, I could become a concert pianist.
6. I know and understand the theological doctrine of predestination.
7. I could play in the NFL if I really tried hard enough.
8. I could learn to speak Mandarin Chinese fluently in a year.

Belief is an amazingly powerful force, but it is not a creative force. Belief can drive us to discover and bring our potential to the fore. A belief that we have Evidence to discover is what LSI's *Positive Forensic*

Process is about. Belief that the Evidence exists is the gateway to discovery. The Evidence is there, so believe it and find it!

One of the elements of discovering your DNA Code is desire. Have you ever thought why you never had any interest in playing in the NFL or becoming a concert pianist? Just for a moment, think about yourself holding a football and standing in the end zone in a football game. What about performing a piano recital in front of a large audience? How long do either of those thoughts stay in your mind? The likelihood is that you were probably never Designed to do either of those things if the thought didn't remain for any length of time. You just are not wired to give piano concerts or play any position in football.

The laws of nature, physics, DNA, and Life apply. There will always be people who will seemingly break the mold, but there are also some realities that no one will ever change. You will never flap your arms fast enough to fly. There are examples in nature that defy our realities, such as hummingbirds, which, from what we know about aerodynamics, should not be able to fly, and ants, which can move objects that outweigh them many times.

There are examples of people who have done seemingly unbelievable things in crisis situations, such as lifting a car to free a trapped person. Those are anomalies, and if we seek those as experiences we want to define and build our lives on, we will find that reality, and maybe gravity, will cause us great pain. Potential never trumps gravity; gravity always wins. If you want to test that reality, pain awaits you.

What I do know personally is that I was never built to run particularly fast. An Olympic coach might have helped me run a little faster, but I could never beat someone who was physically talented at running fast. I know that I have the ability to hit a cricket ball or golf ball a far distance. I have won competitions through the years for doing just that. I have the Evidence. I won a long-drive (golf) competition and was awarded a case of rum. I don't drink, but my friends who consumed the winnings are witnesses to the feat.

There are some things you have and others you don't. No one, including you, can add what God didn't see fit to include in your DNA! That is just a reality. Some people have Talents that others don't. There is great freedom in understanding and celebrating that.

If you keep looking and hoping for Evidence that does not exist, you have a long road of missed opportunity and dreams to follow. What is not, is not. Focus on what is. You will never be disappointed!

I got into a little trouble at a school where I taught LSI. I had told the kids that they could not be anything they set their minds to become and that they could not do anything they wanted by simply believing that they could. One of the kids told his parents, and the parents called the principal, and the principal asked to speak to me. She asked me what I had said, and I told her. She agreed but asked me to think about a better way to explain what I was telling these high-school students so that I did not discourage them or take away any motivation that might push them to explore.

So I did think more carefully about how I needed to explain what I believed about potential. The next week I was able to give a far better explanation as to what I believed about potential to a group of fifteen- and sixteen-year-olds. You may be fifty, not fifteen, yet understanding these factors is just as important for you.

Important Forensic Factors in Discovering Potential

Discovering Evidence of your Unique Design is dependent on some of the following factors:

1. **Age**—Life is growth, yet certain things in terms of your Talents are seen at a young age. A host of research tells us that certain personality traits, Passions, and interests can be seen by the age of three and don't change much at all throughout our lives. The same ones are still part of adults when followed up twenty years later.

    Another aspect to age is that certain Talents are not seen early on. They are there in a dormant state and can only be discovered as other Talents are developed. Each stage must be mastered before the next stage can be attempted and lived. The obvious example in the early stages of Life is simply that a baby first has to sit before crawling, crawl before standing, stand before walking, and walk before running. This applies to other maturational parts (Fields of Evidence) of who we are, such as social, emotional, intellectual, and spiritual. We move through different stages as a natural progression of Life.

    One of the fundamental tasks of parenting is to watch your children and look for clues about their Talents, most of which are obvious. I believe your greatest responsibility is to study your children and look for Evidence of their Talents. Don't wait until they are teens. Start young because that is where you will see them. We are advised to *train up children in the way they should go or in accordance with their unique Talents* if we want them to be successful. That means we work with the grain and groove that is already who they are.

2. **Talents not yet tested or pushed**—It is often said that the best of who we are is not discovered until it is pushed or squeezed out of us. Pressure allows for the expression of latent Talents. I remember being part of an officer selection course when I was in the military. One of the first parts of the selection was to give an extemporaneous speech for ten minutes to the other members of the course and the officers who were running the course. I was always one of the funny guys in class, but if there was a serious issue, such as history or math, I was on mute. So I was given a topic, which I still remember to this day: "*Uhuru* in Africa" (Freedom in Africa). We were given a couple of minutes to prep and gather our thoughts, and I stood up and waxed eloquent. I did well. I loved it, and it was in a serious arena.

I have been a cricket coach for many years and love the coaching process. One of the aspects I love about it is that I get to help people discover natural abilities they never thought they had. As a coach, I have an ability to see athletic Talents. When I instruct a player to try something new and it works better than I ever envisioned, what a blast it is to watch the player come alive! Some say, "I never even thought I could do that," and others state, "I always knew I could—I was never shown how or given the opportunity." I have also watched players who do okay at a lower level of competition, but when they have the opportunity to play at a much higher level, they come alive. When they are only somewhat challenged, they perform, but when they are under pressure, they excel. Pressure often creates the opportunity to bring out the best of who we are and reveal our true potential.

MYLIFESCENE.COM—CROSS NOW—MYLIFESCENE.COM
Life Scene—Vijay

I have known Vijay for about ten years. I met Vijay when he joined a cricket team I was playing on and we became good friends. Vijay was a very talented athlete and had played a number of competitive sports at the college and club levels.

I was the coach of the NorthWest Cricket League regional team. About five years ago, Vijay was chosen not only to represent our NorthWest Cricket League regional team but also to captain it. I knew Vijay would do well because he had talent, was exceptionally fit, practiced hard, and was also an exceptional leader, both on the team and at Microsoft, where he worked.

What I saw in Vijay was a huge leap in Performance. He was a very good player in our local league, but when he had the opportunity to play at a significantly higher level of competition, the real Vijay emerged. He singlehandedly won matches in the toughest of circumstances. He led the team to beat leagues that were never supposed to lose to ours.

The result was that Vijay was selected to represent the U.S. Northwest regional team and also captain them. Again he showed the real athlete he is when his real physical Talents were demanded. There was really no other way for his Talent to be revealed other than for it to be tested at a high level.

One of the ideas I talk about in the chapters on Reliability Testing is that of "flow." When Vijay brings his **High Skill** to meet a **High Challenge**, he excels, and the very best of who he is is brought to the stage.

I have seen students who are bored in school and are marginal students because they are not challenged. When they get to college they become honor students and go on to get their doctorates. There are leaders who have never had the challenge to lead in the face of overwhelming odds, but when they do, they make history. Their social Talents come to the fore when pressure forces them out.

So what about you? Has this been your experience? Did you discover something exceptional and continue to use that Unique Talent as an integral part of your Life? Maybe you need to push your child or someone you manage to possibly discover something by challenging them to do to more than they believe or have shown they are capable of. Imagine what they might discover!

MYLIFESCENE.COM—CROSS NOW—MYLIFESCENE.COM

3. **Not exposed to, so not attempted**—There are some things we have not been exposed to, and so the thought that we are really good at them never enters our minds. We probably have a sense of this force within that is seeking expression, but it remains undefined. I came alive intellectually in college when I found out about psychology, theology, philosophy, political science, and other subjects I had never been taught in high school.

4. **Not given or taken the opportunity**—Grandma Moses, the famous American artist, spent most of her Life raising her children and then her grandchildren. Life was busy and left her little time for anything beyond parenting and caring for children. She had suffered from arthritis as well. In her seventies she started drawing and painting. She never lacked the Unique Design or Talents, she just never had the opportunity or time to sit down and put her way of seeing Life on canvas. When we are too busy, like Grandma Moses, to even stop long enough to think, look for Evidence, and analyze our lives, we will break down eventually. We have some success. We are paying the bills, running fast, and enjoying friends, and Life is somewhat good, but not great. When we stop long enough to think, we feel unsettled and need to get moving again because it doesn't feel good to have time to think and evaluate our unlived Design.

There are daily consequences, consequences that steal the best from Life and that make us ineffective and result in our never living up to our potential.

> *If we did all the things we were capable of doing, we would literally astound ourselves.*
> —Thomas Edison

Evidence Lost or Diminished

There are times in Life where it may seem, and rightly so, that potential is lost and gone forever. Life changes, and as we age, our Talents change with us. Some are enhanced, grown, and matured. Intellect and social Talents should become great markers of old age. Others, such as athletic ability and physical strength, change and diminish with time. In many ways, our late twenties and early thirties are the peak of our physical Talent. That is not the case with all physical Talents, such as musical, artistic, surgical, or other capacities, but generally it holds true.

Life also presents situations where it might seem Talents are gone or hidden due to disease or physical damage. When Evidence is contaminated by drugs, emotional and intellectual Talents can be harmed without the potential for recovery. Life also delivers accidents that disable and take away Design Talents that can never be replaced, such as those I talked about with the soldiers at Tsanga Lodge.

What often happens when we lose one Design Talent is that another is found or others seem to grow. A benevolent compensation occurs.

MYLIFESCENE.COM—CROSS NOW—MYLIFESCENE.COM
Life Scene—My Dad and Double J

My father, André, was a great example of a coach. He was always helping discover and develop talent. He never missed a game I played. He was at many of my practice sessions with a coach he hired for me, picking up balls and doing whatever he could to help me succeed.

My father was a very bright man and a great salesman. He had been a very talented sportsman, and people talked about his physique being like a Greek god's. His rugby career was cut short by a major injury in his mid-twenties. He was also a very good-looking man, a man who looked like a movie star. He had everything that any man would measure as being a symbol of success. He was also a big softie, and his heart was open to every down-and-out on the planet.

On his way to the construction company he owned, he regularly saw a beggar who had lost both his legs and most of the fingers on one of his hands after being robbed and pushed under a moving train. My father stopped to talk to the man, who was called "Double J." The man was dirty, reeked of alcohol, and moved around on his metal stumps and crutches. Double J told my father that before his accident he was a diesel mechanic. My father was not convinced but got him in his truck, and off they went.

My dad had a number of larger diesel trucks, and in no time at all Double J proved what a great mechanic he really was. Beyond being a great mechanic, his disability became an advantage to him. It enabled him to climb under and into the truck engines and do what few other mechanics were able to do.

My dad took a chance, as he often did, and it paid off big for both him and Double J. He saw more in this beggar than others ever did. My dad just had a knack for that sort of stuff.

One small caveat to the story that is also worth mentioning: One Sunday afternoon my father got a call from the local police. They asked whether Double J worked for my father and whether he had permission to be driving a Willy's jeep that my father owned. Double J had wanted to impress a young lady and had "borrowed" the jeep for an outing with her. When the police saw him driving it, they became a little suspicious. There were no side doors on the jeep, and using crutches to shift gears was problematic.

Double J continued in my father's employ for many more years as a valuable member of the company.

Have you had a major change in a Design Talent? Do you know someone who may need your opening a door to give them a chance at displaying something you might never guess they are uniquely able to do?

Do you see Talents where others don't? Do you go to bat for people whom you just believe have what it takes and do what you can to find opportunities for them? Do you look beyond the obvious?

MYLIFESCENE.COM—CROSS NOW—MYLIFESCENE.COM

Cold Case Evidence

Cold Case Evidence Defined

Cold case refers to a crime or accident that has not yet been solved. A cold case is not the focus of an open criminal investigation. It is a case for which new information could emerge from new witnesses or testimony, Evidence that is reexamined, and retained material Evidence. New scientific and technical methods developed after the case was active can be used on the Evidence that has been stored to reanalyze the causes, often with definitive results.

In most police departments they have a room where *cold case* files are stored. These are cases that were not solved for a variety of reasons. Many of these cases date back to the time when DNA and other more recent forensic tests and identification techniques were not available. Almost 30 percent of homicides were not solved prior to DNA testing being available.

I see cases almost every day on TV and in the news of criminals who have now been caught. They are arrested for major crimes, such as rape and murder, that were committed twenty to fifty years ago.

In August 2009, I read in the news about a Kentucky man who kidnapped and killed a young couple in Wisconsin in 1980. They had his DNA, and that Evidence, though almost three decades old, matched Evidence at the revisited crime scene.

I recently read that the Detroit Police Department is going to examine Evidence from more than a thousand cold-case rapes. I wonder how many criminals are having sleepless nights with the possibility of now being brought to justice.

Many women, and some men, quit following a career, profession, or other defined Purpose for many years to manage a home and have and raise children. They were often productive and influential before their detour and now find that after the kids are gone, they can no longer rely on the support of another person; Life demands that they reengage and discover or rediscover their Evidence.

Before they took on this role at home, they ran businesses, were teachers, sold real estate, finished a degree, and so on. Then came marriage and family. Sometimes another responsibility, such as an elderly parent, a transfer to another state or country, a sickness, or some other situation, didn't allow them to continue engaging Life based on Talents and direction known at that time.

When Life changed again, and the opportunity or the demand for income then presented itself, the question was, *"What do I do now?"*

I believe the best answer is to go back and pull out those cold case files that are filled with great Evidence of who you were ten, fifteen, twenty-five years ago and still are today. The Evidence is still good. The Talents you possessed then are the same ones you have today.

MYLIFESCENE.COM—CROSS NOW—MYLIFESCENE.COM
Life Scene—Maren

Maren had gone through a divorce about three years ago. Her daughters were in college, and she had moved into a small house by herself. She had also recently been through a very traumatic experience where she had taken time to help a dying brother settle his business affairs. She was now looking at Life as a fifty-year-old woman essentially alone. Maren was a very attractive, articulate, and energetic woman looking at how to restart a Life and navigate a new future.

Maren has always been a go-getter. She worked from a young age because she loved it. She was involved in fashion, helping her father entertain clients and assisting her mother in a printing business. After high school, Maren graduated from college with a degree in advertising and marketing and then started a successful career as a marketing director. She then got married and for twenty years focused on her family.

Maren now had to start again, so she pulled out the files marked *"Cold Case Maren."* She reread the files, which had all the Evidence she needed to open a new case for a Life of Purpose, Passion, and Performance. She didn't have to start with a blank sheet or without any direction because all the Evidence was already there in those cold case files.

Maren went back to school to build on what she had been successful at earlier in her Life. She completed a graduate certification in marketing management at the University of Washington and then continued with certification as a personal brand strategist. She recently began to build her new business in the midst of a tough recession. Maren stays focused, is Passionate, and knows where she is going because she knows she is today what she was successful at many years ago. She now brings many years of wisdom and experience to those Talents.

So what about you? Are you starting again? Are you asking what you are going to do now because you have to, or because you now have the time to begin a new phase in your Life? Maybe you have an overriding need to find Meaning and Purpose in your Life. You feel a deep sense of doing something significant in this new and possibly final era in your Life. That does not mean what you have done in the past was not significant, only that you are at a new place and the road is open.

This is the time to pull out those cold case files and see what they contain. A history of success and what you were good at is always the best place to start. It tells you that you have already demonstrated Talents, which never really leave. They may need to be dusted off and retooled, just as Maren did in going back to college.

Time to start again? It may seem daunting, but how exciting! Go pull out those cold case files!

MYLIFESCENE.COM—CROSS NOW—MYLIFESCENE.COM

In the *CSI* episode "If I Had a Hammer," the story involved Catherine's first solo case as a CSI fifteen years prior. The convicted murderer from that case was filing an appeal. The Evidence on which he had been convicted was no longer sufficient to convict him if he was granted a new trial. More Evidence was found because Catherine had no option but to find it.

When she went back to look at the old crime scene, she found the one piece of Evidence that had been missing from the original case, a hammer. The hammer was lodged in a tree, and she was able to use the blood and DNA Evidence from the hammer to ensure the murderer stayed where he was, convicted and in jail. Take the time to go back and reexamine the Evidence. You might just find Evidence to open the door to an exciting new future!

When you read the chapter "The Forensic Evidence Timeline" you will be able to use some of the ideas to refresh your memory and rethink all the incredible Evidence from a different stage in your Life. You will also have collected and processed a great deal of Evidence that you can now use to chart a new direction in your Life. This direction will be based on all the Evidence, cold case plus all that you have collected in the LSI Forensic Process.

What I do know is this: when we don't discover and develop the Talents we have, we never reach the potential we do possess. That is a tragedy, the *greatest crime in human history.*

There are two slogans or company mottoes I love. The first is Microsoft's: "Your Potential. Our Passion." Doesn't that just say it all? That is a slogan LSI could live by and really is what we are all about. Microsoft uses software to help you discover; and LSI uses forensics.

The other slogan I love comes from the U.S. Army: "Be All You Can Be," which is possible by joining the U.S. Army, according to the ad campaign. What a great recruiting line! Again, the same is what I believe LSI is all about. We use forensics to help you discover the Evidence so that you can become "All You Can Be." That is my greatest hope—that you will discover all the potential you possess and become *all* you were created to become.

The reality is simple but profound. Our greatest potential for growth exists in the development of our natural Talents and Gifts. We cannot be all we want, hope, envision, dream, or affirm, but we *can* be more of who we are!

Be all you can be, and turn your potential into your Passion!

Chapter 7
The LSI Forensic Formula:
Purpose, Passion and Performance

The purpose of life is a life of purpose.
—Robert Byrne

Life Scene Investigation is easily understood if you understand the LSI formula. It is not complicated. I taught a class three years ago to some ninth-graders. One of those ninth-graders recently became a friend on Facebook and he was so proud because he remembered the LSI formula. I have those who go through the classes and seminars learn this formula by heart. I make them repeat it at the start of every class. I break the class into groups, and we do rounds as each group starts at a different time. I know you can remember it because you are just as bright as that ninth-grader.

The LSI formula is more than a simple formula. It is a philosophy a, belief system and a way of looking at Life.

People define this place in many ways: *Life purpose, my Passion, sweet spot, calling, Life mission, God's will,* and more. It is often talked about but I believe badly defined. I hope as you read this chapter you will gain a far clearer definition of what you seek and what LSI will deliver to you in your quest to answer the question *?RU.*

Happiness, or another word, *Passion,* is what we all want. Many would substitute the word *Passion* for *happiness;* they could be used interchangeably. People talk about finding their *Passion* or state of happiness either in career, geography, relationship, or experience in Life. *Passion* is a state of positive emotion. We want to feel alive, in control, connected, that what we are doing is not just worthwhile but delivers a feeling we call *Passion!* To be Passionate is to be alive and filled with positive emotion!

One of the great tragedies of Life is the distinct lack of *Passion* displayed in so many. Those who seek Passion with cheap, destructive, and very temporary imitations see the great tragedy in the substitutions.

The formula is simple. The better or stronger we are at doing, the greater the feelings we experience. Do those things that demonstrate your Talents. If you want to enjoy the feeling of self-esteem, demonstrate your best and strongest abilities. Talents lived create positive emotions.

Life Scene Investigation is the path you have chosen to investigate. You have made a choice to read *The DNA Code: The Forensics of Purpose, Passion and Performance.* You are taking the time to discover a process that will deliver what those ninth-graders, and probably you, desperately seek. You should desire and demand nothing less!

The LSI Forensic Formula

*Design Determines **Purpose** . . .*
*Purpose Creates **Passion** . . .*
*Passion Fuels **Performance***

Design Determines Purpose

Design—My DNA Code

a. Design is defined as the unique combinations of all my capacities. My DNA is a blueprint of my Design.

b. Design, in my belief system, means there is a Designer. I personally believe that God made me and Designed me for a special plan He has for me. For me, the question, *?RU*, is simply answered, "I am created and Designed by an all-knowing, all-powerful and all-present God."

c. Design is the unique composite or combination of my Five Fields of Evidence, which are distinct and interconnected:

1. Physical Talents
2. Intellectual Talents
3. Social Talents
4. Emotional Talents
5. Spiritual/motivation Talents

Determines

a. The maximum potential allowed by my Design
b. The unique function of my Design
c. I can only live what my Design allows
d. I cannot live outside the boundaries of my Design
e. What I can do and where I can go with my Life is guided by my Design

Purpose

a. Why I am here!
b. The *optimal* and best function of my Design
c. The *intended* function of my Design
d. The *road map* that is defined or prescribed by the Talents in my Design
e. My *reason* for living as defined by my Designer or DNA
f. That internal sense which makes Life make sense and gives it cohesion

Purpose Creates Passion

Creates

a. Results in, by its very nature, when I live my Design
b. Generated by its very nature
c. When used, Purpose produces positive emotion

Passion

a. Passion is positive emotion
   1. Thankfulness
   2. Satisfaction
   3. Joy
   4. Peace
   5. Exhilaration
   6. Alive
   7. Spiritually complete
   8. Strong
   9. In the zone or *flow*

b. Passion is the sense of internal cohesion
c. Passion is feeling complete
d. It is the feeling of doing what I was made to do
e. I am living the "pleasure of God"

The award-winning movie *Chariots of Fire* tells the dramatic story of Eric Liddell's rise to prominence as a sprinter in Great Britain, culminating in victory in the 1924 Olympics in Paris. He won the gold medal in the four-hundred-meter dash and a bronze in the two hundred. His sister worried that athletics would rob him of his fervor for God. But Liddell told her that he believed God had made him to run and that when he ran he felt God's pleasure and affirmation that he was performing the very thing God Designed him for.

Passion Fuels Performance

Fuels

a. We want to repeat what we love and are Passionate about
b. The energy of Passion makes us want to enjoy the positive emotions over and over again
c. We have a full tank of high-octane that drives us to excel
d. We attempt more because we know we have the energy and ability

Performance

a. Perform better
b. Fewer down days
c. Fewer sick days
d. Produce better and more
e. Quality and quantity improve
f. Morale is high

It is so logical to understand this concept. When we do what we enjoy or love, we want to do more of it. We do it well. We want to find ways to improve it.

Life Scene—Mark Fallis

The third part of the LSI Forensic Formula, "Passion Fuels Performance," was created by Mark. Mark is very creative and is always looking for new ways or angles to understand or explain something. He is a musician, marketer, father, husband, and engineer. This continuation of the original two parts of the LSI formula flows so perfectly and is the product of a man who has a unique Talent to see and articulate new ideas.

Famous Forensic Story

I have to tell you a story. It is a great story. This is my favorite parable about discovering the most important information in Life. I am going to apply the LSI Forensic Formula to the Animal Story.

What does a story about some animals that want to open a school have to do with forensics? Everything! It tells us about what happens when people don't focus on the right Evidence. There are daily consequences, consequences that steal the best from Life and make us ineffective and that result in our never living up to our potential.

You will see how important it is for your family, your children, your choice of career, your business. It applies to everything you choose in Life.

The Animal Story

Once upon a time, the animals decided they must do something heroic to meet the problems of a "new world," so they organized a school.

They adopted an activity curriculum consisting of running, climbing, swimming, and flying. To make it easier to administer the curriculum, *all* the animals took *all* subjects.

The duck was excellent in swimming—in fact, better than his instructor; but he made only passing grades in flying and was very poor in running. Since he was slow in running, he had to stay after school and also drop swimming in order to practice running. This was kept up until his web feet were badly worn, so then he was only average in swimming. But average was acceptable in school, so nobody worried about it except the duck.

The rabbit started at the top of the class in running, but he had a nervous breakdown because of so much makeup work in swimming.

The squirrel was excellent in climbing until he developed frustration in the flying class, where his teacher made him start from the ground up instead of the treetop down. He also developed "charley horses" from overexertion and then got a "C" in climbing and a "D" in running.

The eagle was a problem child and was disciplined severely. In the climbing class he beat all others to the top of the tree but insisted on using his own way to get there.

At the end of the year, an abnormal eel that could swim exceedingly well and also could run, climb, and fly a little had the highest average and was named valedictorian.

The prairie dogs stayed out of school and fought the tax levy because the administration would not add digging and burrowing to the curriculum. They apprenticed their child to a badger and later joined the groundhogs and the gophers in order to start a successful private school.

Source: Attributed to George Reavis.

The approach taken by the vast majority of corporations, parents, and educational institutions is the same as these well-intentioned animals. The results are most often negative, the opposite of what was intended. If the person does not have the requisite talent, there will never be a positive outcome. Continued effort in the wrong direction will only grind individuals down to a place of ineffectiveness and misery!

The results in Life are the same as well. Life feels like a "grind," devoid of Purpose, Passion, or Performance. It is cutting against the grain. Running against the wind. Swimming against the current.

Forensic Definition—*Prima Facie* Evidence

Latin for "on its face." A *prima facie* case is one that at first glance presents sufficient Evidence for the plaintiff to win. It means "what is plainly evident and obvious."

It is time to apply the Animal Story to the LSI Forensic Formula, and you will see why I love it.

Design (DNA Code) Determines Purpose

What is the most obvious or *prima facie* about the Design of:

a. Duck?—wings, webbed feet, flat beak, bulky
b. Squirrel?—short legs, tail, claws
c. Eagle?—huge wings, talons, sleek, sharp beak
d. Rabbit?—strong legs, big paws, big ears

Design determines that:

e. Duck—flies slowly, swims and dives, eats plants and small insects (swims like a duck).
f. Squirrel—climbs, jumps, and runs fast (climbs like a squirrel).
g. Eagle—flies high and fast, attacks and kills prey with claws and beak (soars like an eagle).
h. Rabbit—runs fast as well and jumps (run, rabbit, run).

Purpose Creates Passion

Forensic Definition—Stipulate

Stipulate is a legal term that means the prosecution and the defense both agree on a stated fact in Evidence. They don't need a jury to evaluate or interpret the Evidence because it is obvious and accepted by all involved. It goes without saying.

It is *stipulated* that:

- Ducks . . . *SWIM.*
- Eagles . . . *FLY.*
- Squirrels . . . *CLIMB.*
- Rabbits . . . *RUN.*

Now I want you to try and picture these four animals differently. I want you to ask yourself a simple question: "How happy or Passionate would the animal feel if it were to perform the action I describe below?" Close your eyes and imagine the particular animal doing what I ask you to imagine it doing:

1. He ran like a duck.
2. She swam like a squirrel.
3. He flew like a rabbit.
4. She climbed like an eagle.

Immediately there is a sense of "That's not right!" "That doesn't make sense!" "That is just not natural!" "How stupid!" That is the point!

The Animal Story tells us what happened when the animals focused on being what they didn't have the Unique Design Talents to do. How much Passion does a:

- Duck with sore feet have?
  - o Do you have "sore feet?"
- Rabbit experiencing a nervous breakdown have?
  - o Are you on the verge of a breakdown?
- Squirrel with "charley horses" and bad grades have?
  - o Where do you get "charley horses?"
- Severely disciplined and frustrated eagle have?
  - o Do you often get disciplined or written up because you are frustrated and know you are being underutilized?

So what Talents are "stipulated" in your Life? What is "*prima facie*" to your DNA Code? What is so obvious to everyone who knows you? Can you name three Talents to get you focused and started on applying the *LSI Forensic Formula* (I am a duck and I swim! I am an eagle and I soar!)?

_____

_____

_____

Passion Fuels Performance

There is *none*—there is *no* Passion to fuel unnatural, non-Design attempts at excellent Performance! Sustained and excellent Performance cannot be experienced when you don't possess the Talents to do so. That is a stipulated fact!

What If the Evidence Just Isn't There?

An important question needs to be addressed: *What do I do when I am required to do something I don't have a Unique Design Talent to do (work, team, school, Life)?*

I need to start with a correct definition of what a *"weakness"* is.

Forensic Definition—Weakness

A weakness is anything I am not uniquely endowed with a Talent to perform.

A *weakness* is a Common Design component that does not have the potential to become anything more than average.

I am not "weak." I am simply not enabled, Designed, or endowed by my Creator to perform certain tasks.

A state of weakness is the result of not knowing, using, and giving my Talents to experience Purpose, Passion, and Performance.

Weakness is what I am when I do not build character alongside the discovery of and use of my Talents.

Weakness is the attempt to be something I don't have the Talent to perform.

If I am required to participate or perform as a part of my job, a school curriculum:

1. I ask for help. If I am not good at math and need it to graduate, I get a tutor and seek to get a passing grade. The same goes if I am not a good manager or not competent at accounting. I ask for help to do what I need to get done.

What are you not good at and know you will always need help at?

_____

2. I partner with someone who has a Talent in the area I am responsible for. (One of the invaluable parts of the *StrengthsFinder 2.0* Report is a section that helps you identify not only people you should partner with to help you maximize your Talents, but also people who will complement your weaknesses by using their Talents.)

Identify someone you know who has a Talent in your area of weakness.

_____

3. I advise the person who requires me to do an excellent job that I am not the best person for the success of the project. That allows for someone who has the required Talent to step in, experience success, and demonstrate high Performance. That is how great teamwork is experienced.

Who do I need to speak to advise them of the need to change from my current position of weakness?

_____

4. I need to make a commitment to my Design and make a decision to change where I am and what I am currently doing.
5. I change as Life changes. Great players can become coaches. Students become teachers and tutors.

MYLIFESCENE.COM—CROSS NOW—MYLIFESCENE.COM
Life Scene—Sam Acho the Exceptional

I have friends whom I have known since my college days. Dr. Sonny and Christie Acho have four children. Our firstborns attended class together *in utero* in a Lamaze childbirth class back in 1983.

One of their sons is Sam Acho, and he is exceptional! Sam is one of the few people I know who excels at running, flying, climbing, *and* swimming.

Sam is an exceptional physical athlete. He is currently in his second year as an NFL linebacker and plays for the Arizona Cardinals. He played for the University of Texas for four years before that.

Sam is an academic. In 2011, Sam won the "Academic Heisman," or the William V. Campbell Trophy for outstanding college athletes. He uses the intellect God gave him.

Sam is socially warm and funny, and he connects to so many people with ease. I have seen him working in the youth department of his father's church, Living Hope Bible Fellowship Church. Kids flock to him and his brother Emmanuel, another standout college football player. Socially he connects and gives of his time to make a difference.

In the summers, Sam goes to Nigeria to work with a medical ministry his parents run. The ministry, www.livinghopeministries.us, works with thousands of people, and Sam is there, giving of his time and working with the less fortunate. He recruits other NFL players to go along with him as well. His motivation is his faith, and he lives it.

Everything Sam does is at a high level of Performance. He is not just well rounded; he excels in everything he does. There are not many Sams around, and I don't suggest you try and be a Sam, unless, of course, you are.

MYLIFESCENE.COM—CROSS NOW—MYLIFESCENE.COM

Jenifer Fox is a leader in the quest to help people, parents, and specifically children discover their Talents. She wrote a great book, *Your Child's Strengths*. It is a must-read for anyone and everyone who has or works with children.

I was at Jenifer's website recently, www.strengthsmovement.com, and read what it said about the challenge of applying the lessons from the Animal Story to our "New World." I cannot think of a better way to finish this chapter than for you to read and think through what was said:

> *The world lies on the cusp of great global change, and in order to remain competitive, future generations of Americans will have to be more adaptable and inventive than ever. We can't rest on the assumption that we will come out on top. Today, the United States ranks nineteenth in the world in education. Forty years ago, it ranked number one. A country's economic system cannot sustain this kind of gradual decline, especially when technological progress is accelerating and most jobs of the future will require knowledge skills over labor skills. Many people, from economists to CEOs to professors, have accurately described globalism and all its challenges and opportunities, but there has been little exchange*

between the people responsible for educating the future workforce and those who fear there will be too few skilled people to fill the demanding jobs of the future. The future will need us to bring our strengths not our weaknesses.

—Jenifer Fox, *Strengths Movement,* http://www.strengthsmovement.com/ht/d/sp/i/176/pid/176)

Chapter 8
Evidence of Motive

How to gain, how to keep, how to recover happiness
is in fact for most men at all times the secret motive
of all they do, and of all they are willing to endure.
—William James

One of the issues that is fundamental to answering the question of why we behave in certain ways and what makes us do what we do is *motive!* Motive is the *why* behind the action.

What is the motive? Investigators and prosecutors are always trying to establish motive. They know that if they can show a reasonable explanation why a crime was committed, what the moving force to commit the crime was, it is always much easier to get a conviction.

> *The motivations of a man's heart are like deep*
> *waters, but a man of understanding can draw them*
> *out.*
> —Proverbs 20:5

When a motive cannot be clearly established, the chances of conviction often hang in the balance. Unless a defendant is mentally deranged or mentally incompetent, which becomes an explanation for a crime, motive needs to be established in order for jurors to be convinced of a defendant's guilt.

We are not animals who act purely out of instinct. The lion that kills an antelope does so because that is what a lion does. We don't need to think of any motivation other than the lion was hungry. The lion kills without feeling of remorse or guilt. He does so to eat.

When a human kills, we ask why. Was he attacked? Did he kill in self-defense? For instance, while walking down a dark street late at night, a man was attacked; he fought back, managed to grab the assailant's gun, and shot him. The assailant was a known criminal with a lengthy record of assault and battery. The motive? Self-protection.

> It's motive alone, which gives character to the actions
> of men.
> —Jean de la Bruyere

When a wife takes out a million-dollar Life insurance policy a month before her husband "accidentally" dies, we might think she was part of engineering the "accident." Her motive was probably money. Her motive also might be revenge because she found out he was having an affair and felt justified in killing him and being rewarded for her many years of being a good wife.

Motive is just as important in LSI. Motive, or motivation, is founded in what we value and believe.

Motive Matrix

Motive—anything that causes a person to act, be it a need or a desire.

Possible Motives

Money—I want to be able to buy anything I want
Fame—I want lots of people to know and adore me
Status—I want people to look up to me and think I am someone
Acceptance—I want people to love me
Control—I want to control people and things
Power—I want to have power over people
Pleasure—I want to feel good
Altruism—I want to help and give to others
Revenge—I want to repay people for hurting me
Hate—I want to harm others
Achievement—I want to make it big and succeed
Service—I want to do things for others
Love and serve God—I want to please God

What is the bottom line for you? What is your reason for discovering your DNA Code? Do you have one? Can you state what it is? Let me ask it more forcefully: what is your overriding, all-encompassing reason or motivation for living and discovering who and what you are?

- Serve humanity
- Make all the money I can
- Change the world
- Find a cure for AIDS
- Be a great parent
- Become a great teacher
- Become a professional gamer
- Provide for my family
- Influence history
- Some other noble pursuit; you name it:

_____

What is your reason for living, your *raison d'être*? One of the most hopeless and spiritually deficient characters in history was philosopher Friedrich Nietzsche. What Nietzsche did not know personally, a sense of Purpose or motivation, he was able to observe in others. This observation about people and the way they lived was simple, but so profound. He concluded that people who had hope and lives that demonstrated a sense of Purpose were able to face Life with a sense of great resiliency. Nietzsche stated,

He who has a why to live can bear almost any how.

What if you lived your Life based on the Purpose you decided was right for you? You then accomplished what you set out to do. What if you were able to accumulate everything you thought was enough or even more for living the Life you envisioned based on your currently established motives? What then?

Do your motives leave you unsettled? Do you have a relative certainty that the Purposes for which you live are lasting in terms of value and personal legacy? Do you feel that there is an authenticity about what you have done or what you are currently doing to achieve your goals?

I have known people whose motive is seeking revenge for bad things done to them who end up feeling empty and desolate. They win lawsuits but end up feeling let down and experiencing deep despair. Others make millions of dollars and discover that the emptiness they had with an overdrawn bank account is no less than what they experience in their current affluent state. People give their lives in service to the needy and feel cheated and alone because what they did was not always returned when they were in need.

So what if you got what you wanted, motivated by your *raison d'être*? What then? Maybe you are already there and you have reached the goal you set out to achieve. Did it deliver, or are you still left wanting?

King Solomon was reputed to be the wealthiest man of his time and one of the wisest men in history. He was a man who had every material, sensual, and sexual desire fulfilled at his command but concluded his life with these words:

> *Vanity of vanities, all is vanity.*
> *It is like grasping at a cloud/steam.*
> *All is empty.*

- So *?RU* or who will you be when you get to the end of the road guided by the motives you now hold?
- Do you ever question your motives?
- Does it make you feel uneasy when others question your motives and ask you why you do what you do?

The overriding motive in discovery should be to know and use your DNA Code. The motive for discovering your DNA Code should be to develop and use it to affect and serve the world you live in. You should do that in business, teaching, fixing cars, working with kids, developing code for computer programs, selling houses, caring for orphans, styling hair, raising kids, or whatever you do.

MYLIFESCENE.COM—CROSS NOW—MYLIFESCENE.COM
Life Scene—Joel, Ali and Family

My son Adam married Abigail in 2008. Abi's parents are a wonderful and very bright couple. They have graduate degrees, his in economics and hers in education, both from very good universities. Many years ago they decided to leave the comfort and quiet of Minnesota and go to Southeast Asia. They have been there for many years.

Joel and Ali work with people who lack what so many others in the world have: food, clothing, education, protection, money to start businesses, basic health care, and much more. They love people, and they have given themselves to educating, healing, encouraging, and building others.

They do what they do because they believe it is God's will for them. They are motivated to be God's hands to those in need of: education to fill their minds, medicine to cure the most basic but potentially fatal diseases, rescue from prostitution and despair.

I met many of Abi's family members at the wedding. What was so incredible was that most of the family is involved in nonprofit work overseas in Southeast Asia. They are spread across a number of countries. There is no fanfare, no looking for any accolades, just a determined and humble love of service.

They could be back in the United States making good money and enjoying the American Dream. Instead they spend their time separated from their family in adverse conditions. Their son Josiah and daughter Abi are also very involved, just like their parents.

Their motivation? They love God.

What are your motives? Are your motives dictated by your needs and selfish desires? How pure are your motives, or could they be challenged when Life gets tough and you abandon them with ease? What do others see, or what would they say your overriding motive is for living?

MYLIFESCENE.COM—CROSS NOW—MYLIFESCENE.COM

Why do you do what you do? Why do you work? Why do you love family and friends? Why would you give money to someone or something (a cause)?

> *He is no fool who gives up what he cannot gain for what he cannot lose.*
> —Jim Elliot

If I alone am the only reason for my existence, I create my own motives and define my own morality. If God is, then I must know who God is and answer the question "What did He make me for?" If God is the creator and He created me, He must have a Purpose; that would be a reasonable assumption in my way of thinking.

The most pointed and powerful forensic question ever asked, when seeking Evidence of personal identity and motive, was asked by Jesus Christ. He asked His disciples a simple question to see whether people understood who He was and why He was doing what He did. Apply that same question to your Life:

> ### Who do men say that I am?
> ### —Matthew 16:13

When others look at your Life and see what you do, are you willing to have your Life and motivation subject to forensic evaluation? How willing would you be to put that question out in the public forum to be answered by all who know and observe you each day?

In your business contacts, *PRU* and who do people say you are? In your Facebook or LinkedIn profile, who do you say you are?

Nobel laureate Alexander Solzhenitsyn was able to demonstrate his Purpose in the face of distorted and contaminated motive. In writing about his imprisonment in the Soviet gulag, he saw how that system used power. His assessment was that power was a poison if it was not combined with a belief in a higher power or faith to which we are ultimately accountable. He believed that power would ultimately destroy those who used it as if they were accountable to none but themselves.

His was the testimony of a resilient human spirit who remained unshakable in his conviction of a greater meaning, evidenced as he fought to survive physically and spiritually in the Soviet penal system of soul-crushing hardship and injustice. Solzhenitsyn's unquenchable attachment to his belief in God empowered him to endure eight years in Stalin's labor camps and then three years of exile in Kazakhstan. A vital spirit with resolute strength of soul, he believed outer freedom and inner worth nurtured each other in a relationship of miraculous beauty and intimacy.

There is a God-Shaped vacuum in the heart of every man which cannot be filled by any created thing, but only by God, the Creator, made known through Jesus.
—Blaise Pascal, French mathematician, philosopher, and physicist, 1623–1662

MYLIFESCENE.COM—CROSS NOW—MYLIFESCENE.COM
Life Scene—Carrie Raymond

Synaptyk is a vibrant and very successful company in Dallas and is owned by Jett and Carrie Raymond. Carrie is the CEO of Synaptyk.

Synaptyk recently hired Corp-DNA (www.corp-dna.com) to work on developing their leadership team as they prepared for a significant growth. We went in and began doing a *Positive Forensic DNA Profile* of the company and of each member of the executive team. They all went through a series of profile tests, including the Gallup *StrengthsFinder Leadership Profile*, *VIA Character Strengths Profile*, *The Zone Q-10*™, intensive interviews, and 360 Witness evaluations.

The purpose of this analysis was to discover what Synaptyk's success DNA was made of. We wanted to know what the DNA Markers of their success were. We do this with each of our business clients because we believe that if you want a blueprint for greater growth and success, you identify Evidence of what works, is strong, and is successful. Future success is created by building on strength, Talents, high-performing processes, Analysis of Asset, and those characteristics that have resulted in the business's current level of success.

What we found out was that Synaptyk was successful for many reasons. Most of the executive team had long friendships going back almost fifteen years. They had a work ethic that was founded in their West Texas roots that made their word their bond. What they said they would do, they did. What they promised, they fulfilled.

In addition, their DNA Talent Profile listed all the innate markers that one would want in a company that was seeking to become a leader in their industry. From the Gallup profile, their top five strengths were: Achiever, Strategic, Belief, Competition, and Responsibility.

It was during one of the leadership team-building seminars that a defining DNA Marker was identified. My girlfriend and business partner Krisandra was going around the conference room table and getting each member of the executive team to identify and openly state to the other members their personal motives for doing what they did. It was fascinating.

Carrie Raymond, who keeps very close control over the finances of Synaptyk, said it was payroll: not hers, but her employees'. That sounded a little strange at first. She followed up by saying that it made her happy because it was a direct reflection on how well her employees were doing and how hard they were working and supporting their families. Her Motive was to see her employees do well, pay their mortgages, go on vacations, be happy, and perform well in their lives.

What a refreshing change to see a CEO whose motivation is people. Synaptyk is in business to make money and lots of it. The difference between Carrie and many corporations is that she sees money as a means to more for her employees. She sees money as people and not people as money.

If you run a company, what is your primary motive? How you treat your people and the meaning you derive from success will be determined by how you answer this question. How can you as a leader and decision maker genetically re-engineer your corporate Motive?

MYLIFESCENE.COM—CROSS NOW—MYLIFESCENE.COM

Chapter 9
Evidence Contamination Part 1

How to gain, how to keep, how to recover happiness
is in fact for most men at all times the secret motive
of all they do, and of all they are willing to endure.
—William James

The very best Evidence can be thrown out at trial if that Evidence has been contaminated. Lives are no different. When the best Evidence of Life, the greatest Talents and potential are contaminated, their effectiveness and ultimate Purpose can be marginalized or even discarded from Life. A mistrial can be the result.

When great potential and ability are not protected from contamination they can often result in opportunities that are lost and relationships that are strained, harmed, and even broken. The pathways to success and promotions are lost. The possibility of realizing full potential can fade away. The Purpose, Passion, and Performance we seek to discover can evaporate before our eyes.

LSI is not just about Evidence and the weight of that Evidence but how the Evidence was obtained, preserved, tested, and interpreted and how it was used to support and prove the facts of a case. Maintaining the integrity of the Forensic Process is vital.

Who Says You Can't Do That?
Crime Scene Contamination

The contamination of Evidence can both set criminals free and lead to the conviction of the innocent. With the advent of DNA matching and other newer forensic processes, the quality of Evidence in criminal and civil cases is carefully scrutinized. Both defense and prosecuting attorneys look at the manner in which Evidence is collected and handled to bolster their cases.

Many trials involve extremely technical testimony about biology, chemistry, and physics. The best Evidence can be brought into question and even excluded from being admitted when it has not been collected, processed, and stored according to established protocols. It is the responsibility of police, crime scene investigators, and forensic specialists at the crime scene to make sure that everything is done correctly when it comes to the Evidence. People's lives depend on it.

The goal should be to eliminate any question of contamination before it becomes an issue. The aim is to never lose a case because of a technicality. When cases go to court, any unexplained Evidence collected at the crime scene needs to be identified. Evidence that is unidentified, such as latent fingerprints, shoe prints, blood, hair, and DNA swabs will need to be identified. If not identified, the questions as to where it came from will most likely be asked.

There are rules to crime scene investigating just as there are rules that govern Life. When these rules are violated at any stage of the process, problems are likely to occur. In extreme cases, Evidence can be so completely contaminated that it is damaged and rendered useless for Life. How tragic!

Drugs are a prime example of this. Drugs contaminate physical Evidence by destroying brain cells and vital organs, opening our bodies to disease and infection, death from overdosing; killing social connections, causing social ruptures; dulling emotional Passion, flat-lining emotional connections; depleting Performance; jail; and so much more. Even drugs such as steroids, which can enhance certain strengths temporarily, often end up destroying the people who use them. Just ask many of the so-called great athletes of the past twenty years, many of whom are now being reconsidered as Hall of Fame candidates. *Contaminated Evidence!*

Greed is another. Bernard Madoff was a proponent of the *Bonfire of the Vanities* lifestyle. He was a brilliant man who was recently sentenced to over 150 years behind bars. He went from palatial surroundings to a small cell. He was financially and socially very savvy, had a great intellect, and was able to gain the confidence of many very successful and wealthy clients. He ran a massive scam: he lied, hid assets, manipulated financial records, and covered his crimes for many years. The result was the loss of an estimated $50 billion and lives that were shattered. Nonprofits who helped thousands were closed. Families who were retired and seemingly secure were now broke and looking for places to live. Children's college funds were decimated. Others sadly committed suicide rather than face Life penniless. *Contaminated Evidence!*

I knew a forensic psychologist who was a brilliant man. He was one of the leaders in his field and had been elected to national positions in forensic psychology. His testimony had assisted in convicting many criminals, including the worst sex offenders. This brilliant man's Life was out of control and nobody knew it. He was caught doing things that some of the criminals he'd helped convict did, and his reputation and career were over. His embarrassment and loss were so severe that he took his own Life. He was a man with many wonderful qualities and a great family. *Contaminated Evidence!*

The results of this talented man's contaminated Evidence/Life were far reaching. Many of the criminals he had evaluated and helped send to prison could now challenge their convictions because his expert testimony at their trials was now being called into question. The repercussions were devastating and long lasting.

Recently I read in the news that the celebrated baseball player Alex Rodriguez admitted to taking steroids. He admitted that he contaminated his incredible talent with steroids. His talent was and is exceptional, but everything he has done will forever be tainted by the fact that he contaminated his Evidence with steroids. How disappointing to the millions of fans and young up-and-coming players who have another fallen hero. The reason, according to A-Rod, was that he felt the enormous pressure to perform and meet the expectations of his adoring fans. It was their fault. He had to be what his fans believed him to be, one of the greatest players of all time.

His need to measure up to the pressure from his fans and those who paid him the highest salary in baseball history resulted in his choices to cheat. *Contaminated Evidence!*

Design and Talents can be used for moral and immoral Purposes. The chapter on *spiritual Evidence* deals with motivation. That is a distinct *Field of Evidence* in and of itself, but it is also much more than that. The chapter deals with elements of your DNA Code, which must be identified.

Moral Choice—My DPS (Design Positioning System)

There exists within every person a DPS (Design Positioning System). We call this a conscience. Regardless of where we go in any culture or group on the planet, people have a sense of right and wrong. The emotion we feel when we ignore our DPS is called *guilt*. It makes us stop and reevaluate what we are doing. It tells us we need to go in another direction.

This DPS not only guides us in what we know as right and wrong but also tells us how to use a capacity according to the Designer's intended Purpose. That DPS is an internal barometer that tells us by registering negative or flat emotion when we are not living our Talents and Design DNA. When we do live our Talents, it lets us know by the fact we experience positive emotion.

Moral choice can be developed and strengthened, as any other capacity, by making consistent right choices in the face of tough situations. You cannot develop moral Talents in isolation or on top of a mountain. You do it in the course of Life.

This capacity is what distinguishes you from animals. A lion feels no guilt or remorse for killing a baby deer: instinct versus choice.

Moral/Help versus Immoral/Harm Uses of Design

Some of the best businessmen I have ever known are drug dealers. Gang leaders are some of the greatest motivators you will ever find. The former use exceptional managerial, people, and marketing skills to sell death and misery. They do this while remaining invisible. The latter motivate gang members to commit horrendous crimes through fear.

Capacity	Immoral Use
Physical	Drugs
	Physical abuse
	Sexual abuse
	Domination
	Alcohol abuse
Intellectual	Cheating
	Plagiarism
	Creating a computer virus

	Cyber-bullying
	Dominating arguments
Emotional	Manipulation
	Creating fear or anxiety
	Withholding praise
Social	Excluding
	Domination by peers
	Hazing
Spiritual	Taking from others
	Confusing or deceiving
	Dominating

We have choices as to how we use each capacity. We can use a hand (physical) to either pat people on the back and encourage them or hit them in the face and cause physical harm. We can include (social) a new person in our school when we go out for lunch, or we can ignore her. We can use our minds (intellectual) to create a computer virus, or we can create a cool website. The possibilities are endless. In the following exercise, think about at least two other ways to use each of your capacities in moral and immoral ways.

Moral capacity can be strengthened, just like any other capacity. Just like a muscle can be strengthened by repetitive exercise and training; so can moral choice. Making right choices over and over again when it matters, when the option to go the other way is available, results in strengthened capacity. Moral strength cannot be built without the opportunity to be immoral, and real Talents need substantive and real opportunity, Life.

Factors Resulting in Evidence Contamination

Evidence contamination can result for a variety of reasons, all of which need to be examined carefully. You will be asked to develop systems and safeguards to help you avoid contaminating your Evidence. Here are some of the reasons Evidence is contaminated.

Living Based on Untested or Unverified Evidence

A common factor resulting in Evidence contamination is that people attempt to be someone or something they are not. We all have done this at one time or another. When we seek to live each day pretending we are excellent at something that we are no more than simply qualified for, or even average at, and we know it is not based on our Unique Design and DNA Code, we are waiting for a fall. The anxiety robs us of any potential Passion.

This is a common problem among the majority of people in management and positions of leadership. In a recent poll, six out of ten managers believed they did not choose their positions based on what they knew about themselves and their Talents. Beyond that, many were experiencing the anxiety of waiting to be "found out" for what they were not. They were worried someone was going to discover they were not competent to hold the positions they currently occupied and for which they were not qualified.

Often when I speak to corporations, I see the same problem: managers and senior executives living on the defensive and insecure in their positions. One of the major problems is even though they are more than competent and performing, they can't articulate or describe their Talents and why they are performing so well. What we do in our Corporate DNA™ (Corp-DNA™) programs is help them quantify and articulate who they are. The result is greater confidence and Performance. They become leaders who lead from Talents and not insecurities.

Often in Life we are asked to assume a position or role for which we are not qualified. There is nothing in our DNA Code that points to us being qualified for the position. We were simply in the wrong place at the wrong time and the position needed to be filled. We may have been viewed as educated, and so that meant we would automatically be competent to perform a role for which we have never shown any real competence. It could be a major in college, a position on a team, a job in a company—it doesn't matter. The reality is that we just don't fit and we know it.

Many of these managers performed adequately, not excellently. In reality, they had nothing to worry about. What is most important is to understand that the LSI Forensic Process generates the confidence that allows you to walk into your Life with all the confidence that the authentic, tested, and verified Evidence produces. That is a foundation we all need and should have in order to live Life to our fullest capacity.

People sometimes pretend to be something they are not. We have a word for them: *fakes*. That does not mean their reasons for trying to be someone or be something better are always wrong or that they are acting out of evil motivation. The desire to be someone is basic to all of humankind. We seek significance. We all want to be seen. We all want to feel a strong sense of authenticity as well as to stand out.

When people attempt to be someone they are not and someone they were never Designed to be, they live lives filled with anxiety and stress, seeking to protect what they know is not true. They are constantly on guard and are like Hollywood sets, facades without any substance backing them up. It happens in the business world, in relationships, on sports teams, throughout all of Life—people wanting to be more but not knowing who they really are. *PRU*

What I know is that as you continue in your discovery adventure, you will never be disappointed when you find the Evidence. The very core of your being will agree with the Evidence. You will feel and be comfortable in your own, known skin. It is those people who want to be something that they are not who have to live in the fear of being discovered as unauthentic and false.

Have you ever seen one of those intense courtroom dramas where just in the nick of time the course of a trial is altered? Evidence is discovered and introduced that either convicts or exonerates the accused. When Evidence is not known, it leads to a Life of uncertainty and surprises. Unexpected and dramatic changes in the course of our lives often happen. More than that, the unknown leaves us living in a place where we can easily pretend to be what we are not.

Evidence That's Not!

The misuse of forensic Evidence is a very serious problem. There are many examples in recent years of those misuses:

- A police chemist falsified reports and sent hundreds of innocent people away to jail on rape charges.
- Even those we trust to maintain and enforce the law are not always reliable; the main FBI laboratory is under suspicion.
- In West Virginia, a serologist falsified test results in hundreds of cases over a ten-year period, resulting in the sentencing hundreds of defendants to lengthy prison terms.
- In Texas, an extreme case, a pathologist faked autopsy results, resulting in as many as twenty people being sentenced to death.

Those situations are extreme and are found mostly in a world we don't have much to do with. In the world we do live in, resumes are contaminated by being enhanced, listing phony degrees and positions. In a situation in Washington State, ten state patrol officers were accused of buying diplomas to get additional pay. The officers ultimately were not charged, but they had to repay all the extra pay they had received for their "advanced academic standing."

When people contaminate their Evidence by falsely enhancing their lives and pretending to be someone they are not, it usually means they have not discovered and identified the Evidence they really possess. The question is, "Are you who you say you are?" If you have answered the most important question, *?RU*, then you can clearly and confidently state "yes" and live without fear. If you are who you say you are, you have nothing to fear.

Examples of Internet dating nightmares are everywhere. People display photographs that are ten years old and fifty pounds lighter than their current state. They exaggerate their physical, educational, and economic status, often to absurd proportions. When they end up meeting someone in person, they are sometimes not even recognizable as their online counterpart. We all have humorous stories we could share, either from personal experiences or those of friends.

Remember, reality and reputations only go so far and only hold up long term if the Evidence bears them out. One small contamination can ruin a reputation that has taken many years to build and that was built on otherwise solid Evidence.

There have been instances in the show *CSI* when the Evidence becomes inadmissible in court. In one instance, the CSI on the stand knew that the Evidence was wrongly tested or the result was incorrect.

Evidence Contamination Analysis

- Are there any areas of your Life that need authenticating for alignment with your DNA Code?
- Is there Evidence that is "NOT" and that needs clarification by you with a manager or employer?
- Are you waiting to be "found out" for someone you are not or something you may have even falsified on a resume, application, or other information source?

Forensic Contamination Identification

Contaminating Evidence can come in many forms. Crime scene investigators have been known to compromise and contaminate a crime scene with their own footprints or tire tracks. Exceptional care must be taken so as to not jeopardize the integrity of a crime scene by making these elementary mistakes.

Eliminating contamination at a crime scene can make or break a case. New technology, intense media attention, and the popularity of forensics and crime scene television shows have resulted in attorneys and potential jury members being savvy enough to look to the Evidence to prove a case definitively.

The role of the crime scene investigator will be put under the microscope in all cases. Questions about how the Evidence was collected will be asked. Was the Evidence compromised in any way? How do we know that it was collected correctly? When an investigator carefully follows commonsense rules and methods to reduce contamination, it goes a long way in helping the investigator stand up under the toughest cross-examination.

Cross Contamination—Past Cases

In the *CSI* episode "Weeping Willows," Catherine heads to a bar to unwind and ends up having a brief romantic encounter with a stranger, Adam Novak. Later that night a woman from the same bar turns up dead, and the Evidence points to Novak as the main suspect in the murder investigation. Problems between Gil and Catherine arise when she fails to disclose her encounter and her knowledge of the suspect. While that is happening, Mia deals with cross-contamination of Evidence in the DNA lab with confusing results.

The past and past actions have the ability to really mess up the present and limit future opportunities. It has been said that *the past is only the past if it does not affect the present.*

Unresolved issues from our past, such as issues of character, lies told, relationships fractured, forgiveness withheld, sins covered, abuse and pain held deep within, flawed patterns of living, loss, and misuse of Design all of a sudden erode the very ground we stand on, collapsing it, and our lives are thrown into turmoil. Old cases will come back to Life if they are left unresolved! It is what we call "baggage."

One of the important issues in Evidence collection is to make sure all the instruments that were used in previous cases are either discarded or thoroughly cleaned. If they are not, Evidence can be contaminated and confused because Evidence from the last case is carried forward.

Forensic Tip

For six to nine dollars, an investigator can do simple things to maintain the integrity of DNA Evidence. DNA can be transferred from one crime scene to another when tools to collect Evidence are not properly cared for, cleaned, or disposed of. Fingerprint brushes can easily become contaminated as they retain DNA. To ensure you don't transfer DNA from a brush used at one scene to the next, it is absolutely necessary to use a new brush at each scene.

This procedure is vital in homicide cases, where the DNA may be the determining factor. In homicides, the brush that is used should become part of the Evidence. Investigators must remember that it is not only the brush that is used, but even the powder itself that can become contaminated. Magnetic applicators can be cleaned with a bleach solution, or disposable ones can be used. Most fiberglass brushes cannot be easily cleaned and reused. Good, clean Evidence is the currency of forensics.

Essentially, what happens when we carry over Evidence, toxic Evidence, from past cases is that Life becomes muddled or confusing, even small issues. We know where we want to go and grow in our clarity of Purpose, but we keep looking back. We may want to focus forward on the things we want and the direction we see, but we can't effectively go forward while looking back.

We can't go forward while we think about what we want to avoid. We are double-minded. When our vision is clouded because we have not dealt with past issues, their power will be like a ball and chain around our ankles.

A settled past gives us clarity for the road ahead. Design determines Purpose, not bad situations that reflect the wrong use of Design. Design is to be discovered and embraced and is never the result of avoiding bad, misused Evidence.

Many people get out of a relationship, and the most important direction they verbalize is what they never want to repeat. That doesn't get you anywhere. You have not defined direction, only a road you don't want to travel down again. Simply eliminating negative possibilities does not give you any direction.

Deal with issues you must deal with. Forgive yourself and others. Focus on the future and what your Design tells you.

We all carry with us the situations from Life that have contributed to who we are today. These have been both positive and negative. But all of our lives have issues that we need to work on.

We all carry the past, negative issues into our futures in many ways.

Past Pain and Loss

The past is powerful! It has the capacity to contaminate our ability to live strongly and with Purpose, Passion, and Performance today. Life subjects all of us to pain and loss in varying measures. Many of these issues when not dealt with have serious effects on our present and future attempts to live by our DNA Code.

I believe that no matter what has happened to us, we have a choice as to how we carry those issues into our futures. Some terrible things happen to children and adults, things that have never happened to me and that I hope never enter my world. I have met people who have lived through terrible abuse and loss. They have been told they were damaged and will never really recover. That message is true, but only if they believe it.

There are countless examples of people who have lived through the most terrible abuse, loss, and evil. Many of these people are the strongest, most grateful, giving, magnificent people on the planet. Others who have had similar or less severe abuse continue to live subject to their abuser's actions or the heavy losses they have been subject to. They live in a world defined by deficit and refuse to look at the assets they have to give to others.

The difference ultimately, I believe, is choice: the choice to forgive their abusers in many instances; the choice to work through their losses with friends and family or with skilled counselors. Often this involves gut-wrenching therapy, in each case with the option to choose to discover and live their unique God-given DNA Code or continue to hide. They must, more than anything, choose to give and involve themselves in the lives of others, and that takes courage.

Ultimately, I believe those who stay bound to the past and subject to the people and pain of their experiences are those who refuse to discover and prove their DNA Code. You don't get rid of past bad Evidence by blocking it, avoiding those who perpetrated it, hating, and being consumed with how to enact vengeance, but by demonstrating in the present what you are made of. If you ever believe a person can destroy or contaminate your God-given Design so badly that you cannot live it as it was intended by the Giver, you lose, and they (or the past) wins. The choice is yours!

Evidence Contamination Analysis

- Can you identify issues from your past that need deliberate action and must be addressed if you are to move on and live your DNA Code?

- Who do you need to forgive? Maybe that someone is you. Be specific and identify who, what, why, and when.

We cannot focus forward while we are fixated on the past, so make the choice and forgive, regardless of the response of the person or situation that resulted in pain from your past.

Contaminated Beliefs

We all have beliefs that must be challenged and changed. These beliefs often come from sources that are contaminated and are usually external to us.

1. *I can't because I am*: a woman, minority, disabled, too young, too old, too anything. There are always barriers in Life we have to overcome. Some of us have more than others. If you wish to focus on your barriers and deficits, you will lose. If you choose to focus on your Design DNA and Talents, the opportunity to live a Life of Purpose, Passion, and Performance becomes a reality.

2. *I am not worth it.* So many people believe they can't, they are not worth it, or they "just will never." The way we see ourselves is vital. You don't build Life by believing you are worth it or simply having self-esteem. Simply being told, wishing, or affirming daily that *"I am worth it!"* or *"I am a powerful person!"* doesn't make it so. You need Evidence, and you are on your way to discovering all the Evidence you need that when collected, identified, tested, and interpreted will tell you who you are and what you are worth. Your desire and affirmations need the substance of hard Evidence, and LSI will give you that. What are you worth?

3. *An expert told you that you didn't have the right Evidence.* One of the great tragedies is that important people in our lives—teachers,

parents, coaches, managers, and others—have told us we couldn't because we just didn't have what was required. Many of us have believed their words and have defined our lives based on faulty testimony. Words by people who have impure motives, wrong ideas, bad Evidence, are prejudiced or bitter for what they never had the opportunity to experience need to be excluded from the Evidence that really defines our lives. Most often they are people devoid of any Purpose, Passion, or Performance themselves and would deny anyone else the opportunity to live what they don't.

I had a wonderful experience recently when I was training a group of mental health therapists at the Neighborhood Youth and Family Counseling in Richardson, Texas. The nonprofit agency had decided to train many of their staff and have them certified with Life Scene Investigation. We got to this talking about Contamination, and as we began to apply the Talents philosophy to some of the issues they dealt with on a daily basis, they came alive with ideas and new ways to approach these issues.

One of the most important aspects we talked about was how patients or clients defined their lives. Many clients who had substance abuse issues identified themselves by the standard AA (Alcoholics Anonymous) language. Those who belong to AA generally attend meetings on a regular basis and when attending meetings introduce themselves with a simple statement: *"Hi. My name is _____ and I am an alcoholic."* I know that AA has helped millions of people, and I am in substantial agreement with many of their beliefs and practices. They have saved many lives. There are, however, two problems I have with how they approach addiction. They are problems of belief.

We started to rework some of the beliefs and statements common to psychotherapy and addiction theory. One of the best ideas we talked about was integrating the Talents or strengths model into working with "addicts." I suggested that instead of allowing the first statement of someone who subscribed to the classic addiction model to be *"My name is . . . and I am an alcoholic,"* we ask them to make a definitive statement about a hardwired Talent that they possessed. Why should we first be defined by our deficits or perceived deficits? Instead, why not begin with *"Hi, my name is . . . and I am a leader . . . I am an artist . . . I am creative . . . I am a teacher . . . I am a coach . . . I am an exceptional encourager . . ."* These Talents, when lived, result in the same emotions addicts find when they drink, shoot up, or smoke.

We then started to talk about the concept of "flow" and Reliability Test 2 (which you will read about in the chapter on forensic reliability tests just ahead). Almost all the emotional states that are inherent when we are in "flow" or "in the zone" are the emotions addicts and alcoholics seek in external substances.

Read through these symptoms of "flow" and, if you are an addict or alcoholic, be honest and identify which of these you are seeking to have met when you drink or drug:

- You felt particularly strong
- Alert
- In effortless control
- A sense that you were performing at the peak of ability
- Both the sense of time and emotional problems seemed to disappear
- There was a sense that you were living what you were Designed to live

You experience "flow" when you engage your Talents with a task that demands the best of who you are. I posited the thought that one of the best approaches to dealing with addiction and alcoholism might begin with helping these clients discover their Talents and find places where they have experienced "flow."

I believe that addiction and alcoholism are symptoms of Talents not discovered and lived. They are also indicative of a lack of gratitude when or if those Talents are known. We can produce positive emotions when we know and live our Talents. I personally believe this is a much better approach to helping than defining deficit and seeking every way possible to avoid it.

I do not believe that addiction is part of our genetic DNA. Some people are more easily attracted to substances that are then very difficult to rid their lives of. They become dependent, but not powerless. One of the beliefs and basic requirements of those who attend and subscribe to the AA model is a belief that in order to get help, they must admit that they are *powerless* and their lives have become unmanageable. I believe any such statement is wrong and goes against the very fabric of human Design and Talents. To be weakened and feel powerless is a reality, but to be without power to change is just not true. We are not powerless! We comprise magnificent capacities, both hardwired abilities and character abilities that can be discovered and developed.

You have some choices to make as you continue reading *The DNA Code* regardless of who you are, what you have been told, where you were born, whom you were born to, or what opportunities you lack or have been denied. Evidence of *who you are*, the real Evidence, is what needs to define your Life. Focus on and build your Life based on the Evidence. It is your choice to continue to give power to contaminated sources that are seldom accurate. Your Life is your responsibility, and if you want it to be defined by others and not the Evidence, that is a bad choice that will affect every area of your Life as long as it remains your belief.

So as you look at your Life, the great Evidence, as you test your Evidence, as you think through how to apply it to your Life, make sure you are growing and developing your character at the same time. You can reach the top of your field as a professional athlete, business professional, parent, teacher, mechanic, or whatever, only to have the Evidence of who you are and what you do questioned and, in extreme cases, lose more than you ever thought possible.

Evidence Contamination Analysis

- What beliefs do I currently hold or do I know slow me down from discovering and living my Evidence?

- What does the Evidence say that contradicts those beliefs, and how can I reframe or restate them based on the Evidence?

Contaminated Attitudes

Attitudes are our own and originate with us. We own them, build them, and maintain them. They are within our control to challenge and change, and no one else is responsible for them.

1. *"I am not subject to the rules—I am special."* Some people have a sense of superiority and entitlement that gives them the false impression they can do anything they want and it won't hurt them. For years I have worked with children who came from very wealthy families. Their parents gave their kids everything they ever wanted and lavished them with things they never deserved or asked for. Often these people get a sense of being

invincible and think they have a coating of Teflon that renders them immune from bad things ever happening to them. After all, they have never incurred any real consequences because their parents paid their way out of everything that ever happened to them. They committed crimes, but their parents hired attorneys who worked the system, and so there were no consequences. When they received bad grades, their parents threatened to sue the school if those grades were not adjusted upward. Those parents were wrong!

What is interesting is that this same attitude is not found only among the wealthy, but in those who might have lacked or been denied opportunity in the past and have been victims. Often, individuals from these backgrounds feel that opportunity is owed them. They should be given a free pass and should not be held to the same standard as those who had or have it easier than them.

2. *"Because I am talented and successful, the rules don't apply."* As the proverb says, "Pride comes before a fall." No truer words were ever penned. Tiger Woods in his apology on television said he felt he "deserved to enjoy the temptations" that came with his incredible success. There are countless examples of people who, immediately after a success, fall. They do something that seems so out of character, and it often results in great harm. The action will sometimes take away from the success that immediately preceded it. I have known of businessmen who, after closing a great deal, decide that they deserve to celebrate but do so in ways that are illegitimate, and they end up contaminating their Evidence with excesses that bring them down.

I have coached many very Talented people. There are times when Talent can be misused and contaminate Life. Some Talented people have a sense that because things come easily, they don't have to work or practice as hard as others who may have less natural ability. The truth is that the more Talent you have, the more responsibility you have to use that Talent well.

3. *"Small issues and lies don't matter."* A sinkhole is the result of small seepage over a long period that results in a huge problem. Small issues that are left unattended can develop into big problems. Erosion takes place very quietly and often starts with a small trickle. Over time, that small trickle becomes a steady stream and eventually a river that can wipe away the best Evidence

produced over many years of wonderful Talents applied with sweat and tears, hard work, and sacrifice. You can't let small contaminants go unattended and ignored, or you will pay the price. Small resentments grow into giant killers. Remember, it is the little foxes that spoil the vines.

4. *"What others don't know doesn't matter."* The problem is as long as you are putting time, effort, and energy into covering your tracks, you cannot fully give yourself to living with Purpose and Passion. Lies always take away from living free. When your mind is on hiding and covering, it is not on discovery and giving. The reality is we fool ourselves when we think we can hide our lies for any length of time. Be assured, contaminated Evidence will be discovered!

5. *"I am the most important person in the process."* There are people who believe their lives are the most important and that what they want or do has priority over everyone else. It is true that the more you know about your Talents, the more you can serve and significantly touch the lives of other people. Much of the discovery process is founded on our serving and involving our lives in the lives of others by giving to them. *You will never learn more about your DNA Code and Talents than what you are willing to give away.* A selfish attitude does not allow for Evidence to be discovered or developed. Everything you do affects others. You need others to be involved in your journey of discovery, and others need you. We are all members of a team, and when we think the only reason others exist is for our needs, we will lose.

Any good scientist should live with a sense of questioning or healthy skepticism. The Evidence might seem perfect and the processes we have followed correct. The problem is that humans are subject to error. To go through Life with a stubborn belief that we can never be wrong contaminates the entire process. We need to be open to questioning, asking questions, and reevaluating Evidence and conclusions.

Evidence Contamination Analysis

- What attitudes do I currently hold or know are potentially destructive and could result in my Evidence being disqualified or greatly marginalized?

- What do I need to do to change those attitudes and be grateful for the Talents I have been given to serve others with?

Higher Standards Required for Higher Positions

What Michael Phelps, multiple gold-medal winner, did with smoking pot might not have been an issue if he had made another choice. After the Olympics, he was asked to represent a number of companies that would pay him to be their spokesman. He had performed magnificently and was a world record holder multiple times. When he became the spokesman for these companies, he made a choice to be on a platform that requires a different level of accountability. Had he simply wanted to go back to swimming and living and not be rewarded for his efforts with advertising money, his behavior probably would not have been subject to a higher level of scrutiny and responsibility.

Before you take on a higher level of visibility, you need to know that higher levels of responsibility come with it. More people will be watching, and you will be open to criticism. Often that criticism will be unfair, and you will need to be above reproach. The choice is yours. You can stay where you are and the rewards will likely be less; or you can take your Talents to a higher level of Performance and visibility that require greater character and guarding against contamination.

So how do you protect against contaminating your Design DNA? The chapter that follows will help address this fundamental issue. Please read it carefully and with an appropriate attitude of seriousness. You are worth it!

Evidence Contamination Analysis

- Do I believe I can go much further than where I am today?
- What sacrifices do I need to make and what things do I need to do to ensure I can move to the next level of visibility and effectiveness in my Life?

Chapter 10
Evidence Contamination
Part 2

How to Safeguard against Contamination

Guarding against contamination is a constant pursuit. We must have safeguards, principles of operation, personal ethics, and guiding beliefs. It is essential to have the insight and oversight by others to ensure the integrity of the process, the willingness to have our motives challenged and our processes questioned, and, finally, our conclusions validated. All these are vitally important!

What are Your Guiding Ethics?

When I was growing up I had the wonderful privilege of attending an incredible school, St George's College. St George's is located in the small central African country of Zimbabwe. This school had great traditions, beautiful old stone buildings, including a castle turret, and a hint of Harry Potter thrown in.

St. George's is a Jesuit Catholic school. The Jesuit maxim "AMDG" was embedded and displayed on all of the school emblems. The letters *AMDG* stand for the Latin phrase *Ad Majorem Dei Gloriam*, or "To the greater glory of God." What was drilled into us was that before we undertook anything, large or small, we had to think, "Will this be to the greater glory of God?"

Every exercise we did had to be prefaced with the letters *AMDG*. If it was a quick quiz, we had to preface the quiz with *AMDG*. If it was handed in without those letters in the top left-hand corner, before the date, our names, class, and so on, it was rejected out of hand. Even if we got 100 percent, it was not recorded. The same went for term papers, essays, math assignments, anything and everything.

We were sometimes given "lines" as a punishment. Lines were awarded for minor infractions. They had to be written on special paper and usually were the repetition of a long, obscure sentence that had to be copied one hundred times. If by chance all the lines were copied perfectly, without *AMDG* being written on the top left corner they were torn up and the punishment repeated.

St George's required the wearing of uniforms. Our school blazer had a badge that had the letters *AMDG* embroidered on them. Sports uniforms, caps, hats, trophies, anything and everything had *AMDG* on it. That defined the school ethic. Do what you do as if God were watching; He expects you to do everything to the best of your ability, and beyond that, would God receive glory from your everyday thoughts and actions?

There are other great acronyms and slogans, such as the popular "WWJD" ("What Would Jesus Do?") and the more recent one popularized by cancer survivor and Tour de France champion Lance Armstrong, which encourages us to "Live Strong."

Guiding ethics must not be simply slogans or acronyms that we wear or repeat. They must be deeply held beliefs. They are what guides us—a gyroscope of sorts. When we want to go in one direction that is against our Purpose and the best use of our Design/DNA Code, we should feel and sense an inner imbalance. We should immediately question our direction or decision and evaluate whether what we are doing is in line with those beliefs. These beliefs protect and help ensure the most effective Performance and longevity of our Design.

Evidence Contamination Analysis

What ethics or beliefs guide your Life and are the ones by which all decisions in your Life are weighed and measured?

Always Work with a Team

Every *CSI* program shows a team effort. There are those who collect Evidence at the crime scene; identify and test Evidence in the lab; interview suspects and witnesses; interpret Evidence for trials; and perform other important functions. It is always a team effort.

It is important that we have friends whom we know are honest and true and who will talk to us when they see contamination occurring.

These are friends who help guard our lives for the best of reasons and motives. If you don't have people like that in your Life, you need to find them.

If you have a history of contamination in a particular area of Life, there are groups you can join who address those areas: a twelve-step group, Celebrate Recovery, church support and growth groups, small accountability groups that hold confidentiality sacred and others. If you are serious about keeping your Life strong and free from possible contaminants, you need to open your Life to a small select group to help you and come alongside you close enough to observe your Life.

It is also important that the team you have in your Life not simply keep watch and challenge you; they must also be there to help you discover, develop and live your Design. When we live our DNA Code Talents, we need people to celebrate with us and encourage us to live them again. We need their insight to expand and deliver better. We need their perspective based on their Life experiences to give color and greater depth to who we are. Make sure you have people who cheer you on as well as others who referee and keep you true to your Purpose.

Single-focus groups or people who see only either the positive or negative are seldom helpful to anything in Life.

Evidence Contamination Analysis

- List those people who support you and speak objective reality and truth into your Life.

- How have they been able to keep you focused and avoid contamination?

Develop Character to Support and Grow Hardwired Talents

How you do something is just as important as *what* you do. Great Talent that is not supported by equally great character is Evidence waiting to be contaminated and ultimately disqualified. Doing the most outstanding feats of Talent is nothing more than a loud, obnoxious noise void of real, lasting substance.

An integral part of what we do in the LSI discovery seminars and programs is to use a variety of forensic discovery tests and profiles. Two of those tests are the *Gallup StrengthsFinder 2.0* and the *Values in Action (VIA)* profile. (I strongly encourage you to take both these tests.

You can get access to both of them at the www.the-dna-code.com website.) The *VIA* profile is free.

These two tests are similar in the questions they ask, but what they diagnose is very different. When I say *diagnosing*, I am using the word in a positive way, not in the sense of an illness. LSI uses forensics in the diagnosis of Talents. It simply means "through knowledge."

The *VIA* profile focuses on character strengths that exist in everyone to one degree or another, regardless of a person's specific "DNA markers" for various Talents. All twenty-four *VIA* character strengths are part of every person and can be developed through Life and experience, along with various positive psychology "therapies."

The *StrengthsFinder 2.0* evaluation approach, on the other hand, is to bring to light the hardwired, innate capacities that are specific to you, similar to the DNA markers that differentiate you from all other people. Not everyone has all capacities; we are all endowed differently. In this evaluation, you either have a certain capacity or you don't. You can develop your capacities into Talents through knowledge, practice, and experience, but you cannot become talented in an area where you lack a capacity. (In other words, rabbits will never be good at flying.)

I want to share my *VIA* and *StrengthsFinder2.0* results with you. I believe they are very accurate and also very complementary of each other. My top five *VIA* "Signature Strengths" are:

1. Creativity (ingenuity and originality)
2. Spirituality (sense of Purpose and faith)
3. Bravery (valor)
4. Hope (optimism and future-mindedness)
5. Perspective (wisdom)

My top *StrengthsFinder 2.0* Strengths are:

1. Futuristic
2. Maximizer
3. Activator
4. Strategic
5. Achiever

The reason we use both of these tests in LSI is that they help you see the difference between your character, which is something you have greater control over, and your innate Design/DNA Code Talents, which are hardwired. DNA is composed of Codes for Talent that are part of you or not. Your Talents should guide the way you plan your Life, and they generate that sense of Passion and positive emotion.

Character, unlike Design/DNA Code, can be developed. You can desire that your children become more empathetic or generous. You can model that for them and create opportunities for them to develop those character traits by volunteering and helping them learn to give to others who are less fortunate than they are.

Design or DNA is different. Some kids/people just don't possess a sense of rhythm, and no matter who you pay to teach them to dance, play guitar, and so on, they will never be more than maybe average at it. Some people can't hold a tune; some will never become medical doctors or mechanics. They are simply not wired for it.

Design DNA markers must be supported by character. If is not, they will inevitably be contaminated. Character allows us to support not only the use of Talents, but also what results in those Talents becoming all they can be. Character matures Talents and makes them more powerful, meaningful, and controlled. Character allows for the long-term development of our Talents and the security we all seek.

MYLIFESCENE.COM—CROSS NOW—MYLIFESCENE.COM
Life Scene—Phil Dunlap

I had an attorney who embodied both essential elements: exceptional Design DNA and unswerving character. His name is Philip Dunlap. Not only is he an excellent attorney, but he is also a man of exceptional character.

Attorneys are not generally held in high regard in our society. They are often seen as people who can bend the "truth" and stretch reality to their client's advantage. I often use Phil as an example of the most honest and ethical man I have ever met, and he is.

When I first met Philip Dunlap, he told me he would represent me if I would agree to do two things: never lie to him, and show him photographs of my children. His approach was not some clinical procedure or battle about to be waged at all costs and won.

He was a man with exceptional emotional Talents. He saw law as being more than simply getting the best for his client; he had a heart that saw my children as people.

During the course of a very lengthy custody case, Phil often had to litigate with two and sometimes three attorneys on the opposing side, all at one time. The opposing attorneys worked in downtown office towers with all the trappings of material success and resources with which to overwhelm and win against their opponents. Phil worked out of a small office in his house and drove an older white pickup truck.

Philip Dunlap maintained his ethics and honesty at all times, even when the opposing counsel forgot or decided it was not convenient to bring its ethics and honesty into the proceedings. He valued truth and integrity over the win-at-all-costs mentality of the opposition. This was the case more than once.

Whom do you know like Phil Dunlap? Who challenges you to be a better person and support your Life with honesty, character, and ethics? Whom do you know that will challenge you to maintain your ethics when others might cut corners and take the advantage?

MYLIFESCENE.COM—CROSS NOW—MYLIFESCENE.COM

What If?

What would have happened if Bernard Madoff had a large dose of what Phil Dunlap had: integrity, honesty, kindness, compassion, or one of the other *VIA* character strengths? How would Alex Rodriguez have held up under the pressure of his fans and massive endorsements if he had developed a greater sense of fairness, self-control, and appreciation of beauty? His talent was incredible as it was and never needed additional "help."

What about your Life and mine? How have we marginalized our Talents/Design DNA Code because we lacked the right motivation, ethics, and character? Have we pretended we are someone we are not? Have we lied about who we are and tried to pass ourselves off as being people who don't even resemble our real selves?

A final word about contamination. Regardless of what has happened in your Life and the choices you have made; there is more Life to be lived. Life is a journey, and there is Purpose in all the things that happen to you, even from those bad choices and patterns of Life that may have resulted in significant problems. You may have been disqualified from certain positions; some of your relationships might have been gravely hurt and sometimes broken beyond repair; but that doesn't mean you are done. Your responsibility is to focus again on your Talents. Your responsibility is to shake yourself off, get up, and find ways to reengage your Life.

Evidence Contamination Analysis

- Are you willing to make the necessary changes?

- Are you willing to seriously look at where the contamination comes from and seek new ways to eliminate and marginalize future contamination?

- Are you willing to repair the results of that contamination as much as possible?

- Are you willing to seek forgiveness from those who were the victims of your contaminated Evidence and living?

- Are you willing to look deeply and personally and realize that what God has put in your hands is a sacred trust and requires you to use whatever you have been given honestly, openly, and with the integrity God requires?

The reality is that we are all contaminated. We all have issues in our lives that need redemption and grace. That does not mean we don't work hard to be aware of the effects and power of contamination. We need a filter, just like a swimming pool does. The filter is constantly cleaning and purifying the water to control contamination so that we can swim in clean water.

The Unique Design and DNA markers you have been given are still the blueprint for you to discover Purpose and Passion in your Life. You may have to take the time to reestablish your reputation. People are for the most part very forgiving if they sense you are sincere and want to do what is right. Give them a chance.

Remember the Apostle Peter, who denied Christ, was forgiven, was restored, and then became one of the primary leaders of a movement that now has over a billion followers. The man was a coward who was felled by a country girl while sitting around a fire.

Chuck Colson was indicted and convicted in the fallout of the Watergate scandal. He went to prison in disgrace only to use that experience to begin Prison Fellowship, the largest organization in the world that seeks to help those incarcerated change their lives and become good, productive members of society upon their release.

Michael Milken was a junk-bond king in the 1980s. He swindled millions of dollars. Milken now heads up an educational foundation that focuses on building young lives. He is also instrumental in some of the world's most innovative medical and cancer research.

We can all find people in our communities who have made huge changes from where they were and what they did to disgrace their lives to become people who now make positive differences. Maybe you are one of them. Maybe you could become one of those who change and reengage your Purpose to use those same DNA Talents, now supported and infused with character. It is your choice to face the hill, no matter how steep, and do what you were Designed to do!

Your commitment and determination must be to follow what you know you have been given to live and affect your world with, your God-given Design and DNA. Whether people forgive or don't is not always within your control. Living and being faithful to who you know you are and the gifts you have been given is paramount.

The challenge and necessity is for each of us to build a code of personal ethics. We must be able to clearly articulate our ethics, and those ethics need to be known by all who come in contact with us.

?RU when it comes to your ethics? What is at the core of *?UR?*

Rachel Scott was the first person killed at Columbine High School on April 20, 1999. Her acts of kindness and compassion, coupled with the contents of her six diaries, have become the foundation for one of the most Life-changing school programs in the United States, "Rachel's Challenge." Rachel always believed her Life would touch millions of people. That was her fundamental view of her Life, which was ultimately only realized in her death.

What is the message? Rachel believed that "*if one person can go out of their way to show compassion, then it will start a chain reaction of the same. People never know how far a little kindness can go.*" The Rachel's Challenge program is for students who want to understand and use their power to make permanent, positive, cultural change in their schools and communities by accepting the challenge of Rachel Scott to start a chain reaction of kindness and compassion.

Can you clearly explain and articulate your guiding beliefs and ethics? If not, you need to, and soon. Any Life without a guiding set of ethics and principles is going to come crashing down sooner or later. You will be found out.

Take care as you begin the process of discovering your Evidence. Think seriously about Life and know that it is of inestimable value. What you have and are in the process of discovering is a sacred trust. Give it all you have. Follow the rules. Be open and honest. Live with integrity.

Rachel Scott changed the world because of what she believed and lived. What about you? Are you someone who will change the world?

Part 3

How to Discover and Test Evidence

Chapter 11
The Life Scene Lab

Once Evidence has been collected, it must then be identified and tested. In this part of the book, you will be taken into the *Life Scene Laboratory*. Think through any *CSI* episode on TV. The show begins with a crime scene, which is roped off with yellow crime scene tape. The crime scene investigators then begin their search for Evidence within that crime scene. They collect it and place it in Evidence collection envelopes and bags.

All that Evidence is then taken to a forensic crime scene laboratory. In that CSI lab, the Evidence must then be identified. The way that the Evidence is identified is to have each piece subjected to a variety of tests.

Forensic laboratories contain the most up-to-date technology and techniques for enhancing and analyzing fingerprints, shoeprints and tire marks. As specific methods of analyzing Evidence at a crime scene are not practical, the objects are recovered and brought into the lab.

Most CSI labs have a unit known as a "Trace Evidence Unit" where scientists look for clues in Evidence such as hair, fabric, dust, fiber and skeletal remains.

That trace Evidence unit consists of these areas:

- A chemistry unit is present in any laboratory and is used to test samples of blood and urine for alcohol, drugs and poisoning. Chemistry sets are also used in the analysis of synthetic materials such as medicines, dyes and stains. Specialists in the area of chemistry also rely on gas chromatographs, mass spectrometers and microscopes to identify chemicals.

- The serology unit specializes in the identification and analysis of bloodstains and other bodily fluids, as well as DNA sequencing. The most common of the DNA tests, the polymers chain reaction, is now able to be performed in small laboratories thanks to advancements in this area; however, the analysis of mitochondrial DNA is still performed only in large forensic laboratories.

- Material units are used to identify and analyze metals, paints, ceramics, soil and wood in an attempt to trace a crime back to a possible suspect.

- The biology unit is in charge of analyzing all biological Evidence such as seeds and plants.

- Firearms units test weapons to see which weapon made the mark on an object or wounded or killed a person. To be able to carry out these tests, firearms specialists study the spent bullet cartridges and use shooting baths to fire weapons, identify the bullet marks and establish the firing distance.

- Photography plays a vital role in the forensic laboratory, as photography is used to document crime scene Evidence. Digital and computer programs allow specialists in the area of photography to analyze photographs and bring the Evidence to light.

- Computer units are used to gather information from any computer, Internet site or device containing computer technology.

Not all the Evidence you have collected holds the same weight, nor should it be used when defining your Design/DNA Code and Talents. At the end of each Field of Evidence you will find *Evidence analysis* tools. These tools allow you to sift through all the Evidence you have identified and see what is the "Best Evidence."

The Evidence Reliability Tests matrix is one of those tools. It enables you to look at the Evidence you have identified and test it for Strength and Reliability. The more that apply to any one piece of Evidence, the stronger that Evidence is.

RT	Evidence Reliability Tests Quick Checklist
RT-1	"Exceptional," Top 25 Percent, Top 10 Percent
RT-2	Flow
RT-3	Preserved
RT-4	Easily Repeatable and Been Repeated
RT-5	Judged as Exceptional by Witnesses
RT-6	Expert Witness Testify
RT-7	Result of Spontaneous Action
RT-8	By Choice and in My Own Time
RT-9	Positive Emotion
RT-10	Intuition

Please be sure to review each Field of Evidence module and identify as many Talents as you are able to verify. These Talents are what form the basis of your Life Theory or Purpose.

Chapter 12
Forensic Reliability Part 1
(Tests 1–5)

I could have written a book called *The 10 Forensic Discovery Secrets to Finding a Life of Purpose and Passion*. I have given speeches using these discovery tests as stand-alone tools to discover Talents. They are logical, powerful, real-Life discovery tests!

As you begin gathering Evidence from the *Five Fields of Evidence*, you will see certain pieces of Evidence that stand out. Your intellectual, physical, emotional, social, and spiritual DNA markers will become evident. They are everywhere!

How many times have you watched a *CSI* episode and a fingerprint or DNA profile has been sent to the lab? The crime scene investigator is standing, watching a computer compare thousands of currently stored profiles. The computer screen pops up a photo and a profile, and the word *Match* is highlighted.

That's what we are looking to do with these forensic Reliability Tests (RTs). Each time you are able to identify a Talent or strength and one of these RTs is a "match," it confirms the Evidence.

Forensic Tip—Luminol

Some Evidence is not always obvious and needs a little more effort to discover. In almost every *CSI* episode a substance called Luminol is used. Luminol is a chemical that, when sprayed, illuminates blood by giving off a blue glow that lasts about thirty seconds. Even if a criminal attempts to clean up after a murder and the blood is seemingly removed from the scene, its traces can be discovered using Luminol.

After identifying and defining the individual Life Scene, collecting and identifying Evidence is the next important task of *forensics*. The question you must ask is, "Is the Evidence reliable?"

- When put to the test in court, will the Evidence stand up under cross-examination?
- Will the Evidence result in a conviction?
- Is the Evidence solid?
- Can I trust my Life and future based on it?

What you believe about yourself is very important. However, it may not be very accurate. Some people are "legends in their own minds," but not in the real world, where Life must be lived.

Others have a lesser or lower view of themselves than is realistic. Either way, you need an accurate picture of your Individual DNA Code and Talents if you are to really live with Purpose, Passion, and Performance!

When you have well-examined Evidence for personal beliefs, they form the foundation of confidence.

The following tests are meant to test the reality and validity of what you think about yourself and give you good reasons for your beliefs. They help you both *identify* and *confirm* the strength of your Evidence.

If you are both honest and realistic about how you assess your Life, you will only become more confident as you put your Talents through these tests. This is a wonderful process, and as you test your Evidence using these forensic Reliability Tests, you will feel yourself becoming more and more alive! You are discovering the very essence of your Life!

These Reliability Tests (RTs) can stand alone. They can be used as questions you ask of yourself to discover Talents in your Life. That would be a good use, and they are powerful enough to help you on your way to discovering your Design.

Take, for instance, RT-1, "Does the Evidence Reach the Standard of 'Exceptional'?" I could have asked it differently: "What Have You Done in Your Life That Is Exceptional?"

The first way I asked the question assumes you have collected Evidence and you now have to test that Evidence for strength and reliability. In the chapters on intellectual Evidence, you are asked, "What has been your most significant intellectual achievement?" Your response could be that you were in an honors class in mathematics. That reaches the level of "Exceptional." I could have asked a simple open-ended question such as, "What have you done in your Life that was Exceptional?" That is more of a shotgun approach, requiring you to think broadly about your Life.

After verifying the Evidence that you are "Exceptional" at mathematics, you are now required to ask nine more questions, the rest of the RTs. Answering those questions potentially builds a stronger case for you to see how powerful this mathematical Talent really is in your Life. The more RTs that apply, the stronger the Evidence.

RT-6 asks, "Is There an Expert Witness Who Is Willing to Testify to the Validity or Exceptional Nature of the Evidence?" It is possible that a math teacher or judge at a math Olympiad said you were good enough to get an academic scholarship based on your mathematical Talents. The case would continue to be built as you are able to apply more of the RTs to your Evidence.

You will see at the end of each chapter on "Fields of Evidence" a grid for you to review the Evidence you have collected and run it against these ten RTs. You have to establish reliability, and this is one of the easiest and most practical ways for you to do it. The more RTs you can apply to the Evidence, the stronger and more reliable that Evidence becomes.

RT	Evidence Reliability Tests Quick Checklist
RT-1	"Exceptional," Top 25 Percent, Top 10 Percent
RT-2	Flow
RT-3	Preserved
RT-4	Easily Repeatable and Been Repeated
RT-5	Judged as Exceptional by Witnesses
RT-6	Expert Witness Testify
RT-7	Result of Spontaneous Action
RT-8	By Choice and in My Own Time
RT-9	Positive Emotion
RT-10	Intuition

These are "Life tests" and not scientific *per se*. They are based on the observation of people's lives, common sense, and the personal reports of people who have discovered and have been successful in living their DNA Code. As you work through and apply these Reliability Tests, you will see just how powerful they are!

RT-1
Does the Evidence Reach the Standard of "Exceptional?"

Exceptional means above, or better than average, or clearly superior. When you look at the definition of a Talent, could your Evidence be judged in at least the top 25 percent of all other participants? What awards have you won? What superior grades have you been given? What speeds, measurements, weights, and/or awards have you achieved that are better than the vast majority of your peers? What contracts have you negotiated? What examination or board results have you aced?

1. What have you ever done that stands out as being exceptional—not good, but better than the vast majority of others?

2. What have you done that stands out as head and shoulders above what you know is just good, normal, and ordinary?

3. What have you done that, when you think about it, sends shivers down your spine? Can you still picture the Performance, the brainstorm, and the achievement? Can you still feel the exhilaration?

4. What have you done that you still dream about repeating? What happened that you were, and still are, excited about telling others?

This standard of Evidence is important because you'll know, when compared with other similar achievements, there is *no* doubt that what you did was exceptional!

RT-2
Has the Evidence Produced "Flow" or the State of Being "in the Zone?"

Has the Evidence ever resulted in an experience identified as "flow," being "in the zone," or, my favorite, *E'tat de Grace* (state of grace)?

Though this concept is often thought of in a sports context, it applies to every human experience where there is a *high level of challenge* that you meet by using a Unique Talent.

Forensic Definition—Flow

You have experienced flow at different times in your Life and will likely recognize its characteristics: you felt particularly strong, alert, in effortless control, and you had a sense that you were performing at the peak of your ability. Both the sense of time and emotional problems seemed to disappear. There was a sense that you were living what you were Designed to live.

The concept of flow was essentially defined and described by psychologist Mihaly Csikszentmihalyi, a respected leader in the Positive Psychology movement. The experience of flow seems to have at least the following elements:

1. Time just seems to fly, and markers by which time is measured don't seem to exist because we are in the moment.
2. We are completely focused and concentrating due to either innate curiosity or because of training.
3. We know we are fully capable and able to perform the essential task without fear of failure or boredom.
4. We have a sense of ecstasy and are not constrained by everyday reality. Emotional problems seem to disappear.
5. We find ourselves in a place of great inner clarity, possessing the knowledge of how and what to do innately.
6. The end result is not our goal, as we know we will perform without the fear of failing. Our ego is not the focus of our performing.
7. The Purpose of what we are doing is the focus, and we are not burdened by outcomes.

I believe this is the most important of all the RTs and Evidence tests because it involves all of your Five Fields of Evidence to some extent. I believe that flow is when all your pistons are firing in the right order. This does not mean in equal power or capacity, but in the right combination for your Unique DNA Code. It reflects the very best of who you are in the best way possible. It gives you the best Evidence possible as you discover Evidence for your Talents.

When I look at my Life, I have personally experienced flow in the following situations:

1. Cricket is a sport I love and have always been very good at. Cricket is a long game, lasting up to eight hours and often played in very hot weather. I have experienced flow many times while playing. I remember playing hard, sweating in ninety-plus-degree weather. I would be on the field for four hours or more, yet it would seem to be over in a few minutes. It didn't matter whether I won or lost but that I had performed exceptionally well; and that was my reward. (I do love winning, however.)

2. Public speaking/preaching. I discovered my ability to speak when I was nineteen years old and in the military. I was chosen to take an officers' selection course, and one of the first exercises we had to perform was to give an extemporaneous speech for ten minutes. I had never given a speech before in my Life, let alone in a competitive situation. I remember preaching for forty-five to sixty minutes, and it seemed that I had just stood up and I was done. The words flowed; I didn't repeat ideas, didn't "um" and "ah" or use "okay" regularly. Everything worked well and, when I looked at the audience responses, they seemed very positive. I remember recently I had just received news of a very tough situation that affected me deeply. I had to speak, and I did. I spoke as well as I ever had, and there was no thought of what I was going through outside of delivering the speech.

3. Doing photography. I will sometimes go to downtown Seattle, to the famous Pike Place Market or Westlake Plaza, and take photographs of people. I can stand on the corner outside Starbucks for hours and take photographs of all the interesting people who congregate there. Time flies, and I get some great shots. I then drive home so energized, wanting to tell someone about what I have just done.

4. Creative thinking. I don't believe my peers ever saw me as being creative. My creativity is related more to concepts, strategic thinking, and new ways of doing things. That is what LSI is. I have found myself sitting in my regular coffeehouse "office," doodling, writing, and thinking up ideas. I feel alive and productive and come up with some great ideas. I also produce a large amount of work.

5. Writing. I write in spurts. I have ideas floating around in my head, and then, all of a sudden, I need to write and will sit down and go for hours. There are times when time does fly, and I will

only know I have been at it for three hours when the battery on my laptop starts to shut down. I look at what I have written, and sometimes I have ten to fifteen pages that make sense enough that I am willing to let others read what I have just written.

What about you personally? *?RU*

- Where have you experienced flow?
- Where were you?
- What were you doing?
- Who was with you or watching you?
- How many times have you performed this activity and experienced flow?
- What elements of flow can you identify in the Talents you have potentially identified?

The illustration below shows a formula to best identify your flow experience. It is a simple formula but gives a clear description of how flow is experienced.

The Flow Formula

High Challenge (HC)	+ Low Skill/Talent (LS/T)	= Anxiety
Low Challenge (LC)	+ High Skill/Talent (HS/T)	= Boredom
High Challenge (HC)	**+ High Skill/Talent (HS/T)**	**= Flow**

Apply the formula and think about what you have defined as a Talent. Flow can be experienced only when a *High Challenge* is met by a *High Skill* (Talent) in your Life. If you don't possess the *High Skill*, it is unlikely you will ever experience flow. Next, think about when you have had to meet a challenge that demanded the engagement of that Talent. Did you experience flow or being in the zone? If you did, take some time to analyze that experience. Journal about your experience, and see what you can do to remember everything associated with it. That is the most important application of the Analysis of Asset you can engage in.

One of the ways you can really develop this discovery tool as a Life Scene Investigator is to constantly be on the lookout for examples of flow in the lives of those around you. There is a rule to Life that simply says you will never discover more about your own Life than you are willing to show and give to others.

- When have you observed flow in a student or co-worker?
- As a coach, friend, parent, and so on, where have you seen someone experiencing flow?
- Always take the time to tell the person you observed what you saw and what you believe it says about his or her Unique Design.

RT-3
Has The Evidence Been Preserved and Does It Continue to Be Displayed Today?

When we live and use our Talents, we find Evidence that lasts. Talents make their mark and leave a deep imprint.

Forensic Evidence Description—Impression Evidence

People who commit a crime may often leave footprints/shoe prints or tire impressions when entering and/or exiting the crime scene. In many instances, impressions can be positively identified as having been made by a specific shoe or tire. Entire databases of tire and shoe prints are available to crime scene investigators.

Clothing of a pedestrian struck by a motor vehicle can also leave impressions on the vehicle. Examinations of questioned impressions may provide investigative lead information, such as brand and model of tires and footwear.

Vehicle makes and models may also be determined from wheelbase, fender, glass, paint, and track width measurements.

What about the impressions and imprints you have made? Are they representative of Talents in your Life?

- Has the Evidence of what you did been preserved? How so?
- Is there still Evidence that remains? What is it?

- Have your accomplishments lasted over time and made their mark? What did you do?
- There is clear and convincing Evidence to point to your unique involvement. What is it?
- What have you done that really took root and grew?
  - You set a record that lasted a long time: athletics, sales, website hits, sales of Girl Scout cookies, and so on.
  - You started a magazine five years ago that is still going strong.
  - You tutored a pre-college student who was really struggling but who has gone on to do exceptionally well.

I recently was contacted by Bruce, who was part of a youth group I started back in the mid-1980s in Johannesburg, South Africa. He was still living in South Africa and was working with teens and involved in much of the same work that LSI does. He had started a program called "Eternity and Beyond." Bruce was online searching, came across my name, and immediately contacted me. It was a great surprise. I had actually officiated at his wedding to Jenny, who was also part of the youth group. The influence I had in his Life continued and was now growing as he reached other teens.

The time, the effort, and the use of my God-given abilities had borne fruit and many years later was still bearing fruit. I have always worked well with teens. I still work with them today.

One of the things I have continued to do with teens who have been through Teen Discovery, a program primarily for at-risk teens I started in 2000, is to keep in contact with many of them to see where they are and what they are doing years after we have stopped working with them. For many, the involvement has made a lasting change. They continue to grow and engage Life productively. Many are in college, and many others are working in good jobs and staying out of trouble with the law.

Back in 2003, I was held a few months in Homeland Security detention. I want to state at the outset that it was not for any crime—but I was held in civil detention. I was from a country that no longer recognized its citizens who had left the country and not returned after five years. I ended up as a man without a country. I was like the character Tom Hanks played in *The Terminal*. The rules had also changed with how and where paperwork was filed after September 11.

Additionally, my case file went missing for almost a year, causing further confusion.

While in federal detention (it sounds so ominous), I spent a lot of time doing what I have always done; encouraging people who are in tough circumstances. Not only did I talk with people who sought my help, but I found ways to make the situation more positive. Around Thanksgiving, I created a turkey out of a blue rubber glove only to have it confiscated. I played my favorite game, cricket, with a rubber glove wrapped into a ball and a book for a bat. This was my creative side at its best, which sadly was not encouraged or appreciated by the not so creatively endowed prison staff.

One of the people I met "inside" was a young man named Prashant. He was very despondent about being deported from the United States and was extremely anxious about his future. I spent time with him trying to help him understand that his situation was not terminal and that God was still interested in him and had a plan for his Life.

I woke up one morning and Prashant was gone. He was taken in the middle of the night, as were most deportees, and sent to the airport for removal to his country of origin. I missed his friendship.

In 2008 I received a phone call from a number that I didn't recognize. It was much longer than the standard U.S. area code and number; it was from the United Kingdom. The caller identified himself as Prashant. I was not sure at first who it was because I have a number of friends from India named Prashant, with whom I play cricket. He soon reminded me of which Prashant he was. He said he had tried to find me for years and he ran across my website and found my phone number. He wanted to thank me for how I had influenced his Life during the tough time he experienced in Homeland Security detention. He said I had pointed him to God in that desperate time. We talked a little more, and I became his friend on Facebook. His Life had changed wonderfully, and he was now married and living in London. This was Evidence that lasted and had long-term effects.

What about you? What have you done that demonstrates Evidence your DNA Code has made a lasting difference? What have you done that has continued to grow and develop? Is it a business, an organization, a concept or idea, a positive relationship or association, a Life? What do you see now that you have been removed and are viewing with the perspective of time?

When we involve our Talents to effect change, those changes will have a lasting quality. The Evidence will be preserved. Strong influences and actions create and leave Evidence that lasts.

RT-4

Is the Evidence Easily Repeatable? Has the Evidence Been Repeated Numerous Times?

Can the Evidence be repeated again and again with the same or better results? Is there a history of repeated actions?

When you identify a Talent in a Field of Evidence, be confident it is indeed a Talent if you can repeat it easily. If you have a history of repeating it, preferably many times over a long period of time, then designate it as a Talent.

When my son André was about fourteen, we were living in a home that had a large carport with a basketball hoop in it. André was playing basketball at his junior high and was often outside shooting. One weekend he asked me to shoot hoops with him. I am tall and have always been a good athlete, but I had never really played much basketball. I play cricket, tennis, racquetball, golf, and other sports where you hit a ball, not sports where you throw or kick a ball.

The challenge was to see who could shoot as many baskets in a row as possible from a number of places on the court. I would get one or two and maybe three in a row, but never more. All of a sudden, I hit a run of baskets and I couldn't miss. I kept shooting, and the ball kept going in. I kept doing this until I had shot thirty-seven baskets in a row. André was in disbelief, but not more than I was. I kept apologizing because there was no good reason for that run of baskets. The reality was that it was a fluke, an anomaly. The rest of the time playing, I don't think I scored more than two or three in a row.

Some people might think I had great potential to become a good basketball player. But I know the truth, and the truth is this: I am no basketball player, and I have never really enjoyed playing basketball. When I recount the story, I can do so only as an example of a fluke. If I tried to beat that record, it would probably take me many years and thousands of tries to perhaps repeat it. It was not and never will be Evidence of a Talent in my Life.

Many people look back at highlights in their lives and can point to a remarkable feat or action and talk about it as a defining moment in their existence. They build their lives around an *incident*, a one-off demonstration of something that on its face is exceptional. But when you ask them how they have continued to demonstrate and develop that capacity, there is little to no Evidence.

I even know people who talk about what geniuses their children are based on winning an award in elementary school, or what great athletes their kids are because they scored a winning run in a little league game. There are many things each of us has done that are outstanding. But when those outstanding feats have not been repeated and there is no Evidence to show that they were anything more than our own personal shooting stars, seen once, brightly, for a second or two in the span of our lives, we need to assign them to the "not applicable" file. We cannot build a Life or change our direction based on a memory of possible Talent. We need consistency and longevity.

Laser-Induced Breakdown Spectroscopy (LIBS)

Laser-induced breakdown spectroscopy (LIBS) is a relatively new technique for analyzing materials. This technique has been made possible by the advent of very-high-intensity pulsed lasers, which provide enough energy in a brief instant to raise the temperature of matter by thousands of degrees and vaporize it. The excited matter produced by the laser pulse subsequently emits a characteristic visible spectrum as the various elements return to their normal temperature state.

The spectrum can be used to identify many basic elements in a substance and to identify or distinguish the makeup of a substance by means of spectral comparison.

RT-5
Has the Evidence Been Recognized as Exceptional by Your Peers and Other Eyewitnesses?

Have your peers, friends, work associates, or teammates recognized and openly stated that the Evidence meets a standard of being exceptional? Our peers are important in the recognition of exceptional ability. They see us on a regular basis and are able to watch us perform over the long run, in a variety of situations, close up; they can best evaluate whether we are better than they are in a given ability. Evidence based on peer review is essential.

One exercise we ask people to do in our Evidence discovery classes is to send out emails and request that the various witnesses in their lives complete a "Personal/Eyewitness Statement Form."

Recently Helen Meyer, a Licensed Professional Counselor who was completing certification as a Life Scene Investigator, told me how this exercise changed her whole perception of who she was. The replies she got not only confirmed so much of the Evidence she had discovered during her training but had also expanded the view of her amazing Talents.

Look at the "witness" illustrations in the table below and identify the people in your Life who qualify. Make sure you identify them by name. Witnesses need names in order to have credibility, so others, who might question the witnesses' evaluation of our Talents, can see they are real people, not just our pretend friends or names that appear on a resume but can't be found in the real world.

Personal Witness	Examples
Personal witnesses are people who are your peers or who know you and have observed you in action. These can be friends, family, work associates, team members and others who have no other vested or paid interest in testifying. These witnesses are relationally or emotionally connected to you, and at times their objectivity can be questioned. However, their testimony should be assessed and given substantial weight if they are known to desire and have your best interests at heart.	Mother Father Spouse Sister Brother Close friend Girl-/Boyfriend Roommate Longtime teammate Longtime school-/classmate (sits next to you) Business partner

Eyewitness	Examples
An eyewitness is someone who observed the Evidence. They are people who are not connected to you in terms of a personal relationship or people who have been retained by you. They have observed you in action and have important information that is based solely on observation.	Classmate (you don't really know or talk to them) Work associate Casual acquaintance Someone at Starbucks Attends gym with you Someone at school Attendee at a game or performance who watched you Association member

It is important to be able to quote what your peers have said. What statements stand out? Have they been quoted in an article, internal memo, newsletter, or journal? Be clear on what they said, and be willing to verify what they said. Will they confirm what you say they said?

Chapter 13
Forensic Reliability Part 2
(Tests 6–10)

I know as you look at and begin to apply the first five Reliability Tests you will see the incredible value of how they work. They are incisive; they look deep into your Life and experience. They illuminate like Luminol by uncovering Evidence that may have been overlooked or covered up.

Let's continue discovering and answering the question *PRU.*

RT-6
Are There Expert Witnesses Who Are Willing to Testify to the Validity or Exceptional Nature of the Evidence?

Is there an *expert witness* in the Field of Evidence who stated your Evidence meets the standard of being Exceptional? Can you think of "experts" who have made comments or statements about something you have done that made you come alive? Your family, friends, or co-workers may have heard them say you were exceptional or had a bright future. You can quote verbatim what they said with a sense of pride.

Expert Witness	Expert Witnesses
An expert witness is one who has knowledge beyond that of the ordinary layperson, which enables him or her to give testimony regarding an issue	Schoolteacher Manager or boss College professor Superintendent Coach

that requires expertise to understand. In court, the party offering the expert must lay a foundation for the expert's testimony. Laying the foundation involves testifying about the expert's credentials and experience that qualifies him/her as an expert.	Principal CEO Scout (sport, talent, etc.) Youth leader Pastor, minister, rabbi Counselor Doctor Department head Driver's education instructor Tutor

Every CSI outfit has a team of experts who evaluate and test the Evidence. There are experts who evaluate the crime scene and collect Evidence. Other experts work in the morgue, specialist doctors who seek to determine the causes of death. More experts evaluate trace Evidence collected at the crime scene and seek to identify what it is and who it belongs to. Some experts do computer research and DNA testing. So CSI comprises a variety of experts who are all necessary to meeting the ultimate goal of identifying and convicting criminals who perpetrate crimes.

Expert witnesses are witnesses who display special skill or knowledge derived from *training* or *experience* in the Field of Evidence they testify about. Often they are people who have been well educated and then added to that education with years of experience. That combination makes for the best type of expert. Formal education is not an essential element of qualifying as an expert. Much of the time experts are published, or what they believe is out in the public, and their beliefs have been examined and challenged by their peers and other experts.

The same can be said of a coach as an expert. Most coaches have played a particular sport and then pass on not only their personal experience but also their education, observations, insights, and other lessons to become experts in a sport.

The best experts are often a combination of experience and education. Many experts have little to no formal education, but their opinions should not be ignored or discounted because of that. We have many examples of experts who are college dropouts, those who didn't fit a particular mold or even people who are eccentrics. Bill Gates comes to mind. He is an expert and people listen to what he says, even though he is a college dropout.

When I was growing up I had a cricket coach. His name was Jim Cornford. Jim had been a professional cricketer in England for many years before coming to Africa to take up residence at St George's College, where I attended school. Jim was a bowler, or pitcher. What was interesting about Jim was that while he was a great coach of all the elements of cricket, he was definitely best as a batting coach. It was all about perspective. He was a bowler who watched batsmen. He had to constantly observe them and find ways to get them out. Because of that he became an expert practitioner as a bowler but an expert coach of batsmen. Jim was the expert who endorsed my talent to select teams.

You need to find experts in the areas of your Life Scene who can identify, validate, and make specific statements to corroborate the strength of your Evidence. Expert witnesses are a vital part of the reliability process.

We all know the power an expert can have in our lives and the lives of our children. Think back to when you were a teen or in college (or maybe you are currently a teen); think about something you were really interested in. It could be a class, a sport, a sales group, an extracurricular pursuit.

Who is it that you looked up to: an advisor, coach, or head of a department? Who is that individual that you and others on your team considered to be the best and wanted to become like? You respected that person, and he or she was the expert in your opinion. Has that person ever said something that made you come alive, stand taller, and just beam? You can remember what he or she said, maybe years later, as can many of your friends.

Who are the experts in your Life, and what have they said? Can you think about or maybe pull out a report card, job evaluation, article, citation, or other document that cites the expert and what he or she has said about you? Remember, as with your peers, the experts need names, positions, and reasons why they should be considered as an "expert."

Look at the list in the "Expert Witness" box. Completing an "Expert Witness Statement Form" is a great exercise you can perform.

RT-7

Was the Evidence the Result of Natural or Spontaneous Action?

Was the Evidence produced spontaneously—something that you are a natural at?

1. Do you simply perform this Talent without even thinking about how good you are at it?
2. Was the Evidence easily discovered?
3. Was the Evidence easily performed?
4. Was the Evidence easily observed?
5. Was the Evidence produced naturally, not forced?

I have coached cricket for many years. I have had the opportunity to coach kids who have never played or even seen the game before. I often demonstrate the basic elements of the game and then ask them to try and copy what I have just done. There are always a few who just "get it." They instinctively know how while others have no clue.

The same is true with parents I worked with. They describe how their children sat down at a piano, having never played, and just seemed to know how. No instruction was needed to understand the process.

Instruction, practice, and coaching are often needed in order to become better or to excel and take that ability to the level of a Talent; but again, it is a natural process that is obviously wired into an individual.

Think about some of the "natural" things you have done, where the first time you tried, it worked. The process seemed so easy when others struggled, and people looked at you and thought you had done this many times before or had lots of coaching or education.

- Hit a golf ball two hundred yards and thought that was just the way it was done
- Made a speech and the words just flowed
- Went rock climbing and got to the top without any real thought or fear
- Cooked a meal and everything was ready at the same time and tasted great
- Fixed the brakes on a car and the process seemed logical—and they worked
- Understood a foreign language very quickly and was able to converse easily with people who spoke it as their first language
- Decorated a room and everything seemed to fit beautifully, in the appropriate places

Can you list three things you know you are a *natural* at?

1. _____

2. _____

3. _____

Comments or statements like these are all indicators of this RT authenticating your Evidence as a Talent:

1. "I don't know; I was just really good at it."
2. "No one ever taught me. I just did it and did it well."
3. "I was told to do it, and I was better than most of the others who had been playing all their lives."

RT-8

Is the Evidence Something I Perform or Choose to Do Myself? Is It Something I Do in My Own Time?

The choice of what we do with our spare time will show Evidence of our Talents. When we are driven internally and wired with a Unique Talent, we will find ourselves not just using spare time to play or do, but *making time* to enjoy our Talents.

1. Is the demonstrated capacity or Talent something you do by choice or internal motivation?
2. Is it something you do for recreation, in your spare time, and without being required or forced to do?
3. What clubs, associations, or groups do you belong to?
4. Do you receive a lot of emails, newsletters, e-zines, books, or magazines that reflect your intense interest?
5. Do you spend a lot of time on the Internet searching for sites and have websites marked as "Favorites" on a particular subject?
6. Do you have a variety or collection of equipment, articles, memorabilia, and so on that are associated with your Talent (baseball cards, movies, guitars, model cars or planes, plants, cameras, computer games, books, musical scores, etc.)?

Life Scene—HT

Another good indication might be what you watch on TV. I have a good friend, Dave, who has two sons. I was at his condo, and we were talking about our kids and their interests. He remarked about how his ten-year-old son, HT (Henry), loved watching a variety of cooking programs. HT is fascinated by culinary arts and loves to cook.

How cool—a ten-year-old boy who spends his free time not just playing video games or sports but watching cooking channels. I wish more parents would encourage their children in some of these nonacademic loves and pursuits. Watch for HT to have his own TV show somewhere down the road.

So what do you watch on TV? I know a lot of people who watch the history channels, interior design shows, forensics shows, medical shows, military shows, gardening shows, game shows, reality shows, and then the more obvious shows on sports and politics.

- What do you watch when you have the channel changer in your hand and have no one else telling you what to watch?
- What do you do with your extra or down time?
- When you have the time to do what you want without any expectations or restrictions from others, what do you find yourself doing?

RT-9
Has the Evidence Produced Positive Emotion?

In terms of authenticating the reliability of a Talent, experiencing the emotion of thankfulness or gratitude probably carries as much weight as, or more than, any other RT. You cannot use or display a DNA Coded Talent without feeling and needing to express a sense of thankfulness.

You can always identify a Talent by watching the person who lives it generating positive emotion. Happy people are those who know their Talents and live them. Unhappy, anxious, depressed, frustrated people are those who either don't know or are not living their Unique Design and DNA Code. That is as simple as it gets.

Has the Evidence resulted in positive emotions such as gratitude, satisfaction, exhilaration, contentment, happiness, or joy? Different emotions result from different Talents, but again, thankfulness and gratitude are the hallmarks of a Talent that is lived. These emotions are *direct hard Evidence* that this is a Talent!

Parents, managers, coaches, and teachers should be observing what generates positive emotion in those they work with. We are not talking about a short-lived, seldom-repeated emotion, but emotions that are observed on a regular basis, something that makes the person come alive and fill with positive emotion. What is it? Have you experienced positive emotion in the Talent you have discovered or identified?

In the award-winning movie *Chariots of Fire*, Eric Lidle, the hero of the movie, has a sister who is trying to make him feel guilty and stop running in the Olympics because of its eternal futility, in her opinion. She was a missionary to China, and based on her beliefs, he should have given up running and become a missionary like herself. In his response to her, he said that when he ran, he experienced a feeling he described as "the pleasure of God."

That "pleasure of God" is the greatest description I have heard to describe this concept of positive emotion. It is the sense that I am doing what I was made to do and that my Maker, my Designer, is looking down and is pleased, just like a parent who observes his child laughing and enjoying Life to the fullest. It is the synchronization of living what I was Designed to do. It is the unlocking of my DNA Code!

- Have you experienced the "pleasure of God?"
- What were you doing?
- How would you describe that feeling of knowing in a profound way that you were doing what you were so definitely made to do?

Positive Psychology is a relatively new and exciting development in psychology. It has been described as the "science of happiness." The question that Positive Psychology attempts to answer is, "What generates those emotions we define as happiness?" What are those attitudes, activities, connections, and behaviors that produce positive emotion?

Positive Psychology studies people who have defined, positive character qualities. It looks at issues such as how much money is enough to make people happy? What produces optimism that enables people to deal with the tough issues of Life? How do we produce gratitude?

LSI is based on the philosophical belief that when people identify their Unique Talents, develop them, and then actively use them in Life, they produce the characteristics that are studied in Positive Psychology. Design discovered and Talents used produce positive emotion.

How we approach the issue is similar to the way the *Gallup StrengthsFinder* does. The *StrengthsFinder* 2.0 is a test that helps you identify your hardwired Talents. The belief is that discovering your Talents is the pathway to living a happier, more fulfilled Life.

Do you have the opportunity to do what you do best each day?

Do you? *?RU* when it comes to answering this question: someone who answers with a definite "yes" or "no?"

When people are able to do what they do best each day and for a good portion of the day, they are generally happy and fulfilled. That is common sense. Do what you love, love what you do, and the world makes sense.

A number of years ago I started a program similar to LSI for a nonprofit group called the Regeneration Project. This organization worked with children who were orphaned due to a parent having died of AIDS. These were marginalized kids in an extreme sense. Many were minority kids whose parents were often drug addicts, prostitutes, or gay. So in society's view, they were not kids who often engendered the open embrace that many other orphaned or disadvantaged kids do.

There were two sisters whose father had already died and whose mother was receiving hospice care while in the advanced stages of an AIDS-related condition. The oldest girl said she was always so worried going home after school because she never knew what condition she would find her mother in, or that she might even come home to find her mother dead. There was little in her Life that was a source of positive emotion or encouragement.

One of the Talents we had discovered in this girl was her exceptional athletic ability, specifically in basketball. What one of the other Life coaches did was to encourage her to play more basketball. She was not able to play on the school team due to having to care for her little sister and her mother. We got her to take her little sister and some of the other kids in her apartment community and go and play in a small area close to the apartments as often as possible.

What this simple action did was to allow her to use a Talent we knew produced positive emotion and regularly feed her emotional state, which was constantly being drained by her immense responsibilities. We told her that when she really felt overwhelmed, she needed to go and play, even for a few minutes. Not only were there good physical reasons, but she was endowed with a unique Talent to play; it was also a known source of positive emotion.

This example is very important for all of us to learn from, not just in our desire to discover Talents, but also in managing Life when we face a crisis or ongoing, tough situation. Talents help us get through the toughest times if we know what they are and we use them.

When the going gets tough, the tough rely on their Talents to keep going! When the going gets tough, we have the opportunity to discover more Evidence of what we are made of. This is an amazing and fundamental truth about Life if you are willing to learn it.

RT-10

Did You Discover the Evidence through Following Your Intuition or Gut-Sense?

This last Reliability Test could easily be a separate chapter. It is not objective, nor is it based on demonstrated Evidence. Nevertheless, it is an important test that, if identified, may lead to you having the courage to openly attempt what you identify. It does take courage to openly admit to the world that there are parts to you that need to be presented in open court, the court of Life, and then developed.

Many books and theories of self-discovery focus on Intuition as a primary tool of discovery. I would always start with the RTs 1–9 and then go to this last one. Go with what you know, but don't be a coward and disregard what has been part of your Life and possibly your DNA Code and Design all your Life.

LSI is primarily about forensics, which is based on objective Evidence and defined testing and processes. But there are times in our lives when we just *know*. We have what is termed a "gut sense" or "a still small voice." It is not scientifically verifiable or really repeatable, but there are times when great discoveries have been made because an investigator followed his or her "gut sense." The investigator had an intuitive sense where to look for the Evidence or what the Evidence might feel or look like.

It could be described as a shadow, like an outline without substance until you turn around and see the tree that is between you and the sun. It is a sense of internal leading that tells you you're following the right direction.

Intuition can also be looked on as a Unique Talent, what some might call a sixth sense. It must be stated that in the LSI context, if you wish to have any confidence in a Talent discovered by intuition, it must be backed up by other RTs or be looked on with a healthy skepticism. There should be additional Evidence to corroborate it.

MYLIFESCENE.COM—CROSS NOW—MYLIFESCENE.COM
Life Scene—Ben Davis

Ben Davis is one of the most exciting young entrepreneurs in the United States. Ben started a business a couple of years ago called The Gents Place (www.thegentsplace.com) in the Dallas area and then another one in Leawood, Kansas. This year he started another Gents Place in the exclusive Dallas suburb of Preston Hollow.

My company, Corp-DNA (www.corp-dna.com), was hired by Ben to work with his leadership staff as well as do some sales training. As Ben was expanding and about to open his new Preston Hollow location, he asked us to help him in the hiring process. We performed what we call a "Positive Forensic Profile" on The Gents Place's employees and had a DNA Profile of their best performers.

Ben used the profile to begin hiring new employees and did so very successfully.

I had lunch with him recently, and we got to talking about why his business model was so successful and then got onto the hiring process. He loved what we had done for him in setting up the DNA Hiring Profile specifically created for his business.

Ben also went on to say that he used it but that beyond the analytics and processes we had created, he relied extensively on his intuition. He said when he sensed something was wrong, it normally was. He had a number of examples of when he didn't follow his intuition and how it had cost him.

Ben reads extensively about starting businesses, technology, marketing, leadership, sales, customer service, and so on. He is very bright, driven, and always using his amazing business acumen.

Ben's foundation is his bright business mind that is filled with facts, statistics, examples from *Inc.*, *Forbes*, and *Fast Company* magazines, and advice from seasoned professionals. He couples that analytical fact-driven mind with what is not seen but which is powerful and which also guides his decisions to positive outcomes when he trusts it.

At times, even when the facts say "Go," his gut or intuition says "No," and he has learned to trust his inner voice. Great leaders like Ben Davis often have a "gut instinct" and make decisions that matter and that have significant outcomes.

How accurate is your Intuition? How many times have you trusted it to a right decision? Some people have a unique intuitive Talent. Do you?

MYLIFESCENE.COM—CROSS NOW—MYLIFESCENE.COM

Chapter 14
Forensic Evidence Discovery Tests

Most people seem to love taking online tests. They are almost always marketed in an appealing way. I would bet if you have been online for any length of time, you have probably done some of these tests. When I teach classes or give seminars, participants can't wait to take the tests and find out more information so they can figure out new things about themselves. It should always be fun to learn and discover exciting information about your Life.

There is, however, important information about these tests you need to know:

1. Tests are *supportive* of Evidence, but *they are not Evidence in and of themselves.* (They can support the Evidence that an alleged criminal was at the scene of a crime because the criminal's DNA was there. Could there be another explanation?)

2. Tests can *confirm* Evidence. They can be used only after the Evidence has been collected to confirm what we believe to be true or accurate.

3. Tests are *profile Evidence*, which essentially gives us a general picture of possibilities, not of objective truth.

4. Tests are only one part of the process.

5. Tests can tell you that you have a Talent but not how, where, or when to use it.

6. Tests can measure by comparison. The IQ test compares you with others your age.

Some people are fearful of what a test will show. They look at tests from a deficit and "What is wrong with me?" perspective. Remember, deficit is not the focus of *Life Scene Investigation*. Talents and Assets are!

Some tests are diagnostic. We use some of the following tests as a part of our discovery programs and call them "Forensic Discovery Tests." They give you hard, objective information. They also give you a score that is accurate, a profile that is enduring over time, and results that are specific to you individually.

Some tests are very short and simply give a quick snapshot of your current Life situation. They are nothing more than a window into where you are and how you are looking at Life today. They help you get a better perspective on how you are facing a situation that is probably temporary. The "Satisfaction with Life Scale" is one of those. It measures how you look at Life today. It is not a test that reveals a set of personality traits that are very unlikely to change without intensive therapy.

Going to the www.mylifescene.com website will connect you to many of the "Forensic Tests" we use to help people discover and develop Evidence. If you were part of one of our programs, you would learn how to integrate them and apply them to your DNA Code discovery. Go to the www.mylifescene.com site and you can find a list of tests to take. Most are free, but some you will need to pay for.

I want to encourage you to take some of these tests as you work through the Fields of Evidence and other chapters.

Samples of *?RU* Tests and Profiles Used in LSI

- *IQ*, which looks at and measures intelligence (intellectual ability) from primarily an analytical viewpoint. It is a highly focused measure but does not measure intelligence as a whole.

- *Emotional Intelligence (EQ)* measures how well you manage your emotions in a variety of situations. This is as important in making Life a success as an IQ or other measure of intelligence.

- *VIA Inventory of Strengths—Values in Action* is the world's most scientifically validated tool for measuring character strengths.

- *StrengthsFinder 2.0* is the most scientifically valid test for discovering innate, hardwired Talents. The 2.0 version lists thirty-four strengths and gives you your top five in an extensive report, which coaches you on how to use these strengths.

- *Cynthia Tobias* (www.applest.com) is an expert Life Scene Investigator. She studies how people understand and process information, or what we call "learning styles." She has written books on learning styles, developed tests, and knows how to interpret those tests. She also teaches business executives, police officers, and others how to discover and become effective in their professions by applying her *learning styles forensic Evidence*.

We have probably all taken a *vocational assessment* while in school. After taking the tests, we were presented with a list of options such as astronaut, cab driver, nurse, lawyer, landscaper, or teacher. Many of these tests are wonderful and help us in guiding our direction. There are departments of and specialists who do career counseling in most schools and colleges. There are even state government offices that focus on vocational guidance and rehabilitation.

There are also a lot of fun and some, frankly, stupid tests designed to get you to purchase something:

- What sort of animal are you?
- What is your wardrobe style?
- What character are you most like in the movie *The Sandlot* or on the popular TV series *Seinfeld?*
- What sort of dog should you own?
- What is your love style?
- What country do you most look like?

Many of these tests have elements of truth, but don't bank your future on them. The sad reality is that some people do.

Lie to Me was a prime-time forensics television drama focusing on a team of professional lie detectors. They are walking, talking testers who attempt to determine whether people are lying or telling the truth, human polygraphs. They are trained to look for a set of criteria, such as facial tics, eye movement, color of skin tones on various parts of the body, physical movement, and other human physical changes. Again, they might be able to accurately assess whether a person is lying, but they can't know why or specifically what about. They only get a part of the picture. We know people fail polygraphs all the time, and that is why their results are never admitted in criminal proceedings and are used sparingly in civil ones. They are not always accurate.

Marcus Buckingham is one of the pioneers of the strengths movement and the author of three books of the movement's essential reading: *Now Discover Your Strengths, Now Go Put Your Strengths to Work,* and his latest work, *Find your Strongest Life*. He uses a very simple test that is performed and integrated into Life many times a day. It is a two-question positive/negative filter. When I do something in the course of my Life, do I: "Love it?" (green card) or "Loathe it?" (red card). This is a test of perception and a very good way to look at Life broadly but also simply, in small bites. If you have not read these books, you would do well to buy them.

I was writing at a great haunt of mine, Caffe Ladro, in Kirkland, Washington. I looked up at a man who walked by, and he was carrying a book titled *Linear Algebra and Its Applications*. I looked away as quickly as I could and literally felt a negative reaction. I "Loathed" algebra and anything math related. I always have and always will. There is no doubt that a red card notation would have resulted. If the man had walked by with a book on photography, travel, or some sports-related subject, I would have had a very different and positive reaction. I would have "Loved" it and recorded it on a green card.

The Validity of Forensic Discovery Tests

Not all tests and testing procedures are of equal value or carry the same weight, nor are all testing procedures valid.

Many of the teens I have worked with through the years have had a diagnosis of ADD or ADHD. What is obvious to me is that even though they have an official diagnosis by a medical or mental health professional and are now on mind-altering drugs/narcotics, these diagnoses are not always accurate. When I take some time to ask how the diagnosis was arrived at, I find out that the procedures vary greatly in terms of how much Evidence was collected.

Some parents have taken their teen to a family doctor and have answered a few questions. They are sometimes asked to fill out a brief questionnaire, and a diagnosis is given. The process often takes less than twenty to thirty minutes, and the teen leaves with a prescription.

I know a psychologist, Dr. Grant Martin, who will take four to six weeks to form a diagnosis. He will interview the teen extensively, perform a battery of tests, look at report cards, talk to teachers, have parents write journals that are based on daily observation of habits and behaviors of their children, and then he will interview the parents and teen before he will form an opinion. He is responsible, and his diagnoses are usually very accurate—and the clients are greatly helped.

Classic Psychology versus Positive Psychology Tests

One of the great shifts in psychology in the past twenty years is a branch of psychology called *Positive Psychology*. *Positive Psychology* has been called the "science of happiness." Traditionally, psychology has been focused on the "science of unhappiness," based on diagnosing problems, deficits, and attempts to answer the question "Why are people unhappy, depressed, anxious, mentally ill, and expressing hurtful and harmful behaviors?"

The assets-based and Positive Psychology tests are vastly different in the way people engage in taking the tests and embracing the results. I love it when people to whom I have taught LSI come to me after they have done some of these Positive Psychology tests. They love sharing the results. They can't wait to show me what the results are. They come alive because they have been affirmed and discovered something wonderful. Here is a sample of some of the tests and profiles developed by Positive Psychology practitioners.

Look at the lists below and compare the tests. Ask yourself, "Which would I rather take?"

Classic Psychology Tests	Positive Psychology Tests
Beck Hopelessness Scale	Authentic Happiness Inventory
Paulhaus Deception Scale	Values in Action Scale
Eating Disorder Inventory	General Happiness Scale
Childhood Trauma Questionnaire	StrengthsFinder 2.0
Children's Manifest Anxiety Scale	Close Relationships Scale
Psycho/Social Pathology Inventory	Satisfaction with Life Scale
MMPI (Psychopathology)	Meaning in Life Scale
MCMI (Chronic Psychopathology)	Optimism Scale
Depression Inventory	Compassion-Love Scale

The tests we use in our LSI programs are administered by our *Certified Life Scene Investigators (CLSI)*. They have not only taken them during the certification process but have also been trained in how to incorporate and interpret them into the DNA Code discovery process.

Some of the classic psychological tests have a "lie scale" built into them that tests consistency by asking the same question a few times in a slightly different way. The "lie scale" results often describe the rest of the test results as having *limited validity* and states such things as, "The participant attempted to show himself or herself in an overly positive light." People lie when they don't want others to know who they are, they are embarrassed about who they are, or they feel a sense of guilt or shame. Those who know their Talents and support them with character will learn they have no need to lie.

Most of us don't want our lives invaded and the worst of who we are exposed. It is normal and natural to want to hide because the information is often used in the context of a custody case, criminal proceeding, or other type of evaluation where it can harm us.

Bad results on a "deficit test" can result in my being an "every-other-weekend parent" to my children. It can mean having to attend classes such as Alcoholics Anonymous or anger management, which would interfere with my schedule for a long period of time. The results will be used by an attorney to make me look like an evil, twisted person, which I am not. My Life would be classified and defined by a *deficit*. Who would want that? Who willingly seeks out that information, and how much Passion does it deliver to their Lives? How does it help their pursuit of Purpose?

Forensic discovery tests are a very important part of discovering your DNA Code. Take them with a sense of anticipation, and use them appropriately. When used in the right context where they help us discover, confirm, or add a new dimension to our lives and for the right reasons, they are powerful!

Chapter 15
Witnesses for the Prosecution

*The new witnesses, text and Twitter, can make and
break Life in a moment!*

Who has seen you today? What have you done? Where have you been?
From the moment you woke up today to the point where you are
reading these words, who has seen you? You may be surprised at how
many people have witnessed your Life. What Evidence do they have
about you, and what they would say about you?

The reality is that there are people we call "witnesses" who have
been observing us from the day we were born. They have Evidence;
important and valuable information to testify about regarding our lives.
They are our parents, siblings, managers, clients, friends, relatives,
classmates, teammates, teachers, nannies, baristas at Starbucks, people
who have never met us but know us from observing us perform in a
play or choir, fellow travelers on the bus or train, yoga-mat neighbors,
volunteer associates, judges in competitions, chat-room participants,
bloggers, Facebook friends, readers of the comments section in your
local online newspaper, and so on.

You need to know that every person who ever sees you is a
potential witness because he or she has information about you: good,
bad, and everything in between. Be aware.

A witness is someone who tells about what they have seen, heard,
observed, or experienced. In legal proceedings they are generally
restricted to talking about the facts as they know them and have
experienced them. *Hearsay*, or third-party Evidence, is seldom
permitted.

Witnesses are an integral part of any legal case and trial. The power of a witness, especially an *eyewitness* who observed the Evidence or situation being testified to, can never be underestimated. For someone to say, "I saw them," and then talk about what they saw, can sway the toughest jury and result in a conviction.

Your *Life Scene* is observed every day in many different ways. You are being observed, watched, scrutinized, examined, and evaluated in many ways by people you know and others you have never met. To build a strong case, get an affirmative verdict, and build a Life of Purpose, Passion, and Performance, you need the testimony of witnesses, many witnesses.

Some people live their lives based on little or faulty information. They believe things about themselves that are simply not true. Others believe things they have been told by parents or people who love them but which have little to do with reality.

They are told they are good or exceptional by people who want the best for them but who are too close and may be scared to tell them the truth in case it might hurt the person's feelings. Parents will often tell a child that he or she performed exceptionally well because they want the child to feel good. The reality is that the child is no more than average but then develops a view of his or her abilities that is inflated and unrealistic. Life will most often teach such people some hard, unpleasant lessons in such cases.

Other people are told negative things that are not true but that make them view their lives as less than they really are. Powerful messages are conveyed and believed. The result is that these people come to believe less about themselves than they should. They don't attempt new things because they were told they don't have the ability or capacity.

Be aware that not everything a witness sees or states is necessarily accurate or true. My friend Dr. Elizabeth Loftus is known as one of the world's foremost authorities on eyewitness identification. Dr. Loftus was the person who got me interested in forensics. I spent some time helping her catalog a basement full of the cases she had been involved in through her many years as an Expert Witness. I read case files related to Ted Bundy, the Hillside Strangler, Michael Jackson, O. J. Simpson, Rodney King, Nazi war criminals, and other fascinating cases. She wrote a book called *Eyewitness Testimony* that is used in many law schools and police academies around the world. Another book she wrote was titled *Witness for the Defense*, which chronicled some of the famous cases she had been involved in.

I learned the power of a witness in these court cases. That same power translates into your Life in your desire to build a Life of Purpose, Passion, and Performance.

When Witnesses Count

1. *Job Applications.* I am regularly asked by teens or people I have worked with to give them a reference for a job or even a volunteer position they are applying for. I have to be truthful, and I tell the teens/people we work with on a regular basis that they will often need me to go to bat for them in these situations. In order for that to happen, they need to do positive things for me to write about.

I will ask people to go pick up a Starbucks application and fill it out. What would they put in it? How would they fill it out? Who would they list as people to contact to verify their character and work experience? It makes people think.

A few years ago a teen I really cared about asked me to write him a recommendation for a volunteer position at a summer camp facility. He was a great kid with some major problems. What I did was throw the application back at him (not literally!) by asking him to write a testimonial that he believed I could honestly sign my name to. I knew that volunteering would be a good thing for him to do. I believe that anytime teens or adults give their time for the sake of a good cause, they grow and learn great things about Life. The result in this case was that I was unable to write the testimonial, and I was really sad that I couldn't. The good news is he still ended up working there because they decided to give him a chance, and he did a great job.

What about you? If you were to write a testimonial for yourself and ask someone important in your Life who has all the necessary information, what would you be able to confidently say?

One of the realities of the Internet age is that there is information about all of us online for the entire world to see. There was even a recent case of a couple who sued Google Earth because of their property being pictured online by Google's "Street View" map feature. They viewed it as an invasion of privacy. In another case, the Range Rover of a cheating spouse was pictured at the house of his lover. You can be seen from nearly anywhere.

One of the problems many job applicants are running into these days is the testimony they post about themselves on the Internet. Once it is on the web, it is always on the web.

There are things we should take the Fifth Amendment on in all of our lives. You have no good reason to talk in an open forum about things you should forget, are not proud of, and should forever leave behind.

Many of the problems potential employers found when researching online profiles (Facebook, MySpace, etc.) were:

- Drinking or drugs
- Provocative photos
- Poor communication skills
- Bad-mouthing previous managers and jobs
- Overstating and lying about qualifications
- Lewd, extreme, or unprofessional screen name

Enough said? So what is on your Facebook, MySpace, Twitter, IM profile? What can be discovered by searching for you online on social networking or other sites?

Think about how many beauty queens have been stripped of their crowns because it was found out they had posted photographs online that were not in line with the rules of the competition. What about a recent Winter Olympics medalist allowing a fan to "adore" his medal? He never believed the photographs would be seen. Think about relationships that came to a grinding halt when "relationships" that were never meant to be discovered were talked about on websites.

When we testify about ourselves and talk about our associations, friends, likes, dislikes, or political views, use language, display inappropriate photos, or display rank stupidity for everyone to see and then expect a prospective employer to employ us based on what we say about ourselves, we are working against ourselves.

Others have listed associations and causes they support, which though it is their right to do, will define them and give people who are able to view their profile impressions that could hurt them. Marijuana leaves and anarchist symbols posted on your site won't help you get a job. It is your choice. How do you want people to know you?

What does your email address say about you? Words, phrases or numbers, such as "420," that are drug related may be fun to you, but to a potential employer or college they mean something. I remember that a great Life coach who worked for me a few years ago had an email address that began with "federaldeath@ . . . com." I looked past the address because I knew what a great coach he was. Many people won't.

I hope that this book will help you be able to live in the open with all the confidence of knowing your DNA Code and Talents and being thrilled to display them to the world in which you live.

2. *College Applications.* The same goes for college applications. I am sometimes asked to write testimonials and fill in very detailed forms for some of the people have I worked with. You have probably had to ask people to write these recommendations for you or will likely have to in the future. Who would you ask to provide a "witness statement/recommendation" for a college application? What would they say?

3. *Social Inclusion or Exclusion.* Have you ever wondered why you were accepted or even pursued membership in a social group: a team, theater troupe, band, volunteer organization, or other group? Have you ever wondered why you were excluded or excuses were made when you really wanted to join a group?

4. *Court or Legal Proceedings.* Of all the circumstances where the testimony of witnesses counts, in a courtroom may be the most important place of all. Your freedom and or finances could be on the line. People have been sent away for Life or even executed based on mistaken or faulty eyewitness testimony. Evil and despicable people have been caught because they were identified by eyewitness testimony.

If you were in a courtroom, would there be enough Evidence to convict you of your choice to live your Unique Design and Talents?

I have worked with teens who attempted to sell stolen items and illegal substances on the Internet. They used their online profiles as marketing vehicles. You never know who is watching. Private is *not* private, and the sooner you learn that, the better for your future.

Criminals are known to be stupid; they love to brag about what they have done. In fact, most criminals have a sense of pride in what they have done. I taught our first LSI discovery class at a wonderful school, the Environmental and Adventure School (EAS) in Kirkland, Washington. EAS is a charter school and has its facilities at a junior high school. Some brilliant students from another school decided they would burn down a portable classroom on the EAS campus. Great minds that they were, they decided to let their friends know who it was that had done the deed. They shared their exploit on MySpace and were summarily arrested. Case closed.

I encourage you to take the time and look at what you have posted online. Make changes that reflect a new Life defined by your DNA Code and Talents, the best of who you are, the interests you spend your time pursuing, the friendships you value, the books that have made a difference in your Life, the associations you are proud of, the people who have influenced you to become a better person, and the things and people you are most thankful for.

People, employers, potential colleges, new friends, and those who matter to building your Life will be drawn to you for the very best of who you are and will build and support your Life. What you attract is often based on what people see and know of you. What are you attracting?

When You Weren't Watching—Others Were

You never know who is listening. I just have to share this story. Things like this just don't happen, but this did.

Our team at Teen Discovery (a program I started with my sons to work with at-risk teens) had been working with a teen, Jake, who was tough, very tough. He had responded well and had us believing that everything was going great until one day, when I got a call from my son Adam, one of the Life coaches assigned to work with Jake. Adam called me with a big smile in his voice and told me about a voicemail he had just listened to. He was laughing, to say the least.

Jake, who believes he is brilliant, and who is academically very bright, had left school for a short time to work on a drug deal. While away from school and talking to his fine upstanding codealer, Sam, he must have tried to get something out of his pocket and hit speed-dial on his cell phone. He inadvertently dialed Adam, who was busy and wasn't able to answer. Jake talked, which he loved doing, and much of the deal was recorded for a full three minutes. Jake spelled out the name of the young girl he was buying the prescription drugs from. She had been goofing around and spelled her name out on his knuckles, which he repeated to his buddy. He told Sam to go pick up the drugs and pay the girl forty dollars for them, and he even talked about how he was going to sell each pill for ten dollars and make a great profit.

Be Aware, Be Very Aware

You never know who or what is recording or watching you.

The city of London is said to have more than five hundred thousand cameras watching the moves of everything and everyone, good and bad. Chicago has a system that rivals London's watching all the actions of its residents.

Have you ever been caught doing something great? You were just doing what you do, and you had no idea who was watching but later found out someone was. What about someone you observed who had no idea you were watching and enjoying seeing them be the best they could be?

Character has been defined as the good and tough choices we make and actions we do when no one else is watching. Do you have any great examples? There will be times in Life when no one will be watching and you will have no accolades, kudos, or applause, but *you* will be witness to you.

You will know if you followed through, practiced, and became a better person. You will know you used your Talents, and even if you experience Passion possibly in isolation, it will be worth it! That is a great feeling. You should live who you are when people are watching and when there is no one there but you. That is integrity of Design.

The Assessment of Witnesses

The LSI positive forensic investigation process requires the input of witnesses who have observed your Life, people who have watched you in the many facets of your Life, people who know you personally, and others who don't but who have seen you perform and do Life well. I want you to think about people who have something to say about your Life. I want you to identify and make lists of all those who can give you information.

A number of issues are important to look at when determining whether to use a witness to provide testimony about your Life:

- *Credibility.* The most important issue that qualifies a witness is truthfulness. If you want to be confident in what a witness says about you, you must believe that what is being said is accurate and honest and not in any way skewed for any reason whatsoever. You need to be convinced of that. Ask yourself the following questions:

1. Are they known for telling the truth?
2. Do they have an ulterior motive for testifying for or against you?
3. Have they been paid to testify for or against you?
4. Are they known to tell the truth in other areas of Life?
5. Do they have something to gain by testifying for you?
6. Have they been threatened or promised something?

The same is usually true when a plea bargain is offered. The judge wants to know why the person is taking the plea. I have been in court countless times with people who agree to take a plea bargain and admit their guilt in a criminal case. Their guilt is not really in question. They are offered it because it will save the court the time and money to fully prosecute their case, and they accept it because they are offered a reduced punishment. When a defendant accepts a plea bargain, the judge asks a series of questions to make sure that the defendant is accepting the offer freely. The judge asks:

1. Has the defendant been promised any inducements to accept the offer of a reduced punishment?
2. Has he been threatened to take the offer?
3. Is he ready to admit his guilt in open court and accept the punishment?

- *Relationship.* Who is the witness to you? What relationship do you have to the witness? Husbands and wives are not generally allowed to testify against each other. Evidence must be assessed based on the relationship of the person to you. We all know people close to us who love us and would be hard pressed to say anything negative about us. They don't want to hurt our feelings. The reality is those who are closest to us know more about us than anyone else. They see us in all the seasons of Life. They probably have the best information of all the witnesses. Remember, what we are asking them to do is give information about the very best of who we are. We need them to help us discover the very best of our Design.

If your assessment of your unique Talents and Design DNA Code is based only on what your mother or father says, you might be in trouble. I know parents who believe their children are the brightest and best with very little supporting Evidence. When parents, because they love their children, tell their children they are more than any Evidence supports, they often do more harm than good.

Many parents wish for their children to be more than or different from what their obvious Design tells them. This produces frustration, disappointment, pain, and harm. Such parents often lose credibility with their kids because what they say is just not reality, regardless of the motive. These kids know the truth, or will eventually, and will have to deal with the disappointment of reality, ridicule from others, and anger at their parents, who set them up for a nasty fall. Telling a potential employer what your mother said doesn't cut it.

When I do parenting seminars or work with parents, I ask them to look at their children and perform an *Analysis of Asset*. Watch them and study them. Analyze their unique Talents. Look for patterns and track the growth of their Talents. Help expose them to a variety of situations and possibilities.

Each child has Unique Design Talents. Great parenting observes these Talents and helps children develop them. If you want the best for your Life and for others whom you have the ability to observe up close, be honest. Speak the truth. Say what you see. Never miss an opportunity to speak about Talent.

When parents look for the best in their children, not ignoring the choices to be lazy, defiant, and so on, the likelihood that the children will grow and be successful in Life is greatly enhanced. The greatest responsibility parents have is to help their children discover their Talents!

- *Expertise.* What does the witness possess in terms of expertise regarding the situation he or she is giving evidence about? What is the witness's experience? What are his or her credentials? What successes has he or she had? Do peers recognize her/him as being a leader in that field of testimony?

Those of you who have watched *American Idol* in the past few years know who Simon Cowell is. Simon is the originator of the program and also the one judge whom most of the audience and performers love to hate. Simon is honest in his assessment of each performer and performance. He says what he thinks and doesn't pull any punches.

There were two other judges, three in 2009. Randy often gave mixed reviews but was generally accurate in his judgments. Then you had Paula Abdul, who seldom if ever said anything negative about anyone. She was kind and nurturing and never wanted to offend even the worst performer. Paula was replaced.

What most people don't think about when Simon makes his caustic or realistic assessments is the perspective from which he is coming. Simon is an expert in finding the best talent. He is looking to invest millions of dollars in the best of the best. In order to discover that talent, the *American Idol* program was developed. It starts with thousands of people auditioning, performing on an open stage in front of the three judges. After each round, those who are assessed as being good enough are sent through to the next round of competition until they get through to the Hollywood round of the final twelve contestants. From there, it is a process of constant elimination until the final contestant is crowned the "American Idol."

I regularly ask people in the classes and seminars I teach whose positive judgment they would most want: Simon's, Randy's or Paula's. Almost across the board they say Simon. Simon, the hated and despised, but the most honest and accurate in who he assesses as being the best and most talented. He certainly could learn some better ways of expressing his views, but this is a competition where millions of dollars are at stake as well as the reputation of a phenomenally popular prime-time television program.

One thing you know is that when Simon expresses his opinion, you are receiving an open, honest, and almost always accurate statement of ability. When Paula gives her opinion, you will almost always feel good, but you will seldom be sure that you know you have what it takes to be the best.

So think about the people whom you want to get information from. Look for "Simons" who will give you the best information, even if it is not always given in the most emotionally positive and nurturing way. You can bank on what Simon says, and so can he!

The Four Types of Witnesses

Most trials have a number of different types of witnesses.

- Personal (friendly) witness
- Eyewitness
- Expert witness
- Adverse (impeachment) witness

These are witnesses who can provide testimony regarding the Evidence you have collected. They can make or break your case. What is most important is to identify witnesses who will validate your Evidence.

Personal Witness	Personal Witnesses
Personal witnesses are people who are your peers or who know you and have observed you in action. These can be friends, family, work associates, team members, and others who have no other vested or paid interest in testifying. These witnesses are relationally or emotionally connected to you, and at times their objectivity can be questioned. However, their testimony should be assessed and be given substantial weight if they are known to have your best interests at heart.	Mother Father Spouse Sisters Brother Close friend Girl-/boyfriend Roommate Teammate School-/classmate (sits next to you) Business partner Close work associate
Eyewitness	**Eyewitnesses**
Eyewitnesses are those who observed the Evidence. They are people who are not connected to you in terms of a personal relationship or who have been retained by you. They have observed you in action and have important information that is based primarily on observation.	Classmate (you don't really know or talk to them) Work associate Casual acquaintance Someone at Starbucks Attends gym with you Someone at school Attendee at a game or performance who watched you Association member

Expert Witness	Expert Witnesses
Expert witnesses are witnesses who have knowledge beyond that of the ordinary layperson that enables them to give testimony regarding an issue that requires expertise to understand. In court, the party offering the expert must lay a foundation for the expert's testimony. Laying the foundation involves testifying about the expert's credentials and experience that qualify them as an expert.	Schoolteacher Manager or boss College professor Coach Principal CEO Scout (sport, talent, etc.) Youth leader Pastor, minister, rabbi Counselor Doctor Driver's education instructor Tutor

Adverse Witness	Adverse Witnesses
An adverse witness is one who presents testimony that attempts to discredit the Evidence you have presented and or testifies that the procedures you used to collect or assert the reliability are invalid.	Anyone who knows you (not all adverse witnesses do know you or have firsthand Evidence about you); who has seen you; who may not like you; who wants to dispute what you or other witnesses have testified about; and who will give different or opposing testimony to that which has already been testified to.

Identifying the Witnesses in Your Life

As you look through this grid, who are the witnesses you can identify to give valuable Evidence about your Life? Think about what they would say about your Life. If you needed someone to write a recommendation to a college or nonprofit board, who would you identify, and what would they say?

How to Respond to an Adverse Witness (AW)

1. There will always be AWs in your Life. Know that and accept it.
2. The more successful you are, the more AWs there will be in your Life. It is probably a sign of success and an indicator that what you are doing is right and is working.

Use the three areas of credibility assessment on the adverse witness before responding to them:

1. Relationship—Who are they to me?
2. Credibility—What do I know about them and what they have done and said about other people? Is their bias toward Asset or deficit?
3. Expertise—What is their expertise, and what gives them the authority to say what they said?

Don't simply accept what they say, and don't simply reject what they say. There are times when an AW can be a person who loves you and cares deeply about your success. They muster the courage to say what they really believe, and it is most important for us to listen and take what is said to heart. They will tell us even if it means the relationship that exists between us might be strained or harmed.

> *Faithful are the wounds of a friend.*
> *—Proverbs 27:6*

One of the best techniques in dealing with an AW is called "disputing." It is a legal term used to challenge Evidence. When "disputing" the testimony of an AW, you must first complete a full LSI Positive Forensic Analysis. Gather the Evidence before you attempt to dispute. Dispute from a position of Strong Evidence!

When disputing:

- You might have to reject the dreams of your parents for you to follow a profession they have long planned and for which they have put money into a college fund to finance their dream but not your Design.

- You may need to start moving away from a career you are in and begin preparing for one that you know is an honest fit for your Design.

- You will need to exercise great courage to follow your Design if you really want to experience a Life of Purpose, Passion, and Performance!

Be aware that your Life is open to the whole world. No matter how secret you may believe you are, you are being watched, and Evidence is being produced. I cannot think why you would want your Life to be lived in secrecy if you are living or attempting to live the best of who you are. Do everything out in the open; that's a Life of freedom!

Part 4

Where to Discover Evidence

The Five Fields of Evidence

Chapter 16
Cross the Yellow Line—Bag It and Tag It!

The yellow tape reads: "Crime Scene—Do Not Cross." Immediately after a crime scene is identified, it is roped off with the familiar yellow tape. The crime scene is the focus of the most important information in the discovery process.

1. What happened?
2. Who did it?
3. Where is the Evidence?
4. What is obvious?
5. Who was it?
6. When did it happen?

LSI follows the same process, but the differences are huge. *Life Scene—Cross Here!* Cross the yellow line into a Life discovery!

Not all the Evidence you collect holds the same weight, nor should it be used when thinking through what your Purpose is. At the end of each Field of Evidence you will find two Evidence analysis tools. These tools allow you to sift through all the Evidence you have identified and see what is the "Best Evidence."

"Bag it and tag it" refers to the process where a crime scene investigator identifies potential Evidence at a crime scene and then proceeds to:

- Bag it—where it is identified as being Evidence that is possibly useful in solving the crime. That Evidence is then stored or bagged in an evidence collection envelope, bag, or container, which will preserve it as it was discovered at the crime scene.

- Tag it—where information is written on the envelope, bag, or container into which the Evidence was placed. It includes the:
  - Name of the person who collected the Evidence. The person must sign his or her name to the Evidence.
  - Date and time the Evidence was collected.
  - Crime scene where the Evidence was collected.
  - A descriptive marker that identifies the location inside the crime scene where the Evidence was collected. A CSI photographer that covers the entire crime scene will take a series of photographs. Each piece of Evidence will be seen in the context of where it was discovered and identified by a number or letter. Directional signs placed at the crime scene are also photographed.
  - A brief description of the Evidence.

I explained the *Evidence Reliability Tests* earlier. This matrix enables you to look at the Evidence you have identified and ask which of these *Reliability Tests* apply. The more of these tests that apply to any one piece of Evidence, the stronger that Evidence is. In legal terms, this is called the "weight of the Evidence." When the scales of Evidence tilt in your favor, follow the Evidence!

RT	Evidence Reliability Tests Quick Checklist
RT-1	"Exceptional," Top 25 Percent, Top 10 Percent
RT-2	Flow
RT-3	Preserved
RT-4	Easily Repeatable and Been Repeated
RT-5	Judged as Exceptional by Witnesses
RT-6	Expert Witness Testify
RT-7	Result of Spontaneous Action
RT-8	By Choice and in My Own Time
RT-9	Positive Emotion
RT-10	Intuition

The *Best Evidence Matrix* is another way to distinguish Evidence that stands out and that should be looked on as important in helping you discover your DNA Code and Talents. The matrix has four measures by which to analyze the Evidence you collect:

a. What Evidence do you believe stands out?
b. "When?" asks you to identify within a historical context. A date and time stamp is part of all Evidence when it is collected and placed in an evidence envelope. Take time to identify when you demonstrated the Talent. You can identify more than one piece.
c. Evidence Tests include both the *online* and *Reliability Tests*. Please identify and add all tests that strengthen and authenticate your Evidence.
d. Please identify all the main witnesses who have observed or made statements about your Talents. This includes personal, expert, and eyewitnesses.

Best Evidence Matrix

What Was the Evidence? Identify and Specify	When? How Often?	Tests Online and RTs	Witness List and Identify

Chapter 17
Discovering Evidence of Your
Physical DNA Code Part 1

Physical Capacity	• What I look like • My physical characteristics • My physical Talents • My athletic Talents • My physical potential • How I connect and perceive through my senses (sight, smell, touch, hearing, taste); sensory Talents • Bodily-kinesthetic intelligence • Musical intelligence • Naturalistic intelligence

"Where's the body?" is the first question asked at the start of a *CSI* episode. *CSI* shows almost always begin with a body, either a dead body or a person about to die. That body is where the collection of Evidence begins. *What* happened to harm and take the Life from that body? *Who* was responsible? *How* did they take the Life of the dead person? *When* did the victim die? *Who* witnessed what happened?

?RU and what does your physical Life Scene tell us about your Unique Talents?

Our bodies are the way we connect with the world. People see our bodies; they are who we are. They are the vehicle of our Design DNA and Talents and are the most incredibly complex machines on this planet.

Housed within your physical body are your emotional, intellectual, spiritual, and social components and Talents. It is vital that you think about your physical Field of Evidence as being not only a Field of Evidence in itself, but also as a larger field that houses and carries the other four Fields of Evidence.

Great effort must be taken to care for and value your physical Life Scene: your body. When you care for and treat the physical body well, the other Talents housed within have a better chance to reach their potential.

One of the greatest advances in physical forensics is 3-D imaging. What would you look like and what could we see in terms of your physical potential if we could see you through a 3-D imager? Some medical facilities advertise and promise to give you a precise and thorough evaluation of every physical abnormality and potential disease through 3-D scans and analysis. MRIs and CAT scans are accomplished by amazing machines that see inside your physical body and give you unbelievably detailed information.

What do you know about your body, your physical Talents, and how are you using them to live?

Three Basic Shapes of Physical Design

We come in all shapes and sizes. Three basic "types" describe the nature of our external physical shape and size:

Endomorph. Take every offensive and defensive lineman in the NFL (minus nobody) and you'll have yourself a nice collection of endomorphs. Endomorphs are generally what most people consider "stocky" creatures, many of them having short, thick limbs and heavy bones. The likes of Oprah and Rosie O'Donnell would probably also fit.

Ectomorph. This type would seem to consist of every man who ever played in the NBA, minus Charles Barkley and Shaquille O'Neal. Ectomorphs are generally lean and mean but have a hard time packing on the muscle. Cindy Crawford is a female example.

Mesomorph. They, in a sense, are the luckiest of the three. Mesomorphs have the tendency to be muscular and ripped, maintaining the best attributes of both the ectomorphs and the endomorphs.

Components of Physical Movement Capacity

A number of basic components govern physical movement and how our bodies function. They focus on what we do with our bodies and how we can make them do what we want them to. We will look at sensory capacity, which is really instinctual. We don't turn these on and off; they simply are ways we connect with the world around us and process the physical world.

- Speed—the rate at which a movement or activity can be performed
- Agility—the ability to rapidly and fluently change the position of our bodies during movement
- Balance—the maintenance of equilibrium while stationary (static balance) and while moving (dynamic)
- Coordination—the integration of our many separate motor skills or movements into one efficient movement pattern
- Power—the function of strength and speed; the ability to transfer energy into force at a quick rate
- Reaction time—the amount of time elapsed between stimulation and acting upon the stimulus

The physical body is a universe of information.

Fingerprints Can Reveal Drug Use, Medical History

A simple careless touch might be all police or insurance companies need to determine not only your identity but also your past drug use and whether you have handled certain chemical agents or fired a gun. Medical conditions can be diagnosed from small amounts of sweat, hair, body oil, or saliva.

Fingerprints have been the standard way of identifying and differentiating people. Analysts looked at the patterns, swirls, and curls and were able to say with a high probability or certainty who you were. Iron oxide particles in fingerprint powder attach themselves to the tiny bits of water, minerals, and oils that accumulate on the fingers as they touch various objects and other parts of the body.

The new technique attaches the iron oxide particles to antibodies and then suspends them both in a liquid solution. This solution is then dripped over a fingerprint. If the chemical that a specific antibody targets is present, the molecules latch onto it and glow.

Even more recently, doctors have become able to identify individuals by the antibodies found in their blood. It is believed that antibodies hold patterns that could rival DNA in terms of their uniqueness for each individual. These antibody patterns are much easier, quicker, and cheaper to identify than DNA.

For those who work as CSIs (crime scene investigators) this information is invaluable in identifying and convicting a criminal. The world of Evidence that is found when a fingerprint is discovered and lifted from a crime scene is incredible.

Remember Locard's Exchange Principle (from the Introduction), which says:

> *Wherever he steps, whatever he touches, whatever he leaves, even unconsciously, will serve as a silent witness against him. Not only his fingerprints or his footprints, but his hair, the fibers from his clothes, the glass he breaks, the tool mark he leaves, the paint he scratches, the blood or semen he deposits or collects. All of these and more bear mute witness against him. This is Evidence that does not forget. It is not confused by the excitement of the moment. It is not absent because human witnesses are. It is factual Evidence. Physical Evidence cannot be wrong, it cannot perjure itself, it cannot be wholly absent. Only human failure to find it, study and understand it, can diminish its value.*

Simple Evidence that you were there does not prove anything other than you were there. Why were you there? What reason was there for you to be at the Life Scene?

We are ready now to begin the collection of physical Evidence by asking the question *?RU.* What is the nature of this physical body you have been given?

Sensory Capacity

Sensory capacity is how you interpret, connect, respond to, and perceive the world around you through your senses: sight, smell, touch, hearing, and taste. People are described as having an "ear" for music or an "eye" for art or color. These refer to our sensory capacities.

Sensory Forensic Matrix

Which sensory capacities are you exceptional at? Describe that Talent.

Sight	
Smell	
Touch	
Taste	
Hearing	

Think of some combinations of sensory capacity. When two or more senses are combined, what can they produce? Here are some examples:

1. A chef needs a great sense of *taste* because if food doesn't taste great, who will eat it? But what about *smell?* Smell often moves us to want to order a particular dish. *Sight* is also very important because when a chef buys produce, food color can tell what is ripe or of real quality. A chef also needs to make a dish "look" presentable to the consumer.

2. Most musicians have exceptional *hearing*. Those who play instruments are said to have an "ear" for music. Great musicians have to know how to *touch* to have their emotions translated through the instruments they play.

3. Fashion consultants or Designers need to have great s*ight* for color identification and coordination. They also need exceptional *touch* for the fabrics and materials they will use to ensure the quality of the product.

4. One of the first things that happen when we go to the doctor is that the doctor *listens* to our hearts. They *look* in our ears and eyes. They *touch/feel* our glands. Great medical diagnosticians have exceptional sensory Talents. Remember that the combinations are not only of two capacities but often more.

Sight + Smell =	Hunter		
Smell + Taste =	Wine taster		
Touch + Sight =	Musician		
Taste + Touch =	Chef		
Hearing + Touch =	Doctor		

- Do you possess an outstanding sensory capacity?
- What is it? How would you describe it?
- When was the last time you demonstrated that capacity?
- What combination of sensory capacities is used in one of your Talents?

Did you know when one of our senses is less that average, one of our other senses tends to compensate and be higher than average? Some people may lose a sensory capacity such as sight and compensate by having superior hearing. My son Adam had cancer as a child, which resulted in his being totally deaf in his left ear. Adam studied culinary arts and has exceptional abilities with his senses of smell and taste, which are likely heightened due to his diminished hearing capacity.

The soldiers you met in the story of Tsanga Lodge have a great application here. It is not what you don't have or what you've lost, but what you possess and build your Life on. That is what counts. That is reality.

Forensic Tip

Evidence is not always what it seems on the face. People are sometimes misjudged or even prejudged because of what they look like on the outside. It is amazing what some people are able to do when there is nothing on the outside that would lead you to believe they can do anything exceptional.

Many great stories from history, and others of legend, remind us that there are sometimes incredible Talents that lie beneath the surface. Remember David and Goliath? Who would believe a teenage boy could take down a giant warrior? David did it with precision and skill.

There are also examples of people performing a task only once, but with a skill that is almost supernatural. We have all heard of situations where a hundred-pound woman is able to lift a fifteen-hundred-pound car off a child to save the child's Life. And there are people who have survived extreme temperatures or other extremes far beyond their ability to ever repeat under normal circumstances. Those situations are not what we are looking for, but they may give us some clues as to what we really are capable of and able to do when pushed.

Earl Boykins, a 5-foot-5, 133-pound Denver Nuggets player, fought with giants every day. Boykins overcame his size disadvantage with quickness, smarts and hustle. He has uncommon strength; he bench presses 300 pounds, stopping opponents from taking advantage of him in the post. He also had a reliable jumper that kept defenders honest.

What other examples can you think of for people you have underestimated and didn't give a chance? There are others whom you wrote off as never being able to perform or do anything exceptional. We all have examples in our lives of people whom we never believed "could" because they just didn't look the part.

MYLIFESCENE.COM—CROSS NOW—MYLIFESCENE.COM
Life Scene—Paul Potts

Paul Potts was on *Britain's Got Talent*. When you looked at Paul you didn't see any star quality. He was nervous and overweight, had bad teeth and certainly didn't have anything that would indicate he was, or could be, anything more than a cell-phone salesman in a mall, which he was.

He had sung in a church choir and enjoyed it but had never really performed for anyone.

When he walked onstage to audition, he was asked what he was going to sing. He told the judges, one of whom was Simon Cowell of *American Idol*, his song selection. Simon basically put his head down with a facial expression that said, "Here is another idiot who is wasting our time."

It didn't take long; Paul was singing like a star, and even Simon looked like he had undergone a religious conversion, which wiped the almost constant sarcastic smirk off his face. One of the judges had tears and was overcome with emotion. Paul went on to win the competition and become the British "Idol."

A similar story was played out again when Susan Boyle, another "diamond in the rough," competed on the same series. Just look on YouTube and watch the emergence of these two incredible talents. It will bring tears to your eyes.

Don't ever underestimate or discard Evidence because it doesn't seem like it is in the appropriate wrapping. Design and Talents come in many packages.

What is waiting to be birthed in your Life? Maybe the missing ingredient is courage. When Paul walked out onto the stage, he looked petrified. But he walked out and openly declared who he was and what he was going to do. Have courage and try! A new Life might be one decision away!

MYLIFESCENE.COM—CROSS NOW—MYLIFESCENE.COM

My Unknown Talent

Is there something you can do that people would have a hard time believing you had the ability to do because of what you look like physically? (You could also count something fun or odd about you: a double-jointed finger or wiggling your ears.)

Is there something you can do that you have never really taken onstage into Life and shown to others? You believe you are exceptional, but no one knows. Maybe you are too scared to try it and compete with the possibility you may lose. As the saying goes, "You can never win unless you try." I dare you to try. I dare you to show what you have got. I dare you to live!

Exceptional Performance

What have you done, physically, for which you have received awards and significant recognition? Look at the lists below and begin to identify what they are.

You are not looking for an award of participation, but something showing that you stand out and succeed. Participation certificates do say something, which could include courage, endurance, a desire to maintain a level of fitness and other positive Talents. If you participated to be with friends in a race or to run for a cause, that shows Evidence of social and motivation Talent. If you were a part of a group that is committed to maintaining physical health and wellness, that identifies meaning and motivation. Keep that Evidence for a later time and different *Field of Evidence*.

What trophies, ribbons, plaques, medals or awards have you received for your exceptional demonstration of ability? If you have been exceptional, you have likely received recognition, and those recognitions are Evidence of your achievements. Those awards usually have your name, date and the nature of achievement engraved on them. What do they say?

Having a number of awards for one particular sport or activity over a period of time makes the case stronger. That is hard Evidence, and it is necessary in identifying your physical Talents.

Identify a Physical Capacity/Activity	List Recognitions or Awards	When Awarded?

Identification and Analysis of My Physical Capacity

When we think of physical capacity, most of the time what comes to mind is athletics or sports. Those are physical capacities, but there is much more to physical capacity than defining it in such a limited way. We are going to begin there but then expand far beyond that, because your *physical Life Scene* is extensive.

Let's begin with an analysis of what you've done in terms of athletics and sports. Some people have as little interest in athletics and sports as others do in algebra or the periodic table. What we are looking for is Evidence of where you have an interest and where you demonstrated that Evidence in a good to exceptional manner.

We are going to start by having you identify as you look at this lineup of possibilities. I want you to broaden your thinking. This is not an exhaustive list, but the categories should be obvious as you read them. Think about the past few weeks or maybe a long time ago when you were in school or college.

The Olympic Games is the greatest venue for the display of physical athletic and sporting capacity. These games have been around for two thousand years. The Purpose is to provide competition that results in the best athletic capacities being recognized when they win.

My *Athletic* Physical Capacity

Rate Your Physical/Athletic Ability: 1 = Excellent; 2 = Good

Ball Sports—Kicking, Throwing, Contact	Football, soccer, basketball, rugby, Aussie Rules football, volleyball, netball, other	
Ball Sports—Catching, Hitting, Throwing	Baseball, cricket, field hockey, golf, lacrosse, tennis, racquetball, table Tennis, croquet, other	
Athletics—Running	Sprint, hurdles, 100–400 meters, cross-country, marathon, other	
Athletics—Field	High jump, long jump, javelin, pole vault, discus, shot put, other	
Noncontact	Swimming, diving, snooker/pool, darts, archery, target shooting, lawn bowling, curling, weight lifting, other	
Board and Bike	Snowboarding, skating, BMX, wakeboarding, rollerblading, motocross, other	
Gymnastics	Gymnastics, ballet, ice skating, cheerleading, dancing, other	

Contact Sports	Karate, judo, boxing, wrestling, tae kwan do, extreme fighting, other	
Extreme Sports	Skydiving, bungee jumping, white-water rafting, paragliding, other	
Fun/Dangerous	Dodgeball, paintball, pickleball, other	
Riding/Extreme Riding	Horse riding, bicycling, bull riding, other	
Other—List:		

Bag It and Tag It

RT	Evidence Reliability Tests Quick Checklist
RT-1	"Exceptional," Top 25 Percent, Top 10 Percent
RT-2	Flow
RT-3	Preserved
RT-4	Easily Repeatable and Been Repeated
RT-5	Judged as Exceptional by Witnesses
RT-6	Expert Witness Testify
RT-7	Result of Spontaneous Action
RT-8	By Choice and in My Own Time
RT-9	Positive Emotion
RT-10	Intuition

Best Evidence Matrix

What Was the Evidence? Identify and Specify	When? How Often?	Tests Online and RTs	Witness List and Identify

Chapter 18
Discovering Evidence of Your
Physical DNA Code Part 2

Physical Capacity	• What I look like
	• My physical characteristics
	• My physical Talents
	• My athletic Talents
	• My physical potential
	• How I connect and perceive through my senses (sight, smell, touch, hearing, taste); sensory Talents
	• Bodily-kinesthetic intelligence
	• Musical intelligence
	• Naturalistic intelligence

There is a forensics television show called *Body of Evidence*. The show highlights the cases of Dayle Hinman, one of the foremost forensic profilers in the United States. Hinman attempts to crack some of the toughest cases using the latest scientific Evidence and her investigative skills. You will be taught to search for Evidence just like she does.

Another popular forensics documentary is *North Mission Road*, which focuses on the Los Angeles County Coroner's Department. The question to be answered in this show is: *"What does the physical body tell us about who the person was and how he/she died?"*

We will continue to discover what defines the very best of *PRU* and see how they are evident in this physical Life Scene.

The physical Talents listed next are as significant to Life as those we looked at in the previous chapter. We are all different and possess many wonderful expressions of physical capacity. As you go through the list in this chapter, I want you to think of careers that people go into because of exceptional physical Talents.

Let me explain. Jim Carey is a great actor who has developed his craft. The most important element of Jim Carey's acting, that for which he is best known, is his *physical comedy*. He makes faces and moves his body in ways that make people laugh hysterically. Carey has made millions acting physically goofy.

Obviously, when it comes to *vocal expression*, singers can make very good money. Voices that can deliver emotion, that inspire, connect, and generate physical movement are always in demand. From the "Three Tenors" and Michael Bublé to Meatloaf and some of the screaming, growling vocalists, the variety is amazing.

There are many radio and television personalities who, because of their voice tone and quality, found a career doing advertisements, talk shows, news reading, and other on-air slots. The same goes for public speakers, ministers, and sports announcers. Even the somewhat quirky sticks in our minds, like the beloved radio icon Paul Harvey and his "Rest of the Story."

Sometimes, even your mere *physical presence* can change a very tough situation. You can see this in a variety of situations. In the military it is often said that physical presence in armed combat or in leadership can win or lose a battle. Soldiers follow certain leaders because they exude a physical presence that is magnetic. Some people just have that aura. John Wayne and President Ronald Reagan were both men who had a commanding physical presence and used it for good. Hitler was a small man who mesmerized people when he spoke and used his physical presence for great evil.

Physical presence is also an undefined quality that brings calm. Some medical personnel, counselors, and ministers have a way of bringing calm in tough or painful times. Doctors and nurses are known for a bedside manner that relates to positive results of their being with a patient. Are you one of these people? Does that describe you or someone you know?

Physical Talents are obvious in *artistic capacity*. People high in artistic capacity make the world beautiful; they capture Life in a variety of forms. This ability requires many physical Talents, from hand-eye coordination, incredible focus on detail, surgical hand precision, exceptional eyesight, and color recognition to a sense of space and physical proportion, timing, and so much more.

Life Scene—Rhonda Addison

Rhonda Addison is one of the best photographers there is. Her clients are listed as some of the best professional athletes in the NFL and MLB; they include an NFL MVP. Rhonda matches them in talent in every way. She is no less exceptional at what she does with a camera than what one of her Pro Bowl NFL quarterback clients does when he throws a football for a touchdown.

Rhonda brings color to lives. For a number of years I helped Rhonda with many of her photo sessions and saw her in action. I was always in awe of what she did, and much more than just as a photographer. She took her black-and-white photography and added a dimension of color to it with paint and other enhancements of jewelry, gems, and special personal heirlooms.

In one of the LSI classes she attended, we began to analyze the Evidence of what Rhonda did. The verdict was that she adds color to Life. She does it with her photographs of people as well as with her still lifes.

Great photographers have exceptional timing and hand-eye coordination. To "capture" a shot or picture means just that: angles, distances, lighting, exceptional timing, staging, composition—all define what Rhonda does.

Have you ever thought how difficult it would be to capture the perfect shot when you have five children of varying ages and their dog, all with their eyes open, facing the right direction and angle, all the while looking at ease and natural, and without a "posed" look? That is extreme talent!

Part of what made Rhonda exceptional was that she had a great connection with children. Her social Design was witnessed when she needed to get kids to respond with laughter or the appropriate emotion; and so with just the right "pose" she was able to capture the perfect photograph.

What exceptional capacity is in your physical Life Scene? Rhonda is exceptional in her own way, but what about you? Do you know any people like Rhonda, and how would you describe the Evidence you see in their lives?

What do you do that requires a combination of exceptional physical capacities? Can you identify a number of physical elements that, when combined, create an exceptional product or service?
MYLIFESCENE.COM—CROSS NOW—MYLIFESCENE.COM

Musicians who create and play are fine-tuned physical specimens. There are many types of *musical expression* and instruments. Some musicians play solo, such as pianists or guitarists; others are part of a team such as a band or symphony. Lung capacity, mouth and lip strength, fast hands, dexterity, coordination, rhythm, and exceptional *hand-ear coordination* are all important. *?RU*

Some people have great physical pain tolerance. I recently watched my sister Penny go through a third bone-marrow biopsy. The first thing the doctor asked her was what the worst pain she had ever experienced was. He wanted to decide what medication he was going to give her, as the procedure is known to be excruciating. She asked for the minimal amount and endured immense pain, which I know I would never have handled in such a manner. There are people who are able to handle pain to a degree at which many of us would fall apart crying or groaning when we experienced it. Penny is incredible. *?RU*

Yoga is a form of physical exercise for good health, but it requires certain physical abilities. To be good at yoga, flexibility, endurance, and mental control are all essential.

I go to the famous Pike Place Market in Seattle a few times a year. Pike Place is where they throw big fish around and also where the first Starbucks is located. I have been there trying to find runaway teens who often congregate around there for the free food that is available. Many of the vendors give away samples of fruit, snacks, and so on. One of the people I have seen through the years is a unique street performer. He plays his guitar and harmonica, all the while twirling hula hoops. That is exceptional physical coordination. Have you ever tried and demonstrated exceptional physical capacity and *coordinated movement*? What was it? *?RU*

What would happen if a dentist got a reputation of having shaky hands? She would have a light patient load very quickly. Some dental clinics have names like "Gentle Dental," and names like that give us a picture that calms our fears, knowing that the drill or needle will not miss its target and send us flying upward out of the chair. The same goes for a surgeon. I don't know of any patient who wants a surgeon known for having shaky hands. Such professions demand exceptional skills, and one of those skills is having a skilled and steady hand. *PRU*

Cesar Millan, the "Dog Whisperer," has a television show where he demonstrates exceptional *physical dominance* to tame the most savage dog. He is a modern-day lion tamer. What is it about Cesar that makes him exceptional at taming these out-of-control canines? He has a physical capacity that combines physical presence, authoritative but calm vocals, eye contact, the right tug and strategic use of a leash, and no show of fear. Do you have anything that resembles Cesar Millan's exceptional physical capacity? What is it? Where is the Evidence?

Some people possess exceptional *physical endurance*. They can endure great physical adversity and not yield or cave in.

MYLIFESCENE.COM—CROSS NOW—MYLIFESCENE.COM
Life Scene—Michael

I have an older brother, Michael. Michael has always been a natural athlete. I was always amazed at Michael as anything physical he attempted seemed so natural to him.

Michael loved to run. I did anything I could to not have to run. I loved games that required short bursts of effort and running limited to fifty yards or less at one time. Michael took up running long distances, very long distances. Some people go for a 5K or 10K run; I perspire just thinking of it.

Michael ran a marathon called the Comrades Marathon and then the Two Oceans Marathon. I thought that was great until I read that the Comrades Marathon is the world's oldest and largest ultra-marathon, run over a distance of approximately 90 kilometers (55.9 miles) between Pietermaritzburg, South Africa, and the coastal city of Durban. You had to make the run in less than the cutoff time of twelve hours.

What makes this so remarkable was that when Michael was seventeen years old, he left school and joined an elite military unit called the Rhodesian Light Infantry. These were tough foot soldiers who were known for their incredible endurance and superior fighting ability. Michael did well and enjoyed the military. He had a problem, or rather, the military had a problem with him. After two years they discovered he had a physical abnormality that made his intake of oxygen about 30 percent less than average, and so they medically discharged him. They thought he was a liability because he couldn't run far enough and keep up. Running in the Comrades Marathon numerous times was proof positive of Michael's physical endurance with only 70 percent of his lung capacity.

I was on Skype talking with Michael, and he said he had just returned from a 125K (75-mile) bike ride. I broke into a sweat just listening to him. Michael is an example of exceptional physical Talent and endurance.

What exceptional capacity is in your physical Life Scene? Do you have physical endurance like Michael? Where and when have you demonstrated it?

MYLIFESCENE.COM—CROSS NOW—MYLIFESCENE.COM

For each of these physical Talents, there are many more examples and applications than those I have listed and described. Think like a Life Scene Investigator and identify not only where you have Evidence that is identified in those descriptions, but where in your world you see people who demonstrate them every day.

Nonathletic Physical Capacity

Rate Your Nonathletic Physical Ability: 1 = Excellent; 2 = Good

Facial Expression	Smile, scowl, frown, glare, alive, defiant, other	
Vocal Expression	Sing, speech, laugh, shout, scream, imitate, other	
Physical Presence	Commanding, invisible, calming, energizing, other	
Physical Creation	Artistic, drawing, painting, photography, architecture, sculpture, other	
Physical Expression	Hand, body, comedy, twist, contort, glide, animate, other	
Physical Comparison	Large or small when compared with others my age, other	
Coordinated Movement	Dancing, yoga, gymnastics, drumming, juggling, video gaming, other	

Physical Caring Touch	People, animals, friends, bring comfort, other	
Steady-Handed	Minute details, mechanic, artistic, surgery, computer chips, other	
Tactile Hands	Knitting, musical instruments (guitar, piano, trumpet, harp), other	
Physical Pain Management	Great tolerance to little tolerance	
Fun Physical Feats	What weird, fun physical thing can you do? How weird is it?	
Other—List:		

What trophies, ribbons, plaques, medals, or awards have you received for your exceptional demonstration of ability? If you have been exceptional, you have likely received recognition, and those recognitions are Evidence of your achievements. Those awards usually have your name, date, and the nature of achievement engraved on them. What do they say?

Physical Capacity/Activity	Recognition or Awards	When Awarded

My Exceptional Nonathletic Physical Talents

Do you rate yourself as exceptional at a nonathletic physical capacity that sets you apart from most other people? What is it?

Be careful what you exclude from the discovery and development of physical Evidence. Many parents I speak to and whom I have worked with have real problems with their children playing video games or playing what they consider too much. They have a legitimate point. Anything given too much time to the detriment of other essential parts of Life needs to be controlled.

These parents see video games as being a waste of time. They can be, but a recent article showed that there were very positive outcomes for surgeons who played video games. Numerous reports over the past few years have given another perspective on the positive aspects and results of video gaming.

Playing Video Games Makes for Better Surgeons

Researchers have found that doctors who played video games for at least three hours a week made about 37 percent fewer mistakes in laparoscopic surgery and also performed the task 27 percent faster than their counterparts who did not play video games.

Hand-eye coordination is a major element in performing laparoscopic, appendix, gall bladder, and a host of other surgeries that now use instruments very similar to those found in video games. Surgeons who play video games using joysticks become better at their craft.

Minimally invasive surgery involves making tiny incisions and inserting a mini–video camera that then sends images to a video screen. The surgical tools are remotely controlled by the surgeon watching the screen. Surgeons can now practice their techniques through video simulations, just like pilots do when learning to fly.

Preparing to perform surgery is similar to warming up for an athletic event. You go through various warm-up exercises. Playing video games or performing simulations of the surgery now allows for doctors to "warm up" for that surgery.

Kurt Squire is a University of Wisconsin researcher who studied the effects of video game playing on learning. He discovered that gaming can produce improved timing, a better sense of touch, and intuition for manipulating medical devices.

Video games have also been used in rehabilitation facilities. Patients who have had strokes, soldiers who have lost limbs, and crash victims have used video games to recover and learn new skills.

All Fields of Evidence Are Connected

One psychologist in Seattle, Dr. Hunter Hoffman, runs what is called the "Hit Lab." Dr. Hoffman has created a video game program that helps burn victims be able to control their terrible pain by going to a "cold" environment. The interplay and ability of your mind to exercise control over your physical body is just one of the issues you need to be looking at as you collect Evidence.

- You need to ask how, when one Talent diminishes, you support or strengthen it by using another.
- How do Talents in one Field of Evidence strengthen Evidence in another Field of Evidence?
- How do Talents interact with one another and create a total greater than the sum of their original parts?

The effect that each Field of Evidence has on the other Fields needs to be explored with the primary objective of discovering how they can build, support, and strengthen the others.

Are You More Than Carbon?

You are a physical being and possess physical capacities and Talents. But no matter how exceptional those Talents might be, you are more than your DNA, your physical strength, your sensory abilities, and so on. Who you are physically will change: you will grow and develop, depending on your age; some of those Talents and capacities will, at some point, deteriorate, and you may even lose some of them. There will come a time when your physical body will stop being and die.

Never forget that your physical body is vitally important. It is the vehicle of your DNA Code. All the Talents you possess are housed in your physical body. It must be nurtured and protected. Take care of it. Thank God for it. Use it well. Keep it healthy. Feed it well. Don't pollute it, and the rest of your DNA Code will have the opportunity to be discovered and developed to the potential with which the Designer intended.

Bag It and Tag It

RT	Evidence Reliability Tests Quick Checklist
RT-1	"Exceptional," Top 25 Percent, Top 10 Percent
RT-2	Flow
RT-3	Preserved
RT-4	Easily Repeatable and Been Repeated
RT-5	Judged as Exceptional by Witnesses
RT-6	Expert Witness Testify
RT-7	Result of Spontaneous Action
RT-8	By Choice and in My Own Time
RT-9	Positive Emotion
RT-10	Intuition

Best Evidence Matrix

What Was the Evidence? Identify and Specify	When? How Often?	Tests Online and RTs	Witness List and Identify

Chapter 19
Discovering Evidence of Your Intellectual DNA Code Part 1

Intellectual Capacity	<ul><li>My capacity for knowledge or knowing</li><li>How I think (cognitive abilities)</li><li>How I learn</li><li>How I understand or process information</li><li>My intellectual potential</li><li>My capacity to store and retrieve information</li><li>Logical-mathematical intelligence</li><li>Linguistic intelligence</li></ul>

MYLIFESCENE.COM—CROSS NOW—MYLIFESCENE.COM
Life Scene—Danielle

Danielle was a vivacious but rather shy seventeen-year-old student. She was very popular in school and was on the school's cheer team. Danielle had focused on her *physical Talents* and had defined herself by her role as a cheerleader.

Danielle wanted to go into the nursing field, but because she had never excelled in school, she had set her sights on doing a one-year diploma and becoming a nurse's aide. She had already looked at a local community college program and was planning to enroll after she graduated from high school.

Danielle enrolled in the LSI program with another cheerleader. As she went through the program, we were able to find a great deal of Evidence to support Danielle in her desire to enter the nursing field. Her fellow cheerleader talked about how one of the male cheer team members had broken his arm and had the bone sticking out through his skin. Danielle was the only person to take control and assist him while they waited for the ambulance to come. She did not shy away from blood, gore in this crisis situation but demonstrated great *emotional Talent* in handling the crisis. Danielle was also known for being a trusted confidant and counselor to her peers and others on the cheer team.

One of the tests we routinely do as a part of discovering *intellectual DNA Code* is an IQ test. Danielle had seen herself as many other people had seen her, a cheerleader who was pretty and athletic but not very bright intellectually. She had not investigated other parts of her Unique Design.

After taking the IQ test, where she scored well above average, her outlook immediately changed. When she began to understand what having such a high IQ score meant, she began to see her future in the nursing field as much more probable than she currently envisioned. Danielle began to expand her horizons.

Danielle's grades began to steadily improve, much because she believed she was capable of actually doing well academically. She put in more effort and began to use her intellectual capacities as never before. She applied to a number of local colleges to pursue her desire to become a nurse.

She asked me to complete a reference for a local university so that she could enroll in a four-year nursing program. Danielle was accepted and later transferred to another four-year program, from which she graduated.

MYLIFESCENE.COM—CROSS NOW—MYLIFESCENE.COM

Measuring Evidence of Intellectual Capacity

There are many ways to measure intelligence and discover intellectual Talents. Some people measure intelligence by looking at test scores and diplomas or by specific intelligence DNA markers called IQ scores. Before you think you are tough intellectually because you have tested very high on an IQ test, you need to know that other measures and types of intelligence are equally as important to Life. There are some brilliant people with high IQs who have trouble making a simple decision like when to cross the street. They know how to write complex computer codes, but they struggle in reading a simple map or finding their way home.

We call one type of intelligence "book smarts" and the other "street smarts." Both are valuable and necessary in order for society to function. Let's continue the Positive Forensic Process and collect Evidence of your intellectual DNA markers.

Simply, there are unique factors that define you and your intellect. Once discovered, they will help you become the best you can be.

My educational career took a number of turns. I went from public school to private school in fifth grade. The private school I went to was a Jesuit Catholic school known for both its academic and its sports focus.

I started to grow physically and to show exceptional athletic ability. I enjoyed academics a little, with new subjects such as Latin and French, but I loved the athletics being offered, and at this stage of my Life, that is what became important. My father, brother, and grandfather had also attended the school, and my father was an exceptional sportsman. In some ways I was expected to follow in his footsteps.

My singular reason for going to St George's College was to play sports, cricket specifically. I was also very good at athletic field events and regularly won the high jump, shot put, and javelin.

That focus was supported because I was regularly selected for the national junior teams, which was good for the school's image. My desire was to play professionally. My father hired a coach who had played professionally and was recognized as possibly the best coach in our country. I played and practiced throughout the year, often without a break. All the while I was playing, my academics were very much on the back burner. The image of me at school was always that of a jock.

I remember having my annual session with an academic counselor and doing some vocational testing, which determined I might want to look at becoming a dentist. Nothing could be further from who I am than becoming a dentist!

It was only after leaving high school and having a major change in thinking about becoming a professional cricketer that I understood the necessity of academics. I wanted to become a minister and work with people. While in the military, I had to attend night school to technically graduate high school.

After receiving a foreign student scholarship and coming to the United States, I discovered I really had a brain that worked in an academic setting. I was very good at decision making and strategic thinking, as shown in always being a team captain who directed play, determined batting orders, made bowling/pitching changes, set field placements, and so on. I was resourceful and determined. But I was never known for having any outstanding or demonstrated academic Talents while in school.

Once in college and knowing what I wanted to do, I was amazed how well and easily I understood the world of academics. When challenged academically, I did very well. I was exposed to a variety of subjects, and a new world that I began to love was opened to me. I now excelled in philosophy, theology, international politics, psychology, sociology, and other new subjects and ideas.

Forensic Principle—Starter Focus

One of the mistakes forensic investigators can sometimes make is focusing on one element of the Evidence at the expense of the others. Taking time to gather all the Evidence before developing a *Life Theory* is an important principle to follow.

?RU? I have shared with you some of my academic/intellectual history and my DNA markers. They were not seen in any outstanding measure early on in my Life but became clearly evident later on when I changed my focus. We all have different Designs, but we all leave Evidence of our intellectual DNA Code. That Evidence needs to be discovered and our lives guided by what we know and see today.

So how do you start identifying your intellectual DNA Code? What is the *trace Evidence*; who are the witnesses, and where is the hard Evidence? *?RU*

IQ = Intelligence Quotient

IQ (Intelligence Quotient)—A measure of a person's intelligence as indicated by a test; the ratio of one's mental age to his or her chronological age (multiplied by 100)

One of the important things you must understand about the IQ is that it is only one measure of intelligence among many. IQ measures analytical intelligence and, though important, analytical intelligence is only one aspect of overall intelligence.

- A **_higher IQ score_** is never a guarantee that someone will be happy, be productive, or grow spiritually.

- A **_lower IQ score_** does not mean that someone will be unsuccessful financially, emotionally, or morally or fail to perform at a high level of excellence.

There are "high-IQ" individuals in every walk of Life. Many of the traditionally exalted groups, such as lawyers and doctors, can have members who have only a "normal" IQ.

Those people who have a high IQ generally do well in school and in certain types of jobs such as the sciences, engineering, medicine, computers, accounting, and law.

Incredible research has been done in the past few years to identify the variations in the way our brains work to help uniquely distinguish the Talents we all have in the types of brains we have.

What Do I Know about My IQ?

Go to the www.mylifescene.com website, and go to "Forensic Tests." Take the basic IQ test. You can also take the more expanded one and pay for it as well as get an extensive report.

Please remember that these tests are not infallible. They are not perfect. The scores can vary somewhat, depending on when you take the tests, how tired you are, what your emotional state is, where you take the tests, and so on. What is most important is that you have some fun and get more information about your intellectual fingerprint.

Intellectual Olympians

We know the names of Jordan, Phelps, Bolt, and Woods because they are seen on television and are at the top of their athletic game. But other names are just as well known on other fields of play. There are intellectual gold medalists, people, who, if they competed in intellectual competition, would qualify for the NBA, NFL, or Olympics of intelligence. How many of the following names are familiar to you? Do you know what they are known for?

> *DaVinci, Michelangelo, Hawkings, Plato, Solomon, Gates, Socrates, Einstein, Paul of Tarsus, Edison, Crick, Oppenheimer, Ford, Carver, Morse, Pascal, Newton, Jobs, Jefferson, Bell, and Franklin*

Can you name some?

Intellectual Awards, Honors Diplomas, and Degrees

Through the past several hundred years we have developed the concept of universities, places where intellect is not only discovered but also developed along specialized lines. The modern university system, universities that award degrees or diplomas, began in the late ninth century in Morocco, with others in Spain, Italy, France, and England (Oxford, 1167, and Cambridge, 1209) beginning a little later. A university is a place of intellectual discovery and testing where we can demonstrate our exceptional intellectual capacities.

There are many ways by which intellectual capacity is identified and developed in educational institutions. The university model is most basically divided into "arts" and "sciences," accommodating to both basic sides of intellectual capacity.

Beyond the university model we also have the technical and vocational models, which cater to those who want to study the more practical endeavors of Life. We all need mechanics, plumbers, hair stylists, massage therapists, landscapers, coaches, and so on. The emphasis on everyone's being good or great at mathematics and science is sometimes misplaced. Vocations are greatly valued in our world, and those who are excellent at them can be well rewarded.

Societies and Honors	Diplomas and Certificates
National Spelling Bee	Nursing—CNA, NA, RN, PA
National Honor Society	Computers—Microsoft, Cisco, Linux, C++
National Merit Society	Accounting/Finance—CPA, CFP
Math Olympiad	Dental, Veterinary
Quest	Mechanics, Plumbing, Electrical
MENSA	Hairdressing, Beauty, Child Care, Real Estate

Undergraduate Degrees	Graduate Degrees and Beyond
Matriculation—High School	MA—Master of Arts (one–two years)
GED—General Education Diploma	MS/MSc—Master of Science (one–two years)
AA—Associate of Arts (two years)	MEd—Master of Education (one–two years)
AS—Associate of Science (two years)	MPhil—Master of Philosophy
BA—Bachelor of Arts (four years)	JD—Juris Doctorate (three–four years)
BS/BSc—Bachelor of Science (four years)	MD—Doctor of Medicine (four–six years)
BEd—Bachelor of Education	PhD—Doctor of Philosophy (two–four years)
BMus—Bachelor of Music	EdD—Doctor of Education (two–four years)
BArch—Bachelor of Architecture	DSc—Doctor of Science
Degree Honors—*Cum Laude, Magna Cum Laude, Summa Cum Laude*	FACS—Fellow, American College of Surgeons
	ASME—American Society of Mechanical Engineers

Evidence from Report Cards and School

Think of how much time you spend at school. Most of your early years are focused on school, books, teachers, reading, exams, papers, learning new ideas, and so on. Because of the amount of time and activity you spent at school, it is likely that you left as Evidence a great number of intellectual DNA markers during that time frame.

Report cards, transcripts, job evaluations, and certification scores are historical records of your intellectual and academic performance. They also include other good information, such as how you behave toward your fellow classmates, teachers, co-workers, and management. Reports show how well you have done and in which areas of interest.

History of Subject Interest and Accomplishment

Looking at your schooling and academic history, you will find definite trace Evidence that will give you a good sense of your intellectual Design Talents. The matrix that follows asks you to think back to when you were in elementary school and follow to where you are today or have continued with your formal schooling.

Educational Subject Analysis Matrix

As you go through the following list, look for Evidence not only from a subject analysis but from clubs or societies you may have belonged to, past or present. Identifying that you belonged to a club or society would demonstrate Evidence of a Talent. This goes another layer deeper than the previous matrix.

Classes/Subjects	A or B Grade	Loved It! (Clubs, Societies)	What I Loved about It!
English			
Literature			
History			
Geography			
Social Studies			
Languages (Which?)			
Speech			
Sociology			
Psychology			
Business			

Subject			
Philosophy			
Education			
Mathematics			
Algebra/Geometry/Trig			
Statistics			
Chemistry			
Biology			
Physics			
Health			
Physical Education			
Home Economics			
Forensics			
Anthropology			
Politics			
World Studies			
Auto Shop			
Wood Shop			
Technology			
Web Design			
Computer Programming			
Computer Programs— Word, Excel, etc.			
Photography			
Journalism/Yearbook			
Cross-cultural Studies			
Religion/Bible			

Tutoring or TA			
Debate			
Art/Drawing/Painting			
Drafting/Architecture			
Music			
Management			
Environmental Studies			
ROTC			
4-H			
Other Subjects (list as many as you have studied in formal schooling)			

What have consistently been your two or three best subjects at school/college?

_____

_____

_____

I can remember teachers who made learning a pleasure. Some teachers just made sense and knew how to teach. I liked the subject, and I liked the teacher. There were others who were great teachers, but that didn't matter because I just didn't understand the material; it did not compute. Then there were teachers who were terrible at teaching but because I understood and the subject made sense to me, I really didn't care. I would find books on the subject to read. Extra-credit assignments were fun and done not for a better grade but because I wanted to learn more.

I remember being in a sociology class in college early in the morning with a teacher who was not good by any measure. I had never done anything like sociology in high school (Latin and French were high priorities), and it was fascinating to me. That led me to want to study psychology, counseling, sociology, pastoral care, and other related disciplines. I also loved philosophy and political science.

So what were the classes, regardless of the competence of the teachers, which you loved simply because of the subject matter? Do you remember them fondly? What was it that you loved in the class?

Who was your favorite teacher ever? Why?

_____

What in your mind has been your most significant intellectual achievement in school/college?

_____

_____

_____

Forensic Fact

Apple's iPods are so cool. The newest ones can store 25,000 songs, 50,000 photos, and over 150 hours of video. Imagine all that in just a thin piece of plastic! Did you know when you compare an iPod to your brain capacity (gray slop and mush between your ears protected by a thick, bonelike shell or skull), the iPod just doesn't begin to compare? It is *WEAK!* The iPod's capacity is less than 1 percent of the capacity of your Brain!

How Much RAM (Memory) Do We Have in Our Hard Drive?

When we think about buying a computer, the most important issue for many is memory. There are two essential types of memory we look at: Random Access Memory (RAM) and storage (HD).

RAM compares with our ability to think on our feet and process information in real time. We can think through and use what we know to make decisions. The more RAM, the faster we can think and make decisions.

Storage means how much we can store in our memory bank. It refers to how many books and magazines we house or can house. On a computer, this memory is housed in the hard drive.

In the past few years the ability to process information, RAM strength, has developed at light speed. The same goes for HD storage. Most new computers have at least one gigabyte of RAM and anywhere from 50 gigabytes to 2 terabytes of storage.

Quick Forensic Memory Test

- What did you eat yesterday for breakfast?
- Do you remember the name of the person you met at lunch today?
- What were three causes of the American Revolution?
- Can you name five students from your fifth- or twelfth-grade class?

These questions test different types of information. The first two use RAM, and the last two are HD or storage.

MYLIFESCENE.COM—CROSS NOW—MYLIFESCENE.COM
Life Scene—Starbucks Patty

I was writing in a Starbucks and one of the baristas, whom I had met briefly six months earlier, looked at me and said, "Hi Mark." I was shocked that she remembered my name. I remembered her because she purchased a large piece of art from a friend at an art show, and I certainly had more reason to remember her name than she did mine.

I was writing in the same Starbucks, and I watched Patty's incredible memory on display. This Starbucks is very busy; I would estimate it has a few hundred customers who come through every morning during the rush. Patty remembers the usual drinks of most of the customers, their names, their children's names, and more. There are lines of ten to fifteen people at times, and the pressure to move and deliver quickly is intense. Patty handles it so easily, remembering virtually everyone. Patty has great HD (memory) and RAM (memory), and it's on display every day.

Patty is not only gifted intellectually with great memory Talents, she also possesses unbelievable social and emotional Talents. Watching people when they come into that Starbucks is like watching kids come into the classroom of their favorite teacher. Teens, little kids with their parents, grandmothers, everyone wants Patty to see them, serve them, and talk to them. They don't just want some coffee, they want a shot of "Patty Espresso!"

Patty told me how many of her customers who come in share their lives with her. They share the toughest and most private Life situations and struggles with her. In some ways she is like a bartender, but people don't need alcohol to open up; Patty has Unique Talents that invite people, even when sober, to open their lives to her.

What exceptional capacity is in your intellectual Life Scene? What does your memory capacity look like?

MYLIFESCENE.COM—CROSS NOW—MYLIFESCENE.COM

Do you have to study hard to remember information, or does it come easily?

_____

How good is your overall memory for facts, figures and faces?

_____

How quick and productive are your decision-making abilities?

_____

Bag It and Tag It

RT	Evidence Reliability Tests Quick Checklist
RT-1	"Exceptional," Top 25 Percent, Top 10 Percent
RT-2	Flow
RT-3	Preserved
RT-4	Easily Repeatable and Been Repeated
RT-5	Judged as Exceptional by Witnesses
RT-6	Expert Witness Testify
RT-7	Result of Spontaneous Action
RT-8	By Choice and in My Own Time
RT-9	Positive Emotion
RT-10	Intuition

Best Evidence Matrix

What Was the Evidence? Identify and Specify	When? How Often?	Tests Online and RTs	Witness List and Identify

Chapter 20
Discovering Evidence of Your Intellectual DNA Code Part 2

Intellectual Capacity	<ul><li>My capacity for knowledge or knowing</li><li>How I think (cognitive abilities)</li><li>How I learn</li><li>How I understand or process information</li><li>My intellectual potential</li><li>My capacity to store and retrieve information</li><li>Logical-mathematical intelligence</li><li>Linguistic intelligence</li></ul>

As we continue discovering Evidence in your intellectual or cognitive Life Scene, we will be looking at the way you input and process information. This Evidence will guide decisions about the way you study and prepare for important exams; help you choose whether to go to an online college or attend classes in person; enable you to understand the way you see the world and how you can be more effective in understanding others and the way they work; and guide your children or those you manage to perform better.

Forensic Investigation Consideration

When we attempt to or are forced to learn or achieve a level of intellectual success that our minds are simply not wired for, we will pay a price. The same goes for any capacity: physical, social, spiritual, or emotional. It can and does happen to us at different times. We become frustrated and anxious and even melt down when we are expected to produce at a level of capacity we simply don't have the DNA Code for. The problem is that this takes place every day in schools and workplaces all around the world.

Which Way Does Your Brain Lean?

Brain dominance theory is based on research that shows people use different sides of their brains to process different kinds of information.

We all use both sides of our brains without thinking, but most of us tend to prefer learning strategies associated with one side or the other. Such individuals are considered to be *left-brain* dominant or *right-brain* dominant. Some people have about even preferences and are considered to have *bilateral* dominance.

The Left Side of the Brain Analytical	The Right Side of the Brain *Global*
• You process verbal, abstract, analytical information in a linear, sequential manner. • You look at differences and contrasts, seeing small signs that represent the whole. • You concern yourself with reasoning abilities such as math and language. • You are generally very well organized. • You focus on one thought at a time. • You feel energized when you have a step-by-step process to follow.	• You process nonverbal, concrete, and spatial information. • You look at similarities in patterns, forming a whole picture and processing parts in relationship to the whole. • You concern yourself with artistic abilities such as music and graphics. • The "big picture" is what motivates you. • You believe feelings need to be understood. • You enjoy going with the flow and consensus. • You don't need to know all the steps to get involved.

• You like being prepared.	• You can fit in very easily.
• You seek the facts and not emotions.	• You see most of the options.
• You like to know what to expect and don't like the unknown.	

I obviously love forensics or I would not have written this book. What you will notice is that I seldom get very technical. I receive three online forensics magazines, which I scan for ideas but seldom read closely. The reality is I am not a strong science analytic. I love the process of discovery, the ideas that forensics generates and their analogies to Life. I love to discover patterns and see information that others have missed.

Where do you fit on the spectrum?

Analytic_____-_____Global

While we speak in terms of "left-brain analytic" and "right-brain global," please remember that these are extremes. Be objective and identify *PRU* and where you fit on the spectrum, but understand that most of us will find ourselves in both categories.

Evidence of Your Unique Learning Style
Cognitive Input Processor

I know an expert witness in the area of learning styles. Her name is Cynthia Tobias. Cynthia has written books and travels the world speaking and training corporations, educational institutions, police academies, students, colleges, and others by using her expertise in this area. If you want to know more about many of the concepts in this module, have a look at the "Forensic Tests" in chapter 14 to find out more about Cynthia's books and online programs.

Research has found that in some learning style models, your temperament and many of your learning style characteristics are "hardwired" in your brain from the moment you are conceived, *branded* into you as part of your DNA Code. We all learn to adapt and adjust to many different situations and circumstances, but your mind will always possess the basic imprint present in you from birth.

We use three basic categories of Evidence that identify the way you learn or process information:

1. Concentration or focus
2. Remember or retain
3. Interact and process

How You Concentrate—*Environmental Profile*

I need noise, movement, music, and people around me, regular breaks, and the ability to drink and eat if I am going to be productive. When I wrote this book, I spent over a year almost living in Starbucks and St. James Espresso in Kirkland, Washington. I need noise and a variety of other stimuli in order to concentrate. If I am at home, I need the television on or I am useless.

At certain times, though, I am so focused that three or four hours go by when I am feeling creative and I am in the zone. I don't know what is around me for the most part.

For some of you, what I described is everything that doesn't work for you. You have children in school and you demand that they work in absolute quiet, with no distractions, at a time you dictate and in a room you designate, and then you wonder why one child thrives and another is failing. There are reasons, and they are based on the Unique DNA Code each child possesses. Having the Evidence of *?RU* allows you to tailor your parenting or management of your employees for the most effective outcome.

Place a mark on the continuums below the description that best fits:

- **Time of Day**

Early Morning_____Late Night

- **Intake**

  Food___ Snacks___ Candy___ Coffee___ Pop___ Other___

- **Lighting**

Bright_____Mood_____Dark

- **Design Surroundings**

Special features? _____

- **Temperature**

Hot_____Warm_____Cold

Evidence for How I Process and Remember Information

Our brains are incredibly complex. Our minds have three distinct ways of inputting and remembering information:

- *Visual*—what we see and can picture
- *Auditory*—what we hear and say
- *Kinesthetic*—what we feel and do

We all possess and use all three styles, but they are usually not all the same "size" in our brains. In discovering Evidence of *PRU* you need to identify your dominant style. What fires the most easily? What works and allows you to interact with information most effectively and remember it with greatest ease?

Visual Evidence Checklist

When you need to remember something, do you usually get a picture in your mind and need to draw, diagram, or write?

_____ Do you remember faces easily?

_____ Do you make lists and write down what you need to remember?

_____ Do you draw and doodle on almost everything?

_____ Do you make notes in study materials (underline and highlight)?

_____ Do you watch others do things you need to learn and love demonstrations of tasks to illustrate concepts?

_____ Do you take pride in your appearance and in looking good?

_____ Are you are impressed with and do you judge others based on their external appearance?

_____ Do you see pictures in your head of things being described?

My son Adam is very creative as well as being very analytical. I used to look at Adam's backpack, which was normally lying around near the computer, in the kitchen, under my desk, on the floor of the car, and in a variety of other locations. Papers were here, there, and everywhere. I worried about Adam because of what I saw. There was never a page that wasn't filled with cartoon drawings of comedic characters or bizarre creatures with bulging eyeballs. If I had taken him to a psychologist he may have been committed. I saw a small amount of school subject matter on most pages, but seldom was there more writing than there was cartooning.

What was interesting is that he remembered everything. He remembered facts and figures because he was able to associate them with what he drew. Everything meant something.

Adam is into graphics as well as cooking. He went to culinary arts school and is always looking to make Life and food look better. He spent much of his spare time when he was younger taking apart electronic gadgets, radios, and other machinery, attempting to see how things worked.

Where do you fit on the *visual* spectrum?

Visual 1_____5_____Visual 10

Auditory Evidence Checklist

When you have to remember something or study for a test, do you usually need to read the information out loud, discuss it with others, or make a mental noise?

_____ Do you prefer to listen to a book being read than read it yourself?

_____ Do you remember better by making rhymes or songs you can repeat out loud?

_____ Do you think better and solve problems by talking your thoughts out loud?

_____ Do you do better at or prefer performing tests out loud than writing them?

_____ Do you tend to understand a concept better when it is explained rather than having to read and think it through by yourself?

_____ Do you find yourself repeating words out loud when you are writing them?

_____ Do you tend to trust someone by listening to the way the person sounds?

Where do you fit on the *auditory* spectrum?

Auditory 1_____5_____Auditory 10

Kinesthetic/Tactile Evidence Checklist

When I need to remember something, I usually need to move around, take short
breaks, and take some kind of action.

_____ Do you regularly have to move, walk around, and tap your feet or fingers?

_____ Do you need to move or dance when you hear music?

_____ Do you love to watch action movies or television shows?

_____ Do you use your finger to trace words or point as you read?

_____ Do you have to keep notes to help you remember lectures?

_____ Do you understand things better when you are holding or touching them?

_____ Do you gauge people's character by the way they carry themselves, shake hands, or make other physical movements?

Where do you fit on the *kinesthetic/tactile* spectrum?

Kinesthetic 1_____5_____Kinesthetic 10

Forensic Fact IQ and Learning Style

All the research is very clear that there is no statistically significant correlation between your learning style and your intelligence. You cannot use any one test to show you how smart or successful you will be in Life. There is no one predictor of success. What we know is that there are many pathways to becoming successful in our lives.

I said there was no one predictor of success. The greatest predictor, though, is knowing what your Talents are. The more you know, the more you will understand how to succeed and be able to use those Talents to your advantage.

The concept of multiple intelligences explains how each of us can be successful in ways in which our DNA code has enabled us in order to perform at high levels. Real intelligence is the ability to respond to the situation with the innate Talents you have. If your toilet is broken, you need a plumber and not a math teacher. If you are going on a safari, you need someone with naturalistic intelligence and not a chef. How we are successful in any particular environment is dependent on the unique Talents we are endowed with.

Miscategorized Evidence

A great deal of Evidence has been categorized as being deficit, or contaminated, Evidence, but it has been wrongly labeled in American society.

Many components of the intellectual Life Scene have in recent years been seen as problematic. In classrooms across the country we have tried to find ways to make classrooms manageable by medicating the kids who move around, ask too many questions, fidget, finish their work too quickly, and talk a lot. Many of these issues could be dealt with if teachers were given the authority to discipline their students without fear of lawsuits. Kids can often be managed to maximize their Talents by using behavior management tools and greater parental supervision or coaching.

Deficit diagnoses such as ADD (Attention *Deficit* Disorder), ADHD (ADD with hyperactivity), and Asperger's syndrome (normal or exceptional analytical intelligence coupled with very low social intelligence) are Evidence of exceptional intellectual Talents. Many of history's greatest minds are speculated to have had Asperger's syndrome: Albert Einstein, Thomas Jefferson, and Bill Gates are just three of many.

We have medicated many of the greatest minds of our age because we seek to manage them in a classroom of thirty kids. Many great artists and musicians are people of extreme emotional genius. Some of our greatest leaders are diagnosed as having oppositional defiant disorder (ODD) and other mental health deficits. Many of these "deficits" are wonderful gifts, and if we understood and managed people with these gifts like we would an athlete, we would have many more geniuses.

Life Scene—Alan

I met Alan when he was fifteen years old. He was a mess. Alan was a failure at school. He was not even getting just Fs—they were scores in the 20 to 30 percent range, if he even took the time to take tests or do assignments. I spoke to his academic advisor, who believed in Alan and thought he was a great kid. She saw something in Alan that nobody else did.

We tried a number of academic adjustments and accommodations, but nothing really seemed to work. Alan was just not focused and in many ways was too distracted by all that was still going on in his Life, socially and emotionally.

On meeting Alan I was quickly amazed at how bright he was. He knew facts and figures and was able to discuss art history with a friend of mine, as well as philosophy, religion, politics, and a myriad of other subjects most fifteen-year-olds have never even thought about.

What became obvious about Alan was that he was not lacking anything intellectually to be able to do exceptionally well, but he was bored beyond caring. He was intensely logical and basically thought that he was far beyond his age level intellectually and was doing the equivalent of second-grade work.

When he turned sixteen, I took him to a local community college to do a series of tests that would allow him to start college while still in high school. The test was three hours long and consisted of three parts; two were language and English based and the third, a math test.

I took Alan in and got him registered and told him I would go and work in my car and would see him in three hours. I was just getting into my work about forty minutes later, and there was Alan walking up to the car. I was mad. My first thought was, "You idiot, you walked out, you didn't follow through . . ." I was wrong. Alan had finished all three parts in less than a quarter of the required time. I waited a couple of days to get what I thought would be a bad result and another closed academic door for Alan. I was wrong. Alan scored something like 98 percent, 98 percent, and 97 percent.

Alan is in his early twenties now. We have connected on Facebook. I often post thoughts about politics and societal issues. Alan responds, and his ability to understand and articulate his thoughts makes him sound like a professor at Oxford or Harvard. He is brilliant. We don't often agree, but I am amazed each time he posts a response at his intellectual brilliance.

Maybe you are like Alan. You need hard challenges. You are bored. You need your mind to be exposed to challenges where you are no different from an athlete who is playing in a state championship and the best of you is demanded.

Do you have an exceptional intellect? Is there some area of your intellectual Life Scene that is exceptional?

MYLIFESCENE.COM—CROSS NOW—MYLIFESCENE.COM

There certainly are legitimately diagnosed physiological, neurological learning disorders. But don't be too quick to believe you are afflicted with one of them because you struggle to pay attention or learn in certain situations. Take time to think about what you are trying to learn or pay attention to. Could it be the subject matter? Analytics love sciences and globals love the arts. It is vital to understand how much of any difficulty in learning is based on your learning style.

It's important to use a variety of tools and measurements when you're trying to determine your intellectual capacity, your academic Talents, and what you are drawn to do with the rest of your Life.

No one thing will tell you who you are; you are a wonderful mosaic of cognitive and intellectual Evidence factors. You have a "beautiful mind" that needs to be understood, and when you know what the Evidence is of your unique Talents, the world will open up and make sense to you in a powerful way!

Bag It and Tag It

RT	Evidence Reliability Tests Quick Checklist
RT-1	"Exceptional," Top 25 Percent, Top 10 Percent
RT-2	Flow
RT-3	Preserved
RT-4	Easily Repeatable and Been Repeated
RT-5	Judged as Exceptional by Witnesses
RT-6	Expert Witness Testify
RT-7	Result of Spontaneous Action
RT-8	By Choice and in My Own Time
RT-9	Positive Emotion
RT-10	Intuition

Best Evidence Matrix

What Was the Evidence? Identify and Specify	When? How Often?	Tests Online and RTs	Witness List and Identify

Chapter 21
Discovering Evidence of Your Emotional DNA Code Part 1

Emotional Capacity	<ul><li>How I feel</li><li>How I express emotions both internally and externally in a variety of adverse and positive situations</li><li>How conscious I am of inward impressions, states of mind, or physical conditions</li><li>The ability to read and understand the emotions of others</li><li>My emotional potential</li><li>The way I feel internally and how I express those feelings externally</li><li>The way I feel based on how I observe or think about what I see externally in the world around me</li><li>How I respond and feel based on the way I see myself in this world</li><li>The range of moods I express</li><li>Intrapersonal intelligence</li></ul>

There is a time to weep and a time to laugh,
a time to mourn and a time to dance. . .
—Ecclesiastes 3:4

You have been Designed with the capacity to feel or experience emotions. These are internal feelings and sensations that register when we are stimulated by sight, sound, people, memories, positive and negative stimuli, and many other experiences. We are not simply mechanical beings without the capacity to feel and experience joy, peace, depression, guilt, love, Passion, fear, and a collection of other emotions. We have an essential emotional Design DNA component.

Emotions are the way we respond to Life in its many and varied experiences. They are generated by the way we see and perceive Life. They can be pleasant or painful. We seek some because they make us feel good, and we avoid others because they make us feel bad. Some stay for a short time, and others last for a long time. We are sometimes able to control them, and at other times they seem to take control of us.

The word *emotion* derives from the Latin *emovere*, which translates as "to excite, to move, to stir, or to agitate." Emotional states are normally regarded as relatively short levels of arousal and desires to act. Some emotions, such as fear, joy, disgust, pity, and love, are seen as relatively momentary feelings that can motivate us to action and activity and then subside. Other emotions are intensely experienced states, such as rage, anger, terror, grief, and fear, in which our behavior may be erratic or irrational.

Our emotional world can feel mysterious and changeable. Consider the amazing paradox in G. K. Chesterton's observation about the power of emotion:

> *Man seems to be capable of great virtues, but not of*
> *small virtues; capable of defying his torturer, but not*
> *keeping his temper.*

I want you to look for your most commonly expressed emotions, the emotions that make you strong and consistent, those feelings that motivate you to good actions. When others describe you, what do they say?

You are responsible for your own emotional Talents and stability. Your emotions have been given to you to manage, and you have the responsibility to discover and learn how to use them in the most effective and productive ways.

You now have the opportunity to delve deeper and discover Evidence of your emotional DNA markers. Focus on identifying your Talents as you interact with this discovery process.

Some emotions lead a person to feel bad, uneasy, miserable, and so on. Emotions are an indicator of one's behaviors, thoughts, and perceptions of events, people, and situations. The thoughts a person has usually inform his or her emotions, behaviors, and words. If the thoughts are distortions, obviously these will be evident in the way someone feels, acts, and interprets Life's situations. Cognitive scrutiny, followed by alignment with truth and reality, then, is a necessary precursor to accurately discovering your emotional Talents.

Fear may be perceived as a "bad" emotion, one to avoid. The reality is that fear is a protective emotion that can save your Life. When you are confronted with a dangerous situation, fear will cause you to avoid it or prompt you to run away, to escape harm.

Guilt is also an emotion we don't generally enjoy. Guilt is an indicator that we have done something that is wrong. We have violated one of God's laws, which are housed within our conscience, another part of our Design. Conscience is like a GPS (global positioning system) in that it can guide you in your decision making. An even better way of describing it is as a "DPS," or "Design Positioning System."

When we use our Talents based on the Designer's intent, we feel right. When we do what is right, we usually feel good. We experience feelings such as satisfaction, joy, peace, and happiness. Those emotions result from right choices and behaviors. They are rewards that encourage us to continue doing what is good and right.

Marriage and relationship researcher Dr. John Gottman holds a belief that our emotional Design is similar to an artist's palette: a platform with a variety of colors organized in differing patterns, blends, and strengths.

In addition, he divides emotions into two categories: "Appproach" and "Withdrawal." Approach emotions are those such as happiness, interest, anger, amusement, and others. Withdrawal emotions are fear, mistrust, disgust, and so on.

Dr. Gottman believes the greater awareness we have of what our primary orientation is, the more successful we can be in our relationships. Do you know what your primary emotional style is?

As you take your personal inventory using the simplified model (my four basic categories of Mad, Sad, Glad, and Bad), please keep the approach/withdrawal distinction in mind.

You Can't Hide Your Emotions

You need to be aware that everything you do communicates! Absorb this reality. Often your true feelings "leak" through, and you reveal things about yourself that you may believe are concealed from others. How does this happen?

Remember Locard's Principle. It states that we leave Evidence everywhere and all the time. The reality is, you can't *not* communicate. Regardless of whether you smile or hold your best poker face, focus on something so as to distract a watcher, hold your hand out to greet a new friend, stop talking or quit communicating altogether, you are communicating, and people around you will attach meaning to that behavior.

One of my favorite forensics shows is *Lie to Me*. The show begins with a montage of physical responses that are external signs of internal emotional states. They show how people react physically when they are stressed, fearful, angry, genuinely happy, or one of many other profiled emotional states. The show is about a profiler who is hired by law enforcement and other entities to help determine whether people are lying or planning to deceive.

So we are looking for those emotions and emotional states that reflect the best of who you are, your emotional DNA Code.

Your Four Basic Emotion Scenes

We need to understand that *all* emotions are good and have been given to us for a Purpose. All the emotions listed in the four boxes are good and right because they are either a result of choosing and doing what is right or they are an indicator that we need to change certain behaviors and ways of thinking so as not to repeat the same behaviors or thoughts.

My Emotional Fingerprints

Mad

Hated, Angry, Abhor, Bitter, Ripped Off, Contemptuous, Outraged, Annoyed, Furious, Used, Resentful, Frustrated, Insulted, Irritated, Offended, Heartless, Sadistic, Evil, Cynical, Disgusted, Defensive, Vengeful, Sarcastic, Cruel, Ignored, On Fire, Burning, Insensitive, Brutal, Abusive, Destructive, Sabotaging, Jealous, Enmity, Mean, Antagonistic, Indignant, Fed Up, Sullen, Untroubled, Disdainful, Pissed Off, Pissed!, Upset, Bitchy, Selfish, Guilty

Sad

Sad, Despondent, Grief, Sorrow, Martyred, Regretful, Remorseful, Hurt, Empty, Undeserving, Useless, Hopeless, Pathetic, Pitiful, Alone, Upset, Lonely, Unwanted, Rejected, Unloved, Alienated, Depressed, Sorry, Down, In the Dumps, Worthless, Heartless, Insignificant, Tearful, Self-Defeating, Regret, Needy, Inept, Disillusioned, Forgotten, Abused, Left Out, Suicidal, Bereavement, Wounded, Broken Hearted, Blue, Inadequate, Grief Stricken, Apologetic, Discounted, Abandoned, Guilty

Glad

Alive, Calm, Relaxed, Peaceful, Happy, Connected, Inspired, Amused, Pleased, Relieved, Ecstatic, Joyous, Serene, Joyful, Loved, Anticipating, Encouraged, Over the Moon, Excited, Affectionate, Appreciated, Enthusiastic, Patient, Esteemed, Liked, Courageous, Zealous, Cared For, Hopeful, Optimistic, Eager, Proud, Jolly, Friendly, Adventurous, Gratified, Delighted, Sure, Alert, Comforted, Accepted, Content, Helpful, Respected, Consoled, Included, Tender, Capable, Adored, Untroubled, Nurtured, Worthy, Vibrant, Gratified, Brave, Valiant Enchanted, Full of Life, Welcoming, Warm, Benevolent

Bad

Guilty, Ashamed, Embarrassed, Fearful, Threatened, Frightened, Anxious, Dismayed, Apprehensive, Disturbed, Torn, Conflicted, Miserable, Panicky, Humiliated, Shocked, Trapped, Horrified, Afraid, Scared, Terrified, Edgy, Nervous, Degraded, Tense, Worried, Perplexed, Bewildered, Mixed Up, Uncomfortable, Troubled, Alarmed, Shy, Confused, Fed Up, Sullen, Baffled, Dissatisfied, Shaky, Upset, Bashful, Puzzled

Forensic Discovery Tool

The *Johari Window* is a helpful tool in gaining additional information about how you view yourself as well as how others perceive you. The four quadrants offer useful feedback about your personal and interpersonal awareness and how feelings bleed through, despite your best efforts to hide them.

	What you see in me	What you do *not* see in me
What I see in me	The Public Self	The Private (or Hidden) Self
What I do *not* see in me	The Blind Self	The Undiscovered Self

The Public U

The public self is the part of ourselves that we are happy to share with others and discuss openly. You and I both see and can talk openly about this "me" and gain a common view of who I am in this element. *?RU*

1.   *UCU.* How do you see your emotions? What three adjectives would you use to describe yourself emotionally? That is not an easy question. Remember, we are looking for Unique Talents, and there are emotions you know define you and the best of who you are. Don't be scared to openly declare who you are and what you know about yourself. So what are they? Three words:

_____

_____

_____

2. ***UC Me.*** Now think about how others see you and what they would say in describing you. We are often pegged by others who have witnessed us as falling into an emotional category. What do you think you look like to others? If we were to ask three witnesses—your mother, your boss/teacher, and the barista where you buy coffee every morning—what would they say about you emotionally? What are your emotional DNA markers?

Mother _____

Boss/Teacher_____

Barista_____

The Private U

There are parts of ourselves that we believe are too private to share with others. We hide these away and refuse to discuss them with other people or expose them in any way. Private elements may be embarrassing or shameful in some way. One may also be fearful or seek to avoid being discussed for reasons of vulnerability. *?RU*

Between the public and private selves, there are partly private, partly public aspects of ourselves that we are prepared to share only with trusted others. *?RU*

The Blind U

We often assume that the public and private selves are all that we are. However, the views that others have of us may be different from those we have of ourselves. For example, some people who consider themselves as intelligent may be viewed as arrogant and socially ignorant by others.

Our blind self may remain blind because others will not discuss this part of us for a range of reasons. Perhaps they realize that we would be unable to accept what they see. Perhaps they have tried to discuss this and we have been so blind that we assume their views are invalid. They may also withhold this information as it gives them power over us. *?RU*

Forensic Tip
If something doesn't feel right to you, it usually isn't.

The Undiscovered U

Finally, the fourth self is one which neither us or nor other people see. This undiscovered self may include both good and bad things that may remain forever undiscovered or may one day be discovered, entering the private, blind, or maybe even public selves.

Between the blind and undiscovered selves are partly hidden selves that only some people see. Psychologists and those who are more empathic, for example, may well see more than the average person.

Start by picking five or six words from this list that you feel best describe you:

Able	Accepting	Adaptable	Bold
Brave	Calm	Caring	Cheerful
Clever	Complex	Confident	Dependable
Dignified	Energetic	Extroverted	Friendly
Giving	Happy	Helpful	Idealistic
Independent	Ingenious	Intelligent	Introverted
Kind	Knowledgeable	Logical	Loving
Mature	Modest	Nervous	Observant
Organized	Patient	Powerful	Proud
Quiet	Reflective	Relaxed	Religious
Responsive	Searching	Self-Assertive	Self-Conscious
Sensible	Sentimental	Shy	Silly
Spontaneous	Sympathetic	Tense	Trustworthy
Warm	Wise	Witty	

Do you tend to internalize/introvert or externalize/extrovert your feelings and emotions?

It is important that you review how you behave in different situations. I know that when I find myself in a situation or group where I don't feel competent or "strong" I will naturally become an introvert. I sat on the board of a youth program for a few years. When I attended the board meetings I was a very different person than I was known for in most areas of my Life. When I was at the meetings I was probably the quietest person in the room. I seldom said anything other than my "Yea" or "Nay" when a vote was taken on an item of business.

The main business of the group was budgets. I am not a math person, nor do I enjoy or demonstrate any competency at accounting or financial projections. I felt out of place, and if I opened my mouth, I knew I would have nothing to say or I would make an idiot of myself.

I knew I was very knowledgeable in youth issues, but the primary reason the board met was for raising, budgeting, and forecasting revenues. I worked with youth for many years. I counseled and coached teens and raised my own teens. I knew teens and was an expert in teen issues, not financial issues.

So it is important as you look at this emotional fingerprint to see when it is you are an introvert or an extrovert. There are very powerful clues to your Talents found in the situations where you come alive and demonstrate those Talents.

There are people who are extroverts in almost all areas of their lives. The problem is that they are often the same people who make fools of themselves when they enter areas of personal Talent deficit. They make a lot of noise and often put their foot in their mouth. Know what your primary and best approach to Life is.

MYLIFESCENE.COM—CROSS NOW—MYLIFESCENE.COM
Life Scene—Adam

My son Adam is an amazing young man. Adam has always been able to handle Life without the emotional restraints many of us have. When Adam was very young I gave him the nickname "Toughie." That nickname was directed at his emotional Talents.

I ran a large teen youth group in Johannesburg, South Africa, back in the 1980s. We would often take fifty to a hundred teens to a water park, and my kids always went along, even at a very young age. One of the water parks we went to had an extreme slide named the *Kamikaze*. To qualify for experiencing the *Kamikaze* you had to be thirteen years old and also be a certain height. Adam, at four years old, certainly didn't qualify. That didn't stop him, and I remember some of the kids in the youth group pointing Adam out to me as he went flying down the slide. One of the teens christened him the "Kamikaze Kid," indicative of his "no fear" approach to Life.

When Adam was eight years old he had a very rare tumor. After a nine-hour surgery to remove the tumor from facial nerves, salivary gland, and inner ear, he was left permanently deaf on the left side. The side of Adam's face was affected for almost a year. He needed regular steroid and other treatments to restore his facial nerves. Adam was teased at times because his face drooped. I heard about incidents from a teacher at his school. She said Adam never pulled away from his peers and handled the cruel teasing so well.

Fear has never been part of Adam's Life. He connects with people openly and often with a wry sense of humor. He has worked with the toughest at-risk teens we have had in our programs. He disarms them and simply engages and connects with them.

Adam went to New York City as part of a youth group summer program. He was in Central Park and saw the actor Adam Sandler. Most people would feel hesitant to talk to a celebrity like that, but not Adam. Adam walked straight up and talked to him.

We lived on a lake for a few years, and I remember Adam on a Jet Ski. He was flying, hitting waves and going airborne at times. When I went on it I would have fun but seldom if ever put the throttle down and fly like Adam. He always had such a big grin on his face.

Adam and his wife, Abi, now live in Cambodia. He manages a restaurant, and Abi teaches in an international school. They both love new experiences, going and doing things many others are hesitant to attempt.

So what about you? How do you handle fear and other situations that could potentially be dangerous? Adam's emotional Talents allow him to experience many aspects of Life others of us only wish to. He is who he is. What is important is what we know about who we are and how we connect with our world emotionally. *?RU* in the many emotional facets and situations of Life? What defines you and describes your emotional Talents?

MYLIFESCENE.COM—CROSS NOW—MYLIFESCENE.COM

Forensic Definition—Emotional Intelligence

The capacity to understand and use emotions to more effectively manage ourselves and influence positive outcomes in our interactions with others.

Evidence of Emotional Intelligence

Emotional Talents are seen both when we appropriately express positive emotions and also when we learn to control emotions that, if acted on, can harm ourselves and others. Not reacting to feeling as though someone is provoking you to lose control of yourself requires an enormous amount of energy and self-control.

1. When have you managed your emotions well?
2. When have others seen great emotional Talent from you when you have been pushed, taunted, disappointed, or unjustly criticized?
3. When have you had the Talent to express emotions, such as sadness at the loss of someone or something dear to you?
4. When have you openly expressed righteous anger or disgust at others and situations that caused pain and hardship to those who don't deserve it?
5. How strong do you think you really are emotionally?

Emotional Talent is the ability to remain firmly anchored in your fundamental values while nonreactively calming yourself down, self-soothing, as other people are provoking, reacting, and escalating their emotional expression.

Evidence of Your Emotional Intelligence?

Harvard's Daniel Goleman, a pioneer in researching emotional intelligence, wrote a book by the same title: *Emotional Intelligence* (Bantam Books, 1997). He subtitled his work *Why it [EI] can matter more than IQ*. The concept is, in many ways, groundbreaking in redefining what it means to be smart. Goleman lists self-control, zeal, persistence, and the ability to motivate oneself as critical emotional intelligence skills.

The Value of Emotional Intelligence

Heightened social effectiveness is often a benefit of emotional intelligence. Some experts believe there is a correlation between a high score on the "understanding emotions" portion of the emotional intelligence test and higher verbal, social, and other intelligences.

1. The confirmed reality seems to be that within each profession, the best performers have the highest EQs (emotional intelligence quotients). Even the best CEOs have the highest EQs.
2. An added benefit to having a high EQ relates to the effects of stressors, including illness, loss, and various traumatic events.

3. Career selection is frequently a direct outcome of recognizing one's own emotional intelligence. Adept at deciphering and describing aims, goals, motivations, and missions, people with high EQs are often well suited for their chosen occupations— teaching and counseling, which involve social interactions to a greater degree than clerical, technical, or administrative functions. The exercise of tuning into subtle communications, appreciating the full complexity and richness of these messages, skillfully steering through conflicts, away from fruitless altercations, while being present and engaged in promoting harmonious and psychologically healthy living all reveal the employed Talents of a capable, *emotionally intelligent* person.

4. Behaviors considered risky, problematic, and with a high potential for self-destruction, like abuse of chemicals and/or violent episodes with others, are less frequently engaged in by high-EQ individuals relative to others. The positive result of their emotional comfort is likely manifest in their interpersonal ability to show openness and agreeableness, particularly without the "benefit"/hindrance of a social lubricant!

In conclusion, the numerous Life-affirming benefits of having high emotional intelligence become increasingly evident. Managing these gifts well is the key to experiencing their full impact.

Bag It and Tag It

RT	Evidence Reliability Tests Quick Checklist
RT-1	"Exceptional," Top 25 Percent, Top 10 Percent
RT-2	Flow
RT-3	Preserved
RT-4	Easily Repeatable and Been Repeated
RT-5	Judged as Exceptional by Witnesses
RT-6	Expert Witness Testify
RT-7	Result of Spontaneous Action
RT-8	By Choice and in My Own Time
RT-9	Positive Emotion
RT-10	Intuition

Best Evidence Matrix

What Was the Evidence? Identify and Specify	When? How Often?	Tests Online and RTs	Witness List and Identify

Chapter 22
Discovering Evidence of Your
Emotional DNA Code Part 2

Emotional Capacity	<ul><li>How I feel</li><li>How I express emotions both internally and externally in a variety of adverse and positive situations</li><li>How conscious I am of inward impressions, states of mind, or physical conditions</li><li>The ability to read and understand the emotions of others</li><li>My emotional potential</li><li>The way I feel internally and how I express those feelings externally</li><li>The way I feel based on how I observe or think about what I see externally in the world around me</li><li>How I respond and feel based on the way I see myself in this world</li><li>The range of moods I express</li><li>Intrapersonal intelligence</li></ul>

The heart has its reasons that reason knows nothing of.
—Blaise Pascal

Life Scene—Amy

My daughter Amy (fourteen years old at the time and also known as my "Girl-Child") and I were driving one Saturday morning, and a friend of Amy's called in a panic. The friend was hysterical because her mother did not come home the evening before and she was unable to contact her. The friend had been watching her six-year-old brother, and they were both distraught when their mother didn't return and was not there when they woke up on Saturday morning.

Amy went into action. She talked calmly and did not enter the "hysteria" as many girls her age might have done, but instead began to ask her friend very sensible questions to help locate the mother. She asked when she last heard from the mom. Where did she say she was going? When was the last time she talked to the mom? What had she done to contact the mom so far? I was amazed at the calm control she exerted over a very emotional and scary situation her friend was dealing with.

Amy told her to give her brother some breakfast and find his favorite movie to get him distracted. She then asked her friend to call people she had identified might be able to give her more information and then call her back when she had done so. She then made her friend repeat everything she had told her.

The friend called back about half an hour later and told Amy that her mother had just called and was on her way back home. I marveled at my Girl-Child and the emotional Talent she had demonstrated at such a young age.

She has continued to grow and develop that Talent in a very definite way. When she knew I was dealing with some very tough emotional situations she would call me daily and ask me how I was. She would push the case until she was sure I was doing well and managing whatever I was dealing with.

One of the career paths Amy has been looking at is in the legal field, where she can be an advocate for people who have been victims of violent crimes. She also works very well with young children, and in day-care situations she has been able to manage a number of children and the chaos they create when grouped together. She is always in control and able to understand and deal with the emotional needs of these kids in a nurturing but constructive manner.

What about you? How do you handle crisis? Do you need to hand over the phone to someone else when you get a call like Amy did? What is your history of effectively helping people in crisis? Remember, we are looking for Unique Talents, and some of us have the ability to work very effectively with taking the initial call while others of us are exceptional in helping with aftercare and maybe working with a bad situation to prevent it from happening again. *?RU* in a crisis, and how well do you manage it?

MYLIFESCENE.COM—CROSS NOW—MYLIFESCENE.COM

Few men during their lifetime come anywhere near exhausting the resources dwelling within them. There are deep wells of strength that are never used.
—Richard E. Byrd, explorer

In this second part of "Discovering Evidence of Your Emotional DNA Code," we continue to look for and evaluate Evidence. You will experience some DNA Code discovery exercises at the end of the chapter that deal with gratitude and Life satisfaction. These are important and powerful tools to help you continue to discover *?RU* emotionally.

The Agony and the Ecstasy

I love the title of Irving Stone's biographical story of Michelangelo, *The Agony and the Ecstasy*. What an incredible description of the two extremes of the emotional spectrum.

When Have You Been Your Happiest?

- *?RU* when you are happy?
- How does the world see you?
- What does the DNA Code of your happy emotions look like?

Have you ever observed how you express yourself when wonderful things happen to you? I know there have been times when I have laughed and then cried. I remember when my first son, André, was born. I left the hospital and tears flowed. Later that evening I went to Sal's Pizza, ordered a pepperoni and mushroom pizza, and just smiled. After I left Sal's I drove back home laughing, and I couldn't believe I had a son!

I have experienced great joy when I watched my children enjoy their lives, do well, make great friends, serve and talk about how they touched the lives of others; when my sons married; when I see people discover their Purpose; when I see people come alive with Passion; and when I see people thrive by delivering exceptional Performances.

I will feel the same when I have completed this book. My goal in writing this is to change many more lives. I hope to meet many of the people, you included, and find out how your Life has changed because you have answered the question *?RU.*

I can think of other places in my Life where positive emotion was experienced. After winning a national championship, I was elated inside and physically exhausted, but I experienced a sense of deep satisfaction and thankfulness. I sat and just smiled. Others on the team were laughing, shouting, and having a wild time. I translate and experience successes and victories in my personal Life with a deep sense of satisfaction, not external noise. There is nothing wrong with the noise and outward demonstration; it is just not me. I am loud when coaching and encouraging my team. I often walk around the circumference of the field, talking and pushing my team, especially when they are involved in tough competition.

What is important in thinking about this question of your experience of positive emotion is to evaluate and identify the highest expression of your emotional Design. Have you ever really felt emotional exhilaration? What makes you scream, inwardly or outwardly, with incredible happiness or joy? What has been the highest level of emotional ecstasy you have ever felt? This does not mean that you were extroverted in your display, though that is more than possible, but you could have been brought to tears of gratitude or felt something so profound you would be hard pressed to verbalize it.

If you attempted to describe what you have experienced, what would you say? If need be, replay that experience in your mind and "feel" the thrill as best you can. If you look at some of the words in the four boxes from the previous chapter, what words would you use to give a picture to your experiences? Try and articulate as precisely as you can what those adjectives or emotions would be.

When Have You Been Your Saddest?

We have all experienced great emotional pain; it is part of the human condition. There have been times when even trying to give words to what it is we felt seemed beyond our ability. Physically, the response was to groan and feel that death would be a welcome release. Other times we were numb, not feeling the pain we knew was there, but somehow being protected from experiencing it at that time because if we did, it would overwhelm us and render us incapacitated.

The *Sad* emotions are part of an emotional palette. We prefer the other side, the bright, light, fun, and enjoyable emotions. We often medicate people so that they no longer experience these "negative" emotions. What we know is many of the greatest writers, artists, composers, and creative people were subject to a wide range of emotions, which included the *Sad* ones. They often experienced the *Sad* emotions in the extreme yet were able to create the most wonderful and touching music, literature, and art.

How Did You Express Your Sadness?

- *?RU* when you are sad?
- How does the world see you?
- What does the DNA Code of your sad emotions look like?

The greatest emotional pain I have ever experienced was not an experience but a situation that lasted for almost four long years. After going through a divorce, my ex-wife made a decision to leave South Africa, where we were living, and return to the United States without telling me, taking our three children with her. I went to pick up the children for a vacation, only to be told by the man my ex-wife was with that my children were no longer there and I would not see them again. I have never felt such a sense of disorientation and excruciating pain.

I left and soon began a quest to be with my children. I came back to the United States only to begin a court case filled with accusations and lies that were all discredited and exposed over a period of time. The pain of that loss was so extreme; I have never experienced anything like it. To know that my children, whom I had basically raised since they were born, were now being used in such a despicable manner was almost beyond anything I could bear.

After almost two years in litigation and total separation, I went to pick up my children from the office of a court-appointed therapist.

When I got to his office, he looked at me and told me they were gone . . . again. The hope and expectation I had when I went there was again beyond description. My ex-wife and her husband had fled with them again. It took another year before I was able to get them back from an abduction that took them back to Africa. That required another lengthy court case because the South African courts did not recognize a U.S. court order that applied to my three U.S.-citizen children. South Africa was not part of the Hague Convention that applied to child abductions. A South African judge told me that my custody order was not "valid," and I responded in a manner that almost got me sent to jail for contempt of court. I had extreme contempt for that court.

My children had to endure a further abduction to a smaller, war-torn country called the Ciskei, at the end of 1993. A series of events that were nothing short of "miracles" allowed me to find them in a short time and have them placed with me for Christmas vacation. I made the decision that once they were in my custody, I would not return them again to the madness they had experienced the prior three years.

During that vacation I obtained a passport under false pretenses and received unofficial help from the U.S. embassy in South Africa to get replacement passports for my children who had "lost" their U.S. passports. (The South African court was holding my and my children's passports.) I had habeas corpus warrants issued that instructed my children to be returned to the King County Superior Court jurisdiction.

A few days after Christmas 1993, I boarded a train at a small, rural station north of Johannesburg. I had to drug my children so that they would not know where we were going and so that I'd be able to get them through the border at Zimbabwe. After a few days there, we flew back to South Africa on New Year's Eve for a brief stopover. I had made sure we would not have to get off the plane for fear of being caught. We then flew to Amsterdam on our way to Vancouver, Canada, and then to the border, where my children were taken into custody and returned to King County on the habeas corpus warrants.

That required emotional Talents I never believed I had, but when demanded, I discovered them. I had to control my emotions and remain clearheaded to be able to perform in ways I never imagined I would be called upon to do. I had to handle my children's confusion, their fear, their anger at my perceived abandonment of them, and the loss of their mother, regardless of what she had done and allowed to be done to them. I found Talents that were Designed and crafted into me by a God, whom I learned to trust with what I loved more than anything in this world, my children.

I can think of other situations that caused great emotional sadness. I remember the many childhood friends who died in a war. I remember, when I was in college, one of my best friends being blown up and killed by a landmine. There are times I look at photographs from my childhood and remember my friends and those who are no longer here to have wives and children. Many who were in my school yearbooks are not "friends" on my Facebook page because they are gone. Emotions are reflected in these losses.

I did a memorial service for a close friend, whom I have written about, Ellie Moore. The place where the memorial was held was packed. I had not done a memorial for many years, and I was very emotional because of what Ellie had meant to me. I stood up to begin the memorial, and I started to cry. My son Adam was there and I just looked at him and tried to focus. I broke down a few more times, but it was a time of emotional pain.

Evidence of Emotional Intelligence

What is important is for you to see how your emotional fingerprints are displayed in your Life.

1. Are they appropriate in their demonstration? Are they Talents?
2. Are you able to fully and openly express what you feel?
3. Are you able to translate your feelings into actions that are seen as fitting the situation?
4. Are your emotions seen and verified by others as being consistent with the occasion?
5. Are you able to verbalize what you feel in a way that accurately describes your experience?

How quickly do you generally overcome emotional disappointments? Rate your emotional recovery on this scale:

(Very Slow) **1   2   3   4   5   6   7   8   9   10** (Very Fast)

What has been the toughest emotional disappointment in your Life?

_____

_____

What emotional resources did you use the most to deal with it?

_____

_____

It is with the heart that one sees rightly; what is essential is invisible to the eye.
—Antoine de Saint-Exupery, *The Little Prince*

What Are Your Most Effective Emotions?

When people think about you emotionally, how do they see you? What are the most observed emotions that you show to the world around you? When it comes to productive, what I mean is those emotions that allow you to connect with and support those people who are closest to you. What are your emotional DNA markers? *?RU*

What we know about emotions is that we have the capacity to control and develop them. There are certainly people who are born with a sunny disposition. They have always been happy and will always be happy. They walk into a room and the sun seems to shine, emotions are elevated, and people respond positively.

Others are mellower, and there is little in Life that will make them up and bubbly and shouting at a football game. Again, it often depends on the place where you are allowed to demonstrate those emotions. That does not mean they are any less effective with how they connect and how they are able to deeply attach and touch the lives of others.

Forensic Evidence Discovery Tip

A clue to discovering your Talents is to see where you come alive:

Don't ask what the world needs. Ask what makes you come alive, and go do it, because what the world needs are people who have come alive!
—Howard Thurman, theologian

There are people who go to a symphony and are deeply moved. They can be moved emotionally for different reasons. The music or the story of what the composer was going through when writing the music could move them. Again, Life is complex, but there are always clues.

Situations Where I Feel the Freest to Express My Emotions

Have you thought about how you feel differently depending on the situation? Think through those situations where you felt freest to be open and honest about your emotions. This is an important question and analysis. *PRU*

Let's do an analysis. Where was it? Who are those people? What were you doing?

_____

_____

_____

Evidence of Your Emotional Generosity

One of the greatest "cures" for any down or negative emotion is found in actions of looking outside oneself and giving to others. It is important to give from your emotional Talents and not simply look to have your deficits met or understood. Those who give in order to get will find a pit of despair waiting most often down a short road. Give from your emotional Talents if you want to feel a sustained positive emotional lift.

1.   Who have you given your strongest emotional Talents to?
2.   What did you give emotionally?
3.   How did it feel to give away your emotional Talent?
4.   How many times have you repeated that action of emotional generosity and love?

Evidence of Emotional Crisis Management

I have always been able to handle crisis well. I don't know why or how, but if there is a crisis situation, I find myself in the middle trying to bring a sense of control and calmness to it.

I was driving with a friend of mine, Louis, a counselor, in Johannesburg, South Africa, and a terrible accident happened just ahead of us. A school bus was on the side of the road, and a woman decided to go around it at a good speed and killed a small ten-year-old girl, Mia. I parked and immediately identified who the mother was; she had been waiting on the other side of the road for her daughter and saw almost everything that happened. It was a tragic scene.

I was able to call her husband, the police came, and I assisted in a witness report. I stayed for the next few hours, just being with the family. I handled the crisis well, but Louis was far better equipped to do the long-term therapy that the family was going to need to deal with the terrible loss of their daughter.

Crisis Response?

During a Fourth of July party, a girlfriend of mine and I were sitting with a large group of people, enjoying the evening watching fireworks and eating food. All of a sudden, someone shouted "Fire!" and both of us jumped up and began to take charge of the situation. The fire was so quick in igniting, and it grew very quickly. I threw a bucket of ice and water at the tree, which was under an awning by the side of the house, and then found a hose to get the water going. My girlfriend ran to the house of a firefighter who had recently moved in, and he came out and called his fire station, which was just around the corner.

Handling crisis well runs in the family. My sister, Penny, is a psychotherapist in Dallas. Penny works with the crisis response team of a large Texas police department. She enters scenes where there have been suicides, deaths, rapes, and other horrendous situations. She goes in and, with her presence and training, she touches lives and manages crises resulting from tragic Life and crime situations.

Fight or Flight?

When faced with a tough or frightening situation, what is your first tendency? What would you have done in this "fire" situation?

Flight   or   Fight

Run Away   or   Run for Help   or   Feel Flustered but Stay   or Calmly Take Control

Personal Emotional Strength Assessment

Rate how strong you believe you are emotionally. Be realistic and honest. Don't overrate and don't underrate. Give Evidence that can stand the harshest cross-examination.

Rate your emotional strength on this scale:

(Very Weak) **1   2   3   4   5   6   7   8   9   10** (Very Strong)

MYLIFESCENE.COM—CROSS NOW—MYLIFESCENE.COM
Emotional Evidence Discovered in Crisis

In September 2003, I went into Homeland Security to renew my work permit and ended up being detained and held under a civil detention provision. I spent three months in a large cell with criminals who had been released from county jails and federal prisons and others who were being deported to their countries of origin because of immigration violations. I met some wonderful people as well as some undesirables, whom I was more than happy to see exported.

Immigration procedures had become so convoluted since 9/11, and though I was in the United States legally, I had received custody of my U.S.-citizen children and a judge had restrained me from leaving the United States with them. So I was stuck in the United States and very happily so. I love the United States and am now a permanent resident and soon to be citizen.

Prior to being held in detention, I was scheduled to lead a small study group from the church I was attending. Being held in a cell, awaiting removal to a country that was officially recognized as having the lowest Life expectancy on the planet, the longest-living dictator, the highest inflation (in the millions of percent), and the highest unemployment on earth was not a pleasant prospect. Beyond that, and more pressing on me by far, was the possibility of being separated from my children, whom I had come to the United States for and had parented for the past ten years. There were other very deep, emotional attachments that moment by moment gave me a consuming emotional fear of possible loss.

After a few weeks of being held, I was struggling emotionally. The possibilities of being sent back to Zimbabwe and not seeing my family for years was bearing heavily. The group I was supposed to lead was scheduled to meet on a Wednesday evening. I asked to speak to them by phone and see whether I could share for a few moments.

I had spent a couple of days, with pen in hand, thinking of all those things that were reasons for being thankful. At first it was a little difficult. As I kept going, however, it became so much easier. From the people whom I had met and whom I had become friends with, to those who were working so hard outside, contacting senators and political officials, to the many who had written letters on my behalf, to the food that was available three times a day, the candy bar a friend left me as he was leaving to be flown back to his native India, and on and on.

The list grew longer and longer. I wrote pages that reminded me of small, and often what seemed insignificant, issues of Life, but they became nuggets of great joy and were incentives to rejoice.

There were also huge landmarks that caused me to be thankful. Rhonda, a former girlfriend, displayed incredible courage and managed to walk into Homeland Security and find the regional director with whom she pleaded my case successfully. Her family had been so incredibly generous and paid thousands of dollars for an emergency motion to be heard in federal court. I was so blessed.

I led that group from my "cell phone" attached to the wall and costing almost two dollars a minute. I spoke about what I had written and all the reasons I had the Evidence to be thankful for. I was amazed how it had transformed my attitude and given me strength to think clearly, focus on others who needed my encouragement, and look forward, knowing I could face whatever possibilities might present themselves.

Those three months were a short time, but without doubt, I learned that when pushed to face incredible potential loss, I know I have the emotional Talents to do just that. Many times in Life we don't discover until we are faced with the necessity to do so, because we have to or else face the other option, which is to fold.

?RU emotionally? When you have faced a situation you were emotionally devastated by, *?RU*? What emotional resources did you discover and draw from to work your way through it? What did you discover about the emotional Talents that describe who you are emotionally? *?RU*

MYLIFESCENE.COM—CROSS NOW—MYLIFESCENE.COM

Evidence Is Discovered in the Production of Satisfaction and Thankfulness

I love old books, and a few years ago I found a great old book called *The Anatomy of Melancholy*. Robert Burton, who lived from 1577 to 1640, wrote the book. This 670-page book was focused on melancholy, or what we commonly call depression. This massive work was forensic in focus and looked at melancholy from a philosophical, medical, and historical perspective. I often found myself paging through this book and wondering how incredible it would be for someone to write a book on *The Anatomy of Gratitude or Joy*.

I have discovered a simple formula that I see work without fail. It goes like this:

Talents Discovered = Gratitude

Talents Developed = Gratitude

Talents Deployed/Used = Gratitude

If you want to be happy, as defined by a Life of gratitude or thankfulness, start by discovering your Talents. If you want to continue to be happy today, develop those Talents. If you want to maintain and be happy in the future, continue to use those Talents. The more you discover, the happier you will be. The more you develop, the happier you will be. The more you use, the happier you will be.

The converse is also true. The less you know or discover, the less you can develop what you don't discover, and obviously you can't effectively use what you don't know you possess.

You have the opportunity to work on a forensic analysis of your Life that will look for thankfulness and satisfaction. Who knows how much you will discover of your emotional Design/DNA Code? Hopefully you will be able to discover and write far more than the small boxes provide for.

Start today by being aware of what experiences, actions, social connections, people, classes, and so on, generate positive emotions. Specifically map two emotions: satisfaction and gratitude/thankfulness. As you go through this next week, keep track of where these two emotions are seen in your experience of Life.

Satisfaction Output/Production	Gratitude/Thankfulness Output/Production
What Produces Satisfaction in Your Life?	What Produces Thankfulness in Your Life?

Bag It and Tag It

RT	Evidence Reliability Tests Quick Checklist
RT-1	"Exceptional," Top 25 Percent, Top 10 Percent
RT-2	Flow
RT-3	Preserved
RT-4	Easily Repeatable and Been Repeated
RT-5	Judged as Exceptional by Witnesses
RT-6	Expert Witness Testify
RT-7	Result of Spontaneous Action
RT-8	By Choice and in My Own Time
RT-9	Positive Emotion
RT-10	Intuition

Best Evidence Matrix

What Was the Evidence? Identify and Specify	When? How Often?	Tests Online and RTs	Witness List and Identify

Take some time to do an analysis of the people who have given to you and been part of your Life in a way that has produced positive emotion. I believe that the highest emotion that Evidences Talent is gratitude. Here is a way to be more aware and start looking at your Life Scene from that perspective.

My Gratitude Log

Who	What Did They Do?	When	Why	My Response
Dad	Spent time helping me learn how to drive	Thursday night	He wants me to drive	I forgot to say thank you so I am going to let him know how much I appreciate his taking the time and risking his Life . . . me driving!
Manager	Spent time showing me how to work the new program	Wednesday morning	He cares that I do well	Said thanks for making time for me and being so patient. It took time for me to understand it and he is a great teacher. I need to share that.

Chapter 23
Discovering Evidence of Your Social DNA Code Part 1

Social Capacity	• How I relate to others • How I associate with others • How I connect with others • How I give to others • My interaction with individuals and groups • My capacity to understand, appreciate, and get along well with people • My social potential • Interpersonal intelligence • The range of moods I express • Intrapersonal intelligence

MYLIFESCENE.COM—CROSS NOW—MYLIFESCENE.COM
Life Scene—"Nelope"

I mentioned Penny earlier in this book when I talked about how she drove a car from Dallas to Virginia. Penny, or as I like to call her, "Nelope," is the best sister a brother could ever have.

Nelope is a tall, beautiful woman. She is articulate, brilliant, and engaging and could be a brilliant talk show host if she wanted to. Maybe she will be down the road.

Nelope sees everyone who needs to be noticed and affirmed. I was in a thrift store with her recently, and as we were looking around she noticed a little, old, African American woman who was in her late sixties pushing a load of shoes in a trolley. She was very shy and probably didn't want to be noticed. Nelope asked her how she was doing, and she very quietly said she had just started working that day. Nelope said she knew she was going to be very good at her job and commented on how competent she seemed. The lady just beamed and came alive as we left. Everywhere we go it is the same story. The gym, the grocery store, the dollar store, at a seminar, she notices people who want to be seen.

Nelope came to visit me in Seattle and stayed with a girlfriend of mine who had a twenty-year-old daughter. Within an hour of being there, her daughter wanted to know if Nelope could be her counselor and wanted her to move in.

Nelope looks at those who need to be seen and validates something very deep and real in their souls. They have no way but to respond and feel validated and affirmed by her.

She rescues animals that are in dire circumstances, her three dogs included. She has rescued many more and does everything she can to ensure animals are not treated in a cruel manner. She buys large amounts of bread to feed the birds in her garden every morning. I told her she could be renamed "Nelope of Assisi," which would fit her perfectly.

Nelope supports orphans in Africa and Haiti. She cares deeply about how she spends her money to make sure it reflects her love for those less fortunate than herself. She is always looking for and finding incredible deals.

Nelope brought my (basically) refugee parents to the United States as soon as she became a U.S. citizen. They had lost almost everything in the tragedy of the once vibrant central African country of Zimbabwe. They live with her, and she provides for them in so many caring and thoughtful ways.

Nelope does all this while living with a potentially Life-threatening condition. She has incredible stamina because she loves people and all those, animals included, who need someone to notice them, and do what they need, in whatever circumstances they find themselves.

What about you? *?RU* when it comes to connecting with people? Do you see those people whom others seldom notice and affirm their lives and dignity? Do you see potential and help people develop it? Do you come alongside leaders and enable them to change situations and lives because they can depend on you and your support of them? *?RU* and what about your social Design/DNA Code is exceptional?

MYLIFESCENE.COM—CROSS NOW—MYLIFESCENE.COM

You interact and connect with people. Those interactions are called relationships or social connections. We each relate and associate in different ways.

- How do you connect with other people?
- What types of people are you most likely to connect with?
- Where do you fit in a group when you connect?
- How often do you need to connect?
- Do you connect deeply with a few people or more broadly with a lot of people?
- What do you do in a group that normally makes you noticed or effective?

As we investigate this Field of Evidence we will look for and collect Evidence of your social DNA Code. You leave social DNA everywhere. Think back over your day and try to calculate every human interaction you had today. Your family, your school, your classes, your lunch friends, your conference call, your small group at church or a club, a friend you talked with on the phone, the prospective employer you interviewed with, your girlfriend, your teacher, your teammates, the grocery store checker, and on and on and on. You connected in person, online, on the phone, sometimes deliberately, sometimes by accident, and other times because you were required to.

Forensic Definition—Social Intelligence

Social intelligence is the capacity to observe and notice variations in other people, more specifically their emotions, moods, and why they make the choices they do. It is the Talent to manage these people and/or direct them to be successful. It is the capacity of being aware of how we fit in different social situations and our ability to manage both our effectiveness as well as that of others.

Let's begin the process of looking for the social DNA that you leave in the course of your Life with this description in mind. Let us discover what reflects not just your Common Design but what shouts loudly of your Individual Design/DNA Code and Talents.

Most of us will generally see ourselves as more likely to belong to one of two groups. This is a general division, but it is based on how we connect to our world. Think through these categories and see where it is you usually fit.

Living Loud or Living Quiet

Introvert	Extrovert
Introverts like getting their energy from dealing with the ideas, pictures, memories, and reactions that are inside their head, in their inner world. They often prefer doing things alone or with one or two people they're comfortable with. The following statements generally apply to me: • I am seen as "reflective" or "reserved." • I feel comfortable being alone and enjoy things I can do on my own. • I prefer to know just a few people well. • I sometimes spend too much time reflecting and don't move into action quickly enough. • I sometimes forget to check with the outside world to see whether their ideas really fit the experience.	Extroverts like getting their energy from active involvement in events and participating in a lot of different activities. They get excited when they are around people, and they like to energize other people. They like moving into action and making things happen. They generally feel at home in the world. The following statements generally apply to me: • I am seen as "outgoing" or as a "people person." • I feel comfortable in groups and enjoy working in teams. • I have a wide range of friends and know lots of people. • I sometimes jump too quickly into an activity and don't allow enough time to think it over. • Before I start a project, I sometimes forget to stop and get clear on what I want to do and why.

?RU in Social Groups

Social connections are made in varying sizes. We can be in groups varying in size from one to the thousands. Finding social Evidence of DNA Talent requires that I understand where I am most comfortable and effective. How do I best connect when I am with other people or in social situations?

We all need to do an *Analysis of Asset* of each group we are in. We need to look for Evidence of where we currently exist and what is working well. It is interesting when I ask people to estimate how many social groups they are in; they so often go to the low side. They fail to see the importance of, the effect of, the crossover nature of so many of the groups they exist in.

Generally we begin by thinking of our peer groups: classes, sports teams, religious groups, and groups at work. The reality is we are in scores of groups, but it is necessary to define what a group is.

Forensic Definition—Social Group

A social group is a collection or group of people (more than just you) that exists and interacts either formally or informally for mutual benefit and/or to effect change.

Some are passive and based on your choice to involve yourself to a greater or lesser extent. If you live in the United States, you likely are part of the social group "citizens of the United States of America." Making changes in how you are governed is accomplished by your choice to vote or not. Your involvement can become greater or lesser than simply being a citizen. You can become involved in local politics or even a parent-teacher association. You can run for mayor of your town. The choice is yours.

What is important in discovering Evidence of social Design is to look at the groups you are in and have been involved in and begin to think about the places where you fit the best, places where you felt at home and places where you brought about real, substantive change because of your involvement and/or leadership.

Digital Fingerprints
?RU

One of the first actions law enforcement engages in when investigating a case from white-collar crime, murders, child pornography, kidnappings, abductions, drug distribution, and so on, is to get a search warrant for the computers and cell phones of the alleged criminals. Those two areas of potential Evidence yield more information and can provide a profile of the alleged perpetrator better than probably anything else in an investigation. Investigators get the warrants as soon as they can and begin to retrieve the information as quickly as possible.

The computer is the brain that mirrors the user's brain, revealing personal thoughts, ideas, motives, and possibilities that only the user is aware of. The computer is the DNA profile of the user. Who you are, an incredibly clear and precise description, can be constructed without ever seeing you.

Facial reconstruction experts take a skull and are able to develop a face from the simple bones. The picture and profile of who you are physically, emotionally, intellectually, spiritually, and socially could result in a wanted poster that would describe the most intimate details of your Talents.

What is in your virtual, cell, and microchip world that gives Evidence of your Talents? What can others discover by knowing you, even if they have never met you?

The Virtual World
?RU

One of the realities of the world we live in, particularly in the past fifteen years, is that the "real" world has changed. People meet online and end up marrying. Many of the most profound connections humans make, originate, and consummate is in a world where there is no physical contact. That world is the *Internet*.

I recently signed a legal trademark agreement online. A few years ago I would have had to meet my attorney in person and sign with witnesses present in order to effect a legal document; not anymore. Virtual signatures are now legally recognized in many professions and areas of Life.

Groups, colleges, teams, relationships, parents and children, any type and every type of group can be found online. Literally millions of new groups have been formed with the advent of the "virtual world." Millions of students from elementary school to doctoral programs are completing their education online with professors and teachers they may never meet in person.

I train and hold conference calls using online services. I have talked to many people in an online class and then ended up meeting them in person. Often they are just what I envisioned, and sometimes they are completely different. The differences can be wonderful and sometimes not what I imagined.

Then again, many people who have communicated and connected online in a romantic relationship discover, when they meet, that the virtual reality was not what they thought. Sometimes they were either deceived or they simply constructed a persona of the individual that was far from accurate. The virtual world does not always translate into flesh and blood the way we think.

Where, who, how, why, what is the positive gain, value, and growth from these connections? A forensic analysis of your social Design needs to be performed.

On Facebook, kids from a youth program I started twenty-five years ago connected with me; two were living in Germany within a few miles of each other. They connected via Facebook not even knowing they were living on the same continent. My father, who is eighty years old and now living in Dallas, has connected with people he went to elementary school with in Africa. His one friend now lives in Australia. There seem to be no limits to communicating and finding groups who we want to connect with. The once stated *six degrees of separation* might be more like three or four degrees now with the advent of the virtual world.

?RU Online—Social Networks

The online world of social networking and connecting is exploding. Social-networking junkies, people who are consumed with tweeting, blogging, emailing, texting, podcasting, and videoing saturate our existence; you can't escape them. Maybe you are one of them! College students, soccer moms, jurors in court, salesmen, journalists, students, and preschoolers are all part of this reality. Many of these people are either attention-seeking extroverts and/or anxiety-driven introverts. They are who we are, and they are here to stay.

The number of minutes users spent on Facebook over the past years has increased from 1.7 billion a month in 2008 to 700 billion a month in 2011. Over 900 million people are now connected. Most Facebook users spend an average of eight hours a month connecting and reading about the lives of their "friends."

So where and how do you fit in this world? What Evidence can be found about you? How many contacts or friends, causes, associations, and applications do you have in your virtual world?

- MySpace
- Facebook
- Twitter
- Linked In
- Classmates
- Biznik
- Fixter

- Qzone
- Habbo
- Tagged
- Xanga
- Windows Live
- Friendster
- hi5

- Orkut
- LastFM
- Bloggster
- Netlog
- Beebo
- Meet Up
- Pinterest

Many of us have a number of online connecting points. As you think through what they are, whom you are in contact with, and why you associate with them, I want you to look at your digital fingerprint and collect some basic information to answer the question *?RU.*

1. How often do you connect on social networks?
2. How many connections or "friends" do you have online?
3. How many online groups, organizations, clubs, movements, associations, or causes do you belong to?
4. How much of your social life is conducted through these sites?
5. How much time do you spend in the virtual world?
6. How many visits have you made?

?RU Email, Online Presence, Chat, Blogs, Yahoo, Gmail, Hotmail, MSN, Comcast, Verizon, SBC, Other

- How many email contacts do you have?
- How many emails do you send per day?
- How many emails do you receive per day?
- How long are you online connecting with other people each day?
- Who, when, and why did you email and connect with people today?
- Do you write a blog?
- Who follows that blog?

There is a whole world of ways to connect socially in the virtual world. The virtual world has become so much more personal and is starting to seem almost as real as the holodeck in *Star Trek*, where reality and the virtual are almost indistinguishable.

Why don't you take some time to see what social connections you have as a part of your virtual world? Within a few weeks of getting a Facebook account I became part of numerous groups. These were schools I attended, associations and groups I had belonged to, places where I had lived, sports teams I had played on, and countries I had lived in. Some were political groups, where I met new people and became associated with them based on a common cause. These are all fingerprints of who I am and the social connections of my Life. *?RU*

?RU When Gaming or Playing Wii—Xbox—PlayStation—World of Warcraft— The Sims

- How often do you game with other people?
- How many online gaming groups do you belong to?
- How long do you play each day?
- What do you enjoy most about connecting though gaming?

I have spoken to many parents who are worried about their teens' lack of social interaction because they spend a lot of time on the computer, playing online in a variety of video game and other communities. We need to look for and embrace the many positive aspects of this brave new online world and not live on the defensive.

These Internet associations are legitimate teams with real positions, players, leaders, coaches, and so on. They are played on a new and different field from grass or other surfaces, but they are no less real and legitimate social interactions. We need to value them for what they are and ask ourselves how we best connect. Could playing in these Internet or virtual worlds give us Evidence of incredible Talents?

They can have problems, just like any other social interactions. Real-live, breathing people form gangs and commit real flesh-and-blood harm to other real flesh-and-blood people. Sometimes online, social connections have a far smaller likelihood of causing physical damage and harm.

Strong Social Evidence and Talents Discovered in Gamers

The value of these connections has been the subject of much criticism, especially from parents, who see time spent in these online groups and gamers' guilds as wasted. What we are learning is that there are many great advantages to gaming. When we look forensically, we are looking for what it means to be good at these online ventures/connections. Recent research has discovered that those who excel at gaming often possess:

1. Exceptional memory
2. Exceptional executive functioning
3. Excellent strategic thinking
4. Exceptional dexterity

We have also discovered that video gamers share many of the characteristics of outstanding CEOs. These Talents include:

1. Collaboration
2. Self-organization
3. Risk taking
4. Openness
5. Influence
6. Knowing how to earn incentives linked to Performance
7. Being flexible in the way they communicate

MYLIFESCENE.COM—CROSS NOW—MYLIFESCENE.COM
Life Scene—Personas and Avatars

I worked with a young man who was going through some very difficult Life issues. He was facing the divorce of his parents, their bankruptcy, moving from the family home he had always lived in, and at the same time caring for his mom and two sisters. He was tall, good looking, and athletic and also a very emotionally caring person.

One of the things I learned about him was that in his *World of Warcraft* guild (team), he had identified himself as, and taken the role of, a "Healer." A "Healer" is responsible for helping teammates when they need assistance with war wounds, supplies, and getting back into the battle. The "Healer" persona he had identified with and created was exactly who he was in Life. It reflected both his social and emotional Design Talents.

This young man wanted to become a firefighter. The "Healer" was such a perfect fit for who he was and how he saw himself. Even more was seen in his being a defender on a select soccer team. That position required being the last line of defense for his team. Ultimately, he saw himself as protecting and caring for others in crisis.

Do you have an online persona or avatar that reflects who you are socially or in some other Field of Evidence? What is it? How does it reflect your Unique Design or an Individual Talent? The same is true of many of the email names we choose to reflect how we perceive ourselves. Does your email name reflect a particular characteristic that would help people know who you are?

MYLIFESCENE.COM—CROSS NOW—MYLIFESCENE.COM

?RU on Cell Phones—Talk, Text, Multimedia

1. How many names are in your address book?
2. How many minutes do you use each month (average)?
3. How many calls do you make per month?
4. How many text messages to you send and receive per month?

It is so important for parents, managers, teachers, and coaches to know what types of social fingerprints are possessed by those they are responsible for motivating and, at times, disciplining. Being effective requires having at least a basic profile of those social fingerprints.

There are many management and other personality inventories that help organizations build effective teams. The inventories match people based on social profiles. The popular dating website eHarmony promises to match people based on twenty-nine areas of compatibility. The research and science behind these profiles is very sophisticated, but again, you must rely on a variety of Evidence. Never define yourself or your relationships based solely on Evidence gathered from a test. Humans are unique and can never be defined by a test. You are incredibly complex and not subject to definition by a test, no matter how sophisticated it claims to be.

Life Scene—Parenting

I have two sons who are very different people socially. André, my oldest, has a small group of close friends he has known for many years. Adam is totally opposite. He connects broadly and has many friends.

If you looked at the cell phone bill, you would see Evidence of who they are socially. André uses about 200–300 minutes a month and uses 100–200 text messages. Adam is quite different and uses 3,000–4,000 minutes and texts at least 4,000–5,000 times per month. (That is nothing like my dear daughter, who texted 9,877 times in a month, which is certainly not a record, but I think she might want to compete at the national trials.)

When it came to discipline and their social fingerprints, I had to tailor my discipline based on those unique capacities. If I sent André to his room, it wouldn't faze him in the slightest. He didn't need constant human connection and would be happy to read and study for hours on end. Adam, on the other hand, had to be in contact with other people all the time. He had to be connecting on his cell phone, online, and in person. If he was sent to his room, he was like a caged lion, and it got his attention immediately.

Parenting is never easy, but when you parent using the information about your child's Unique Design and Talents, you parent with power and Purpose.

Management and leadership's primary way of motivating and getting people's attention must be tailored to fit the individual Design of people. If we want to create exceptional and sustained Performance, we must use that most powerful path to change.

How can you tailor your parenting, social interaction, and management of people to utilize their specific Talents? What do you need to change in the way you approach people to reflect your leadership style?

What's My Size?

Social connections are made in varying sizes, from one to the thousands. Finding social Evidence of Talent requires that I understand where I am most comfortable and effective. How do I best connect when I am with other people or in social situations?

Have you ever thought about where you are most comfortable? To some extent, it depends on the Purpose of a group. The question here is what type of group do you tend to gravitate toward and feel most comfortable in? It would make sense to want to be where you feel most accepted and wanted, where you demonstrate your greatest effectiveness and feel most energized.

We can look at this question from many different angles, but again, the question is where do you most often find yourself and feel most comfortable? Some people feel anxious in a large crowd while others are most anxious in a small group.

Evidence of My Effectiveness in a Group

Rate your effectiveness (far-right box)
Very Effective = 1   Effective = 2

Social Capacity	I am most *alive* in a group when I am . . . I am most *effective* in a group when I am . . .	1 or 2
Developing	. . . helping people take their Talents to a higher level of effectiveness and competence.	
Encouraging	. . . telling people that who they are and what they have done was worthwhile.	
Inspiring	. . . infusing people with the belief they can do and be more.	
Commanding	. . . helping people find direction because I see a clear goal and articulate it clearly and convincingly.	

Activating	. . . helping people turn their thoughts into actions by getting them started and moving.	
Cheerleading	. . . rallying people behind a cause and cheering them on.	
Managing	. . . planning, directing, overseeing, and correcting people toward the fulfillment of a specific task or goal.	
Supporting	. . . making sure that the leader has what he or she needs to succeed.	
Lone Ranging	. . . getting things done by myself because that is the way things get done best.	
Communicating	. . . helping people understand important information.	
Analyzing	. . . helping people to think through a tough or complex situation.	
Arranging	. . . helping people find their place within a group so that they can work at maximum potential.	
Backstage	. . . helping get things done without the need to have people know who I am or without any fanfare.	
Comforting	. . . bringing calm to people in tough or crisis situations.	
Connecting	. . . helping people who have similar or complementary abilities to connect for greater effectiveness and gain.	
Focusing	. . . helping people see what is most important and then keep to the task.	
Umpiring	. . . helping people to deal with disagreements and issues of fairness.	
Including	. . . helping people who are outside the group to find a place in the group.	

Valuing	. . . helping people see that no matter what their position is, their input within the group is vital to the success of the group.
Judging	. . . helping the group by being able to deal with complex issues and make open value judgments so that the group can move forward.
Restoring	. . . helping people who have been excluded from a group, often by their own antisocial behavior, re-enter and find a place on the team.
Others	

Bag It and Tag It

RT	Evidence Reliability Tests Quick Checklist
RT-1	"Exceptional," Top 25 Percent, Top 10 Percent
RT-2	Flow
RT-3	Preserved
RT-4	Easily Repeatable and Been Repeated
RT-5	Judged as Exceptional by Witnesses
RT-6	Expert Witness Testify
RT-7	Result of Spontaneous Action
RT-8	By Choice and in My Own Time
RT-9	Positive Emotion
RT-10	Intuition

Best Evidence Matrix

What Was the Evidence? Identify and Specify	When? How Often?	Tests Online and RTs	Witness List and Identify

Chapter 24
Discovering Evidence of Your Social DNA Code Part 2

Social Capacity	• How I relate to others • How I associate with others • How I connect with others • How I give to others • My interaction with individuals and groups • My capacity to understand, appreciate, and get along well with people • My social potential • Interpersonal intelligence • The range of moods I express • Intrapersonal intelligence

As we continue to investigate this *Field of Evidence* we will look for and collect Evidence of your social DNA. You leave social DNA everywhere. We are going to be looking at leadership, teams, ethnicity, age, and other ways of connecting socially and discovering Evidence of *PRU*.

Leader or Follower?
?RU

Some experts say that leaders are born, and others say leaders are made. Regardless of how or why, think about your experience. Social groups need both leaders and followers for anything to get accomplished. Where have you left your social DNA? How is your social DNA displayed?

I was watching the Super Bowl a couple of years ago, and they had two commentators who were recently retired coaches: Tony Dungy of the Indianapolis Colts and Mike Holmgren of the Seattle Seahawks. Both these men had been at the top of their game by being coaches who had won the Super Bowl. They were both recognized as being exceptional leaders.

What was so good about having them as commentators was that they were very different in their coaching and leadership styles. Dungy was a quiet, calm man who motivated and encouraged but seldom showed any excessive emotion. Holmgren was the opposite. He led through loud, demonstrative behavior, and you knew when he was mad. He shouted, he fumed, and he was never reserved in giving his opinions. Both were good, decent men with deeply held beliefs and faith, but they demonstrated their leadership in vastly different ways.

How do you see yourself in a group? Often when a new group or team is formed, it only takes a little time before people start finding their place within the group.

In most contexts I find that I am the leader probably 90 percent of the time. I am creative and love to innovate. Theresa Callahan, a coach friend of mine, sent me a test called the "Kolbe A™ Index," a one-of-a-kind, online behavioral assessment that quantifies an individual's instinctive makeup. The profile identified me as a "Quickstart"—an "off the charts Quickstart!" . . . according to Theresa. Theresa is an expert and knows what she is talking about. If you don't believe me, read her book, *Managing for Performance: Building Accountability for Team Success.*

She was absolutely right. I jump in and start things, often without a lot of detailed information to get me where I think I'm going! I use my sense of innovation and adventure to get things done and to lead. And I often do it through experimentation and by improvising as I go, by taking a risk without necessarily knowing the outcome.

I know that sometimes others have a hard time keeping up with me, and they don't always know where I'm going because, frankly, neither do I! But what I *do* know is that I follow this mantra: just go for it! And I know that if "Plan A" doesn't work out, there is *always* another way!

Unlike personality tests that suggest what's wrong with you and tell you how to change it, Kolbe focuses on what's right with you and tells you how to build on it. The Kolbe A Index measures your uniqueness by quantifying your *Conative Talents*, the very nature of who you are and how you take action. I highly recommend that you take this deeply insightful test. (You can access Theresa and the Kolbe A Index by going to the www.mylifescene.com website and clicking on "Forensic Tests.")

I use a great book when speaking to corporations on leadership and Talents-based management. The book, *Strengths-Based Leadership*, was written by Tom Rath and Barrie Conchie. The books also contains a code for you to access and take a "Strengths Leadership Profile." The strengths that are diagnosed fall into what the authors call the "four domains of leadership strengths." My strengths are: *Futuristic, Maximizer, Activator, Strategic, Achiever.*

I have found this strengths test to be very insightful and right-on when defining how I approach Life and leading others. Those who attend my Corp-DNA™ seminars have also given the test rave reviews about its accuracy and the way it has enabled them to become more effective in their leadership positions. I highly recommend the book and our Corp-DNA™ program if you want your corporation to focus on what makes for success: Talents and strengths (www.corp-dna.com).

Does this mean I am a leader just because this is verified in a test? No, but it is more likely, especially as I look at my history, what I have done, where I have led, who has seen me lead, and what successes I have had when I did lead. Tests verify Evidence, and sometimes we can look more seriously at a potential Talent if it is listed or highlighted in a test or profile.

I am a big man and love to talk to people and groups. Taking the lead is sometimes done reluctantly, but most of the time, I end up assuming the position of group leader. I have been a leader as a cricket captain, pastor, coach, innovator, and creator, in small groups, in business, and in many other areas in my Life.

I have an ability to see Talent. That is why I am a *Life Scene Investigator.* I have always loved watching people at airports, sidewalk cafés, sporting events, waiting rooms, and any public setting. I love photographing and writing about people. I am always looking for the Unique Talents in people.

Leaders need people to lead. Leaders must have support and people who are willing to follow and fulfill a vision or goal.

1. Do you find great energy in following?
2. What have you been a part of that made you know you didn't want to lead or be in a position of leadership?

Your DNA as a leader will be obvious by the groups you have led. What groups or other people have you led? More prints can be seen in asking what you achieved as a leader. If you are a leader, you will have demonstrated leadership by leading someone or a group from one place to another. There must be verifiable change, and you need to know what part you played in leading the change.

How often are you asked to lead by others? There are some groups that are originated by the leaders themselves. I started a church in South Africa, and people followed; a church was formed. I have started cricket teams and leagues. I helped start the Northwest Cricket League in 1995, and it now has more than twenty teams. I coach the league's regional team. I have created youth programs and businesses.

Leaders are sometimes recognized from within a group, and they are elected to assume the role of leader. At other times, a board or other group of leaders such as an officers' selection committee selects them. Recognition can come from your peers (eyewitnesses and personal witnesses) or from those in authority and positions of power (expert witnesses).

1. What grade would you give yourself as you review your leadership?
2. How effective are you or have you been?
3. How would others grade your leadership?
4. What specific achievements resulted from your leadership?

These are all important forensic questions that will help you answer this question. Try and answer these:

1. Do you feel like you are chomping at the bit if you are in a group and you are not leading?
2. Are you constantly questioning why and what the leader of the group does?

3. Are you regularly challenging the present leadership and have ideas you share with leaders for a better outcome?

Individual or Team?

An important indicator or Evidence of who you are socially is identified in what sort of groups, sports, or other associations you seek out and participate in. There is no hard and fast rule, but there are certainly traces of Evidence.

I have played various sports through the years. They have been both team and individual sports. What I have found, though, is that when I am on a team, I most often have a leadership role, and I am also a specialized player. I take responsibility for the success of the team very personally and am always doing whatever I can, in the role of an on-field coach, to encourage and help my teammates.

On balance, though, I would say I am more of an individual player. I swim and play cricket, golf, tennis, and racquetball. I have an attorney friend who was in a solo legal practice. He loved racquetball, a solo game.

Some people see the result of their success or failure as being either an individual venture or a team effort. What about you? Where do you best fit in competition? *PRU*

MYLIFESCENE.COM—CROSS NOW—MYLIFESCENE.COM
Life Scene—Mom

My mother, Ruth, was always very social. She entertained a lot in a beautiful home and always loved being around people. As I was growing up, she regularly had friends over for tea and to swim in our pool.

One of the things my mom did was create a magnificent garden. We lived on a property of about one and a quarter acres, which was fully walled. We had a large, sprawling ranch-style home, and we lived in probably the best climate in the world. Our home in Harare, Zimbabwe, was situated at about five thousand feet, and the average annual temperature was around seventy-four degrees.

For more than twenty years my mom and our gardener, a fellow named Mardoni, who also practiced as the local herbalist-cum-witch doctor, developed and created a beautiful garden. The most vaunted feature of this garden was a rockery that ran down one side of the property and measured probably 200–250 feet in length and around 10–15 feet in width.

I have no idea how many varieties of plants were included in this landscape masterpiece, but it was amazing. Part of building this rockery was, of course, lots of rocks. My mom and Mardoni traveled far and wide collecting rocks, big and small, in her car and a pickup truck we owned. I am sure there were hundreds of rocks and boulders.

I have used Google Earth and looked at the rockery from space, and it is still there, at 103 The Chase, Mt. Pleasant, Harare, Zimbabwe. Have a look sometime at a masterpiece of cooperation and endurance that was constructed by means of patience, creativity, and a social relationship between my mom and our old friend and gardener, Mardoni. There was most often laughter, sometimes shouting, and always Mardoni's endless whistling of a monotonous tune that never changed in the twenty years I knew him. They made a great team and built a monument one can see from space!

MYLIFESCENE.COM—CROSS NOW—MYLIFESCENE.COM

Age Groups and Social Fingerprints

It has always interested me how people tend to congregate in large family gatherings. In situations where there is a wide age span of people, who do you find yourself drawn to? People around your age, those who are older, or those who are somewhat younger or much younger?

A friend of mine and I loved working and hanging out with kids. They always seem to have fun when we lead their classes. We loved teaching four-year-olds in church and Sunday School. She led the music and made it fun. And she seldom followed the rules. She loved it, and so did I. She had a blast, and I would sit back and watch the circus—sometimes I was a part of creating the organized chaos.

I have watched teens who are very comfortable with older people. They look for and sit with people many years older and who really have nothing in common with them. What it is that draws them together?

Regardless of what it is that draws you to a particular age group, ask what it is that makes you feel comfortable, what the good reasons are, and what defines and displays Evidence of your unique Talents and capacities. Identify what those social connections are and celebrate them. *?RU*

Evidence of My Cultural and Ethnic Connections

Who Do You Think You Are? is a prime-time series that began in 2010. The forensically based show attempted to trace the ancestry of famous actors and actresses to find interesting people they were related to. Genealogy uses a collection of forensic elements such as birth certificates, newspaper or witness statements, criminal records, marriage certificates that include signatures of witnesses, military records, and much more. The show attempts to discover the genealogical/ethnic roots of these individuals, and the results have been startling in some cases.

I love different cultures and people who speak different languages, eat different foods, see the world in ways not common to me. I have always loved to travel and have been to more than thirty countries and all fifty U.S. states. Whenever I get the opportunity to travel and go somewhere different, I do.

I have photographs of teams I have been a part of that reflects my love of cultures. One photo of a cricket team I was on had players who came from Australia, Pakistan, England, Afghanistan, the Caribbean (one of East Indian descent from Trinidad and one of African descent from Barbados), and then me, from Zimbabwe.

Most of us feel more comfortable when we are with others who look like us, talk like us, support the same local sports teams, and eat the same type of food. This is normal, but what about people who are different from you—who speak another language, have a different skin color, eat different foods, wear different clothes, and think about the world and ideas differently from you? Do you seek them out? Do you want to know more about them? Do you love learning languages?

MYLIFESCENE.COM—CROSS NOW—MYLIFESCENE.COM
Life Scene—Jimmy

Jimmy is his twenties and loves everything that is different in terms of culture. He gets excited about what is not common and comes alive when he gets to experience something out of what is "normal" or "common" when compared with his experience growing up.

I shared an apartment with Jimmy for about six months and learned how his social Talents are demonstrated by his love for foreign cultures. Jimmy and I got on well because I had been born in a foreign country and had also traveled extensively. He was always asking questions and was genuinely interested. He wanted to know about how people spoke, common phrases, favorite foods and places, and the weirdest things I had experienced traveling. Jimmy loved all things foreign.

Strewn around the apartment were Fodor's travel guides, ethnic recipe books, foreign clothing, posters of foreign cities (London, Tokyo, Paris), foreign roommates (me), and foreign beer, and it smelled foreign with all the spices and foods Jimmy consumed. He either ordered out and brought home foreign food or made a lot of dishes himself. He loved to cook. I sent him to a restaurant, owned by an Indian friend of mine, that had an extensive menu. Jimmy began to work his way through the menu to see how many of the dishes he could experience and what he liked.

Jimmy would be up at all hours of the night talking in chat rooms to people in foreign countries. He loved trying to converse with "foreigners." He wanted to learn and had a real hunger for languages. He had studied a number of Far Eastern languages; that takes some serious intellectual Talent.

Jimmy had traveled to China and then wanted to attend a university that had a large population of Eastern students, such as the University of Hawaii or University of British Columbia. He then planned to go to Brazil and study in language school for a summer studies program.

What about you? Are you fascinated with and want to experience other cultures? Have you ever had a strong desire to go on a "mission" or cross-cultural experience where you build houses, run community schools, help kids who live on the streets of a foreign country? Do you listen for other accents or languages? Do you enjoy ethnic foods? What fascinates you about people who are different from you? What do you see in other cultures that you love?

?RU when it comes to different cultures?

MYLIFESCENE.COM—CROSS NOW—MYLIFESCENE.COM

What Types of Evidence Does Learning a Language Require?

Some of us simply love other languages. Have you ever wanted to learn another language? Did it make sense to you? How easy was it to learn? Do you possess a unique Talent in learning another language?

Learning a new language is not for everyone. It requires a combination of a number of Talents:

1. Intellectual—thinking differently, learning new concepts, different grammar, syntax.
2. Physical—being able to hear accents, verbalize sounds, and use physical gestures.
3. Social—being open, accepting, interested, welcoming; choosing to include and reach across frontiers.
4. Spiritual/motive—helping other cultures, missions, and education.

The Melting Pot
?RU

Do you know what is in your melting pot? What I mean is which nationalities or ethnic backgrounds can you identify in your makeup? Most of us are more than one ethnicity. My grandfathers were Greek and Scottish. My grandmothers were Swiss-German and Scottish. I am a good mix, like most Americans, and I was born in a small African country called Rhodesia, now Zimbabwe.

Possible Ethnic Identifications—*?RU*

English Irish Scottish Welsh French German Russian
Italian Dutch Swedish Persian African Arab Jew
Chinese Japanese Korean Mongolian Serbian Spanish
Icelandic Polish Croatian Brazilian Mexican Spanish
Eskimo Pacific-Islander East Indian American Indian Slavic
Greek Turkish Berber Egyptian Other

What is in your melting pot?

I am most comfortable when I am with people of my own or similar ethnic origin:

Comfortable_____**Uncomfortable**

Bag It and Tag It

RT	Evidence Reliability Tests Quick Checklist
RT-1	"Exceptional," Top 25 Percent, Top 10 Percent
RT-2	Flow
RT-3	Preserved
RT-4	Easily Repeatable and Been Repeated
RT-5	Judged as Exceptional by Witnesses
RT-6	Expert Witness Testify
RT-7	Result of Spontaneous Action
RT-8	By Choice and in My Own Time
RT-9	Positive Emotion
RT-10	Intuition

Best Evidence Matrix

What Was the Evidence? Identify and Specify	When? How Often?	Tests Online and RTs	Witness List and Identify

Chapter 25
Discovering Evidence of Your Spiritual DNA Code Part 1

Spiritual Capacity	• How I know and relate to God, serve God, serve other people • The capacity for reflection, meditation, faith, and belief • My *raison d'être* • How I transcend the physical • How I understand Life and Afterlife in terms of meaning and Purpose • The choice to engage in virtuous behavior such as: forgiveness, gratitude, humility, compassion, and wisdom • My motivation to serve and give of my abilities to others • How I determine morality and make moral choices • What I believe about the origin of my existence

Personal Forensic Bias and Belief

The following two chapters on spiritual Design are written primarily from a Judeo-Christian perspective. That is my framework and belief system. I have written this book from that perspective as this is a book that shares my Life and experience. I encourage you to think about your beliefs in a way that seriously integrates these concepts into your desire to answer the fundamental question being addressed in the book. *?RU*

> *God designed the human machine to run on Himself.*
> —C. S. Lewis

You might think looking for Evidence of spiritual DNA and motive would be a little more difficult than looking for physical or intellectual DNA. It isn't! The overwhelming majority of people believe there is a God. This belief is part of every culture on the planet. People attribute their existence to God and find ways to connect with God in what we call *religion* or *spirituality*.

Forensic Definition—Spirit

Spirit/spiritual is the animating or essential element in man that distinguishes Life as more than the physical or material elements. Those elements of experience that relate to, affect or concern the spirit or higher moral qualities, a calling to live beyond selfishness or self, particularly as regards religion or faith, is spirituality.

Spirituality goes beyond just an attempt to reach God; it helps us think about the way God would want us to act or behave toward others and how to live our personal lives. We call that morality. These are the questions of right and wrong.

There are also questions about Individual Design.

- If I have been created by God, why did He make me?
- What is my Purpose for living and being here on planet Earth?
- If God made me for a Purpose, He must have Designed me with the capacities to fulfill that Purpose. What is it?

The most popular book written in many years, *The Purpose Driven Life*, by Rick Warren, addresses how we can live with that sense of connection and direction guided by God. People are hungry and are demanding answers to questions of meaning and Purpose. We all strive for fulfillment in our lives.

The author A. W. Tozer wrote a classic of the Christian faith called *Knowledge of the Holy*. This profound book attempts to help us, finite beings, have a rudimentary understanding of an Infinite Being. It is about the limited and confined grasping at an understanding of the *Unlimited* and *Unconfined*.

- What is it you believe about God; the nature and character of God?
- Who defines God for you?
- What one word would you use to describe who God is to you?
- How do you conceptualize God, the source of Life, the Creator?
- *?RU* in relation to God?

These are basic questions related to our spiritual Design, but they are necessary in helping us understand the nature of that Design.

Where Does the Evidence Originate?

MYLIFESCENE.COM—CROSS NOW—MYLIFESCENE.COM
Life Scene—LeBron James

I believe that when we don't have a clear sense of where our Design originates, we are more likely to lack a deep sense of meaning and Purpose. I also believe we are more likely to misuse or not use that Design to the fullest potential because we have no foundational value system.

LeBron James is already destined to become one of the greatest athletes of this generation. He is still a young man but seems to have a very well-defined sense of where he believes his Design originates.

Imagine if you were a teen, and before you ever even played as a professional you were given a $90 million contract. Many teens and adults I know would be screaming "PARTY!" LeBron was different and with a demonstration of exceptional maturity did something out of the ordinary that was quoted by the *Seattle Times*.

In 2003, after signing a $90 million contract with Nike, LeBron invited his inner circle of friends and family to the famous El Gaucho in Portland to celebrate. Before anyone began to eat, LeBron stood and asked everyone to hold hands. He then prayed and thanked God for the "gifts" given to him.

MYLIFESCENE.COM—CROSS NOW—MYLIFESCENE.COM

Just like LeBron James, I believe that my Design is a gift from and originates with God. I believe that God created me for a specific Purpose, which He wants me to discover and live. God in His infinite wisdom and with His infinite resources and power created and crafted me. His desire is for me to know how He made me. He wants me to discover all the unique and wonderful capacities He has built into me and with which I can live and touch the lives of others.

David, in Psalm 139:14, said:

> *Thank you for making and designing me so wonderfully complex! Your amazing workmanship is incredible—and how well I know it!*

David marvels about the wonderful complexity of his Design and construction and attributes it to the Designer, God. He sees God's fingerprints on everything he discovers about himself. He says, "How well I know it." That statement defines my mission and the reason I wrote this book. It is about discovering and knowing the depth and breadth of God's personal construction of my Life. What is the Evidence of God's complex workmanship in my Life, and how well do I know it? That begins to answer the question, ?RU, for me.

Steven Curtis Chapman wrote a great song a number of years ago called "Fingerprints of God." The words talk about the sense of wonder and gratitude for how Chapman sees God's craftsmanship as he looks in the mirror and thanks for what he has been gifted with to serve others.

One of the most puzzling questions I often think about is, why are more people not living their Talents? If this approach is so obvious, why are people so much more compelled to talk about their weaknesses and what they need to fix?

The reality is most people simply are not aware of them, nor can they accurately describe them. In addition, many people don't want to be viewed as being proud. I believe that if you get the question of origins answered, meaning a belief that everything you have is a "gift," then gratitude and a deep sense of Purpose will come from that belief.

I believe that when you understand you have been given these abilities by a God who loves you and who makes no mistakes in what He has chosen to bless you with, you will hopefully use those Talents well. It is an attribution of value. There is a definite connection between knowing, valuing and using our Design.

The Greatest Crime in Human History

Have you ever thought what "The Greatest Crime in Human History" might be? There are many possible crimes, the magnitude of which might qualify: the Holocaust, Mao and Stalin's destruction of millions, and many others. Individuals committing serial killings such as Ted Bundy and Jeffrey Dahmer would also come to mind.

I believe the "Greatest Crime in Human History" could potentially be the Life you might not live. You have been given a magnificent Design composed of incredible Talents. That Design is meant to be lived and lives changed because of it, because of you!

What if you—a teen, a mother, a salesman, a teacher, a lawyer, a college student, a landscaper, a barista—were to really discover the Evidence that answered the question, *?RU?* How could the world be different because of you?

"The Greatest Crime in Human History," your history, would be your failure to discover and live your potential! You stand accused of potentially committing the "Greatest Crime in Human History." How do you plead?

In the Judeo-Christian belief, a command, a law of Life, can help this statement make more sense. The command comes from the Old Testament, from Moses, who not only delivered us the Ten Commandments but also clearly stated this *Great Commandment*.

Jesus Christ restated the Great Commandment from the Old Testament in the New Testament with one addition, which gave a new social component to it.

I believe that the Great Commandment sums up the Purpose of Life for us. This commandment separates Life into five distinct parts.

*You shall love the LORD your God with all your **Heart** [emotions], with all your **Soul** [spiritual], with all your **Mind** [intellectual], and with all your **Strength** [physical].*

This is the first commandment. And the second, like it, is
*this: You **shall love your neighbor** [social] as yourself.*
There is no other commandment greater than these.
—Mark 12:30–31

I believe that my Purpose in this Life, my Life, is to love God with the totality of who I am. Before I can even attempt to fulfill the Great Commandment, I need to know what God has given me to love Him with. It is a measure of quantity and quality. What do I possess to fulfill that Great Commandment? *?RU*

In The Spiritual Life Scene Lab

A 2004 article detailed how Evidence was discovered that showed how religion and religious activities literally enhanced and positively changed the ways teens experienced Life. The Evidence was discovered by a commission convened by the Dartmouth Medical School. One of the aspects of this commission was that it had no religious affiliation.

Religious congregations made a positive difference in teenagers by affirming who they are, expecting a lot from them and giving them opportunities to show what they can do. Many of these teens were required and encouraged to volunteer and give of their time to those less fortunate. Adolescents, said the Dartmouth commission, are "hardwired to connect" to people and to God.

The commission studied years of research on kids, including brain-imaging studies. It concluded that religious young people are significantly better off than their secular peers.

Religious teens were physically healthier because they are less likely to smoke and drink, more likely to eat well, less likely to commit crimes, more likely to wear seat belts, less likely to be depressed, and more likely to be satisfied with family and school.

But one is tempted to smile at the reasons given by this secular organization for the social benefits seen in religious activity. The study talked about how young people's brains were impacted and influenced by spirituality and that spirituality had the effect of reducing stress hormones such as cortisol. It also noted that sincere personal devotion was twice as likely to protect these teens from risky behaviors as it would adults.

Spiritual Design Evidenced by Changed Lives

The Bible and other religious books speak directly about how God wants us to experience Him and be in a relationship with Him. The experience of coming to realize that God wants to have a relationship with His creation, with me, and then responding to God's invitation to enter into that relationship is described in a number of ways in the Bible. Some of the more common phrases that describe this experience are:

Born again

Conversion

Regeneration

Redemption

Salvation

Each of these terms talks about a definite change in behavior and direction in Life. They also talk about a fundamental change in our spiritual composition. There is always Evidence if there has been a spiritual experience as described by these concepts.

When we look at spiritual Evidence, we have reason to look for discernable change. Evidence of change is what a forensic detective would need to see to prove there has been a spiritual experience. Has there been a change in your attitudes, behaviors, motivations and value systems as well as a growing relationship with God? Where is the Evidence? When God enters the picture, there is change; if not, we need to challenge the validity of the experience.

I Peter 3:15 says we are to give an answer to every man who asks about the faith we claim we have. We should be able to explain what we believe. This defense of our faith should be done in a controlled and loving manner. These are legal terms that require definitive answers.

Victor Frankl, who survived the horrendous conditions of Auschwitz, concluded that the meaning of Life was/is to be found in every moment of living; Life never ceases to have meaning, even in the dire circumstances of suffering and death. He talked about how sensing a friend, a family member of God, in the midst of suffering and engaging that friend often enabled courage and perseverance in hard times.

His belief was that the inner hold a prisoner had on his spiritual self relied on having a faith in the future. If you had someone or something to live for beyond your situation, you were much more likely to live beyond whatever it was you were facing, no matter how difficult or extreme.

So how do we find DNA that gives Evidence of our moral behavior; of our spirituality or desire to connect and have a relationship with God; of our need to find meaning and Purpose in our individual lives?

Evidence of My Spirituality and Faith—Breathing

When I begin to think about my spiritual fingerprints, probably the best place to start is by looking at what many would call the breath of spiritual existence, prayer. Prayer is spiritual communication between the created and the Creator. If there is spiritual Life, there should be Evidence of spiritual breathing. The first response in a Life Scene Investigation is to establish Life, and if the body doesn't breathe, there is no Life. Check for a pulse. If there is a pulse, breathing should be taking place.

Where is prayer in your Life? Is it an essential part of your Life? How often do you pray? For some it is a regular, scheduled practice that is part of a spiritual regimen. For others it is as regular as breathing. It is part of seeing that God is present in everything I do and that it is a spiritual walk. Every step I take, God is with me, and I walk and talk and breathe with God.

It is said that there are no atheists in foxholes. The idea is that when we face a crisis in Life, the first response we humans have is to pray. "God help me!" "If you get me out of this I will do anything for you! Help!" The imagery is similar to that of a drowning man whose head momentarily breaks the surface of the water. He gasps for a possible final breath and pleads to the only source of ultimate rescue. Many times after a perceived rescue, we revert to where we were before the crisis and forget that gasp of breath and the promises we made to God.

There is a variety of Evidence of what we term prayer:

1. *Asking* God for assistance in terms of material support, for wisdom in a perplexing situation, and for something that seems beyond our ability to supply.
2. *Thanking* God. When we believe God is the source of everything and Creator of everything, we should take the time to recognize His supply. That is one of the reasons for saying

grace before we eat: thanking God for the most necessary of human needs, food.

3. *Praising* God for all He is and has done, looking at creation and being in absolute awe of the beauty of this world displayed in both the macro- and microspheres.

4. *Experiencing* God's presence and allowing God to speak to us. This is often identified as *meditation*. It is allowing God to communicate to us.

5. *Confessing*. Most people believe God is the ultimate lawgiver and judge. When we do something that is wrong, we feel guilt. The way we make Life and relationships right again is to confess, and that is done to God in what is called confession.

I have many friends in India who practice meditation, of which breathing is an integral part. I have learned and attempted to incorporate some of their techniques into two areas of my Life in which the techniques have been very helpful. The first is simply regenerating when I am tired or just worn out mentally or emotionally. I can close my eyes and breathe for about ten to fifteen minutes, and it gives me what I would get from a few hours of sleep. I don't sleep but will close my eyes and simply start to breathe in a controlled manner until I actually sense I have reached a fill-up point and I know my batteries are recharged. I do it at Starbucks, in airports, on the side of a cricket field or after speaking.

The second application is in sports coaching. I teach breathing in a rhythmic manner to all my players, especially my fast bowlers. I know that endurance and "flow" are best experienced and maintained when we are keeping hydrated, or rather oxygenated, by the very essence of Life. That may not seem very spiritual to you, but having a clear mind and an ability to endure physically and emotionally is often the determining factor in making good moral choices.

I hope you have been challenged to discover the spiritual and motivational Talents you possess. This Field of Evidence is as important as any and all of the others. If you fail to fully think through and gather Evidence and continue to develop that Evidence, your Life will never reach its full potential.

What are your spiritual Design Talents? Share what you know with someone close to you today and see whether you can clearly articulate them and then be open to discussing and answering questions. *PRU* spiritually?

I am convinced that God is more interested and invested in helping you discover your Design than you will ever be. He created you and Designed you. He knows the Purpose, Passion and Performance waiting for you to experience. Ask the Designer to help you discover His Purpose in your Life. He has no greater hope than you will discover and live what He made you for!

Bag It and Tag It

RT	Evidence Reliability Tests Quick Checklist
RT-1	"Exceptional," Top 25 Percent, Top 10 Percent
RT-2	Flow
RT-3	Preserved
RT-4	Easily Repeatable and Been Repeated
RT-5	Judged as Exceptional by Witnesses
RT-6	Expert Witness Testify
RT-7	Result of Spontaneous Action
RT-8	By Choice and in My Own Time
RT-9	Positive Emotion
RT-10	Intuition

Best Evidence Matrix

What Was the Evidence? Identify and Specify	When? How Often?	Tests Online and RTs	Witness List and Identify

Chapter 26
Discovering Evidence of Your
Spiritual DNA Code Part 2

Spiritual Capacity	<ul><li>How I know and relate to God, serve God, serve other people</li><li>The capacity for reflection, meditation, faith, and belief</li><li>My *raison d'être*</li><li>How I transcend the physical</li><li>How I understand Life and the Afterlife in terms of meaning and Purpose</li><li>The choice to engage in virtuous behavior such as forgiveness, gratitude, humility, compassion, and wisdom</li><li>My motivation to serve and give of my abilities to others</li><li>Who I give my money to</li><li>How I determine morality and make moral choices</li><li>What I believe about the origin of my existence</li></ul>

If Design Originates with God, Then . . .

It is very important to understand that all we have has been given to us and we had nothing to do with what we possess. We didn't go online to order from a vast catalog of options, we didn't pay for what we have, and we had nothing to do with what we possess.

I Corinthians 5:7 reminds us of a fundamental truth about who we are if we believe we have been created by God:

> *For who has made you different from anyone else?*
> *What do you possess that was not given to you?*

Understanding this truth will help to ground you. Three important concepts flow from this:

1. *The first is that each individual is unique and different.* God Designs differently by endowing each person with unique capacities that are necessary for His Purpose in that person's life. We are different because God has made us different. Our DNA is an incredibly complex architecture made up of essentially the same framework but distinctly different elements. We must embrace and develop a deep sense of gratitude for what we possess.

2. *Second, everything we have we are given.* We didn't buy it, order it online, go shopping for it, sit down and choose what it is we thought would be good to possess in terms of unique Talents. Our DNA codes our essential makeup, and now we need to discover what that uniqueness is and develop it. We did not earn it. We had nothing to do with what we have because it has been given to us by God or is the result of chance. Everything means just that—*everything*. There is nothing we have that was not given.

3. *I am responsible to develop and use what I discover.* The results of discovering, developing, and using our Talents are greater emotional health, happiness, social and relational connections, satisfaction with Life, hopefulness, and ultimately a good Life.

Motives Create Actions

Faith without works is dead!
  —James, the brother of Christ

The Evidence of faith is action! Faith or belief must have actions that support it or, according to James, it is not faith at all or it is deceased faith. It is useless. James says the converse is also true. Simply doing good, without faith as the motivating force or factor, means nothing. We do for a reason. We act *because*. We are motivated to serve and make a difference because we hold certain beliefs.

It has been said that real faith is faith that is communicated. It is a belief that changes the way we not only live but behave. True or authentic faith makes a difference in the way we live. There are witnesses who look at our lives: personal, eye-, expert, and adverse witnesses who have something to say about the quality of our behaviors.

One of the Evidences of true or Life-changing faith is that it is communicated. The best communication is a Life that follows the tenets of that faith. The most basic common tenet of faith is the belief we should treat others as we would want to be treated, otherwise known as the Golden Rule. That is the simplest form of belief for behavioral change.

We are not all Mother Teresas, but faith demands we look outside of our own needs and desires and give to the needs of others. Faith means giving and serving if it is to have any relevance. Faith without works or deeds is dead.

The very nature of the Christian faith, my personal belief, is that the Creator gave us the ultimate example of giving and serving, in that God became a man and gave the greatest gift, His Life. He did for us what we had no ability to do for ourselves. That was the ultimate model and greatest act of service. No acts of service can be compared with that, but all acts of service should be motivated by that. Serving God is discovering how our Creator has endowed us and then seeking to use those *endowments* (Talents) in the most effective manner. He endows each individual with a Unique Design for a Unique Purpose.

Beyond that, what is our responsibility to God?

- How does God want us to live and show we believe in Him?
- Do we treat others differently?
- Does our message synchronize with our lives?
- Do we walk our talk?
- Do we seek God and His will?

- Do we seek God's leading in our lives to discover and live our Design?

Spiritual Life Is Evidenced by Spiritual Hunger

Every living thing needs food to live, thrive, and grow. Jesus Christ said, "Man shall not live by bread alone but by every word that proceeds from God." He was emphasizing that in order for spiritual Life to continue, it must eat and receive nutrition. An anemic or starved spiritual existence doesn't work well. The spirit must be fed in order for it to develop and grow.

- Where is the Evidence of your spiritual hunger and consumption?
- Where do you eat spiritually?
- Who feeds your soul?
- How does your spiritual consumption make you stronger?
- What books feed you spiritually?
- What places do you go to that help you grow and develop spiritually?
- What groups do you belong to that challenge you to grow spiritually?
- What seminars, retreats, or conferences do you attend that help you grow spiritually?

Christ talked about those who *hunger* and *thirst* after righteousness as being happy or blessed. Those who seek to fill their spiritual hunger and thirst will be filled, according to Christ.

Spiritual Life Is Evidenced by Your Giving

There is a very important place to look for Evidence of what you value in your Life. Money is the bottom line. It is Evidence of what you believe. How do you use your money to influence or change the lives of other people?

1. Who do you give to?
2. Where is the Evidence of your giving on your tax return?

3. Why do you give?
4. If we were to look at your bank accounts, where would we see money given?
5. Where do you volunteer and give of your time for no monetary reward?
6. Who knows about your giving and volunteering?

My sister Nelope has photographs on her refrigerator of children she supports through World Concern and World Vision. She gets letters and updates on what her money is doing in the lives of these children.

Many people tithe and give 10 percent of their income to their churches. They believe that by doing so it is a recognition that everything they possess in terms of Talents and their Unique DNA Code comes from God and has allowed them to create and earn income. Tithing is an act of thanksgiving to their Designer for allowing them to provide for their lives.

Bill Gates has probably become the greatest example of financial giving in history. He started out creating software and now runs the Bill and Melinda Gates Foundation, changing the lives of millions. His original mission of building a great software company has changed.

You don't have to be Bill Gates or Warren Buffett to make a difference. The story in the Gospels talks of a widow who gave two small coins consisting of a few pennies. That offering represented a portion of her possessions and wealth that far outstretched the large gifts given by the wealthy and pretentious religious figures who gave alongside her. It was a representation of gratitude by her to thank God for what He had given to her. It meant something sacrificial, substantial, and meaningful. That is what giving is about.

Evidence of Morality

Forensic Definition—Morality

Morality: A code of conduct; demonstrates externally what we believe internally.

The Ten Commandments are the foundation of moral law as defined in Western civilization. If you walked into the U.S. Supreme Court, you would see a copy of the Ten Commandments on the wall of the court.

They symbolize that the court finds its ultimate authority in higher law, which is defined by God.

All societies have laws, and these laws are almost always attributed to a deity. To be civilized essentially means you believe in laws that govern your conduct and the relationships you have with others.

- What spiritual or moral laws do you subscribe to?
- What moral laws or body of law do you hold to as a guide for your Life?
- How consistent are you in following these laws and beliefs?
- Does your Life consistently demonstrate your adherence to these laws?
- How does violating one of these laws make you feel?
- How do you view people who don't follow the same spiritual laws you do?

Evidence of Practicing the Golden Rule

Do to others what you would have them do to you.
—Luke 6:31

The Golden Rule is a standard of behavior that most religious traditions believe and have versions of. Essentially, the rule is based on selflessness. It states that we should put the needs and best interests of others ahead of our own. When have we done that? How often do we practice the Golden Rule?

Character has been defined as what we do when no one else is looking. It is what guides us when only we alone know what happened. This can be related to how we respond to issues of temptation and morality. What is our moral compass, and what have we done when we had the opportunity to gain for ourselves through a process we knew would be wrong? Did we say no and resist, or did we take the easy way? Did we hold strong and know we did what was right?

- Can you identify a situation where you made the right choice and it may have cost you professionally, financially, or in some other meaningful way?
- Why did you make the choice?

- What motivated you?

Character also relates to what we do when we know there will be no reward but know the decision or action is simply right. It is our secret, but we did it because it is right.

Evidenced by Grace and Forgiveness

Forgiveness is giving to others what God has given to you. I want to ask you some important forensic questions about forgiveness. Don't rush through these, but take the time to process them and answer them honestly and fully.

- What has been your greatest act of forgiveness?
- What did they do to you that hurt you?
- Whom did you forgive?
- When did you forgive them?
- Why did you forgive them?
- What did you lose by forgiving them?
- What did you gain by forgiving them?
- Who has forgiven you?
- Why did you need their forgiveness?
- What did you gain by asking for forgiveness?
- How do you define *grace* and how do you demonstrate it in your everyday Life?

Many twelve-step and other recovery programs require those who participate to do a thorough moral inventory. They ask each participant to look at his or her life and itemize all those actions that have hurt others. Once that is done, the participant is *required* to go and ask forgiveness of all those he or she has offended, harmed, used, or sinned against.

Whose Evidence Do You Try and Copy?

History has many examples of lives that have demonstrated exceptional spiritual, moral, or motive Talents. Whom do you want to be like?

Sometimes we are asked about people we would most like to meet throughout history. Who would that be?

- Who are the people you admire most because of their morality, faith, beliefs, standards, giving, love, character, selflessness, and attitudes?
- Whose attitudes, behaviors, and examples of lifestyle do you seek to copy or model your Life after?
- Who stands out in history as someone you don't simply admire but want to be like because that person is the epitome of virtue, forgiveness, grace, devotion to God, love, and sacrifice?

A number of years ago a movement was started that asked the question "What Would Jesus Do?" (WWJD). There were bracelets with the acronym *WWJD*. People would add the letters *WWJD* to their license plates and email signatures, or they would put bumper stickers on their cars, all helping people think about a way of living and behaving. Lance Armstrong also created a similar challenge to Life with his *LIVE STRONG* yellow wrist bracelet. He challenges people to live beyond their tough circumstances and be more than ordinary.

What Groups Do You Belong to That Support Evidence of Your Spiritual Fingerprints?

A spiritual group is a collection of two or more individuals who have developed a common social identity relating to serving others and/or helping others grow in their relationship with God.

1. What groups do you belong to?
2. What is the Purpose of those groups?
3. What have those groups done to change the lives of others?
4. What is the Evidence that your motives for joining these groups is being fulfilled?
5. How have these groups changed your Life?
6. What spiritual Talents have you discovered or used to help these groups fulfill their mission or make it more effective?

Which Test Results Confirm Evidence of Your Spiritual Talents?

Forensic Discovery Test
The Values in Action (VIA) Character Strengths Survey

The VIA Survey of Character Strengths (VIA) is the world's most scientifically validated tool for measuring character strengths. There are several versions for different age groups and situations. The questions help you discover your unique grouping of strengths and identify your top five "Signature Strengths." Signature strengths are those you most frequently express.

(If you want to take this test for free as well as have a DNA Talent Profile and Report, go to www.mylifescene.com and click on "Forensic Tests." You will be given a special code that will allow you to get a free DNA Talent Profile and printout.)

If you have taken the VIA, how did you score? Did any of the following character strengths list high on your profile?

1. Appreciation of beauty and excellence
2. Gratitude
3. Hope/optimism/future-mindedness
4. Spirituality/sense of Purpose/faith/religiousness
5. Forgiveness and mercy

All the strengths on the VIA are character strengths. They all reflect issues of meaning, Purpose, and values. They also are essential to supporting all elements of your Design, as described in chapters 9 and 10 on Evidence contamination.

Evidence in Others Following Your Life

Another well-defined spiritual relationship is that of a disciple. There are various modern versions of this ancient relationship, such as coaching, mentoring, and discipleship. The disciple is one who, because he or she sees Evidence of Purpose, Passion, and Performance in your Life, desires to enter into a relationship with you, to become like you.

When others see you living your Talents and Design/DNA Code, they want what you have.

The Apostle Paul told others to follow him as he followed Christ, and then, just before his death, he told his followers:

> *Whatever it is you have learned by observing me, received by instruction, heard me tell you, or seen me model to you—put it into practice.*
> —Philippians 4:9

1. Who is following your Life and example?
2. Who has said he wants to be like you because he sees your beliefs and Life making a difference in this world?
3. Who wants to have a deeper relationship with God because he sees the authenticity of your faith and Life?
4. Are you in a formal relationship with someone who is coaching or helping you to discover and develop your Talents?
5. Is there someone in your Life whom you are teaching to discover his God-given Design and Talents?

Where is the Evidence of your spiritual Design? I hope as you have taken the time to look deeply and be challenged with these most important questions of Life and the possibility of more beyond what is seen and can be scientifically verified, you will live with greater Purpose.

There are many magnificent people whose lives have reached the greatest pinnacles of success, fame, and wealth because they discovered and lived their Design and Talents to the fullest. Many of these same people failed to answer the question posed by the greatest asker of questions in history:

> *What if you were to gain the whole world but lose your soul?*
> —Matthew 16:26

That is the ultimate question you must answer as you complete this Field of Evidence. What if? If you have *reasonable doubt*, go back and answer the questions asked throughout this chapter. "What if?"

I hope you have been challenged to discover the spiritual and motive Talents you possess. This Field of Evidence is as important as any and all of the others. If you fail to fully think through and gather

Evidence and fail to continue developing the Talents shown by that Evidence; your Life will never reach its full potential.

What is your spiritual DNA Code? What are your spiritual Design Talents? Share what you know with someone close to you today and see whether you can clearly articulate those Talents, and then be open to discussing and answering questions about *PRU* spiritually.

Bag It and Tag It

RT	Evidence Reliability Tests Quick Checklist
RT-1	"Exceptional," Top 25 Percent, Top 10 Percent
RT-2	Flow
RT-3	Preserved
RT-4	Easily Repeatable and Been Repeated
RT-5	Judged as Exceptional by Witnesses
RT-6	Expert Witness Testify
RT-7	Result of Spontaneous Action
RT-8	By Choice and in My Own Time
RT-9	Positive Emotion
RT-10	Intuition

Best Evidence Matrix

What Was the Evidence? Identify and Specify	When? How Often?	Tests Online and RTs	Witness List and Identify

Part 5

How to Interpret Evidence

Chapter 27
The Forensic Evidence Timeline

When did it happen? What time? How old were you?
When was the first time you . . .

Many of the questions asked in CSI relate to time. What was the estimated time of death (ETD)? Based on various physical characteristics, a time of death can often be determined.

What time did the witness see the shooter? When was the last time the victim was seen alive? Tracing alleged criminals' movements in an attempt to tie them to crimes has CSIs looking at phone records, ATM withdrawals, time clocks at work, and video camera Evidence that has date and time stamps.

History is about a timeline of demonstrated capacity and ability. It is about the how, when, who, what, and where. Objective data says if you have demonstrated the capacity and done something once, you can do it again. The next question becomes whether you can identify that capacity as a Talent.

One of the most important forensic procedures in building a strong case for your Life is developing an Evidence Timeline. It talks of your roots, where you have been, what you have done. Remember, Evidence is what has happened. Evidence needs to be identified as having a time and place; that is history. You are your history.

Evidence needs to have a context. Without a timeline, Evidence is simply a random set of data that could mean anything. When put in a timeline, Evidence begins to tell a story, and that story might be far more powerful and fascinating than you ever imagined.

When Evidence is connected, it becomes powerful and persuasive. Without a timeline, it is like reading a misprinted book. Have you ever been reading a book when suddenly it didn't make sense? You look at the page numbers and realize that several pages, or even an entire chapter, are missing. You lose the thread or plot, and from there on, you either attempt to fill in the Evidence in your own mind or stop reading in frustration.

So again, Evidence needs to have a context, a place in history. You will be taking all the Evidence from the Five Fields of Evidence, the Forensic Tests, Reliability Tests, and Witness Statements, corroborating the information, and developing an Evidence Timeline.

This timeline is your personal history, your Life from day one to the present. You will now begin to connect the dots. You will be able to see how your Talents (your Purpose) have developed and grown, how they have been lived and demonstrated.

> **What we do in life echoes in eternity.**
> **Maximus—from Gladiator, the movie**

Santayana's Forensic Principle Revised

Philosopher George Santayana made one of the most recognized remarks about the importance of studying history. He said:

> *Those who refuse to learn from history are doomed to repeat it.*

It is a wise admonition about bad choices, wrong decisions, and negative behaviors. It tells us to think about what not to do, where not to go, who not to negotiate with, and who not to ally with. Applying this wise admonition can certainly help us in not repeating destructive and harmful decisions, but it *cannot* help us learn how to live. It eliminates negative possibilities but does not help us discover positive realities. It gives no directions to follow. You *cannot* build a Life by knowing what not to repeat.

What we have learned and focused on in the LSI process are your Unique DNA Code and Talents. As part of understanding the best use and context in which to view our personal history, I have chosen to revise Santayana to read,

Those who choose to learn from their (Analysis of Asset) successes, wise choices, engagement of their Talents in Life, and right attitudes and responses are destined to repeat them.
—Mark R. Demos—LSI creator

What a great way to learn about history! That is LSI Positive Forensics.

Remember when I talked about *AoD* (Analysis of Deficit) versus *AoA* (Analysis of Asset)? That is precisely what I am saying here for the way we should look at history. We need to maximize the strengths of our demonstrated Talents as opposed to attempting to minimize the weaknesses of our histories.

When We Maximize Talents . . . We Minimize Weaknesses

There are two reasons for performing the *AoA*. The first is to see the Evidence in context; the second is that it provides the best Evidence on which to build a Life of Purpose. What are we to do with the Evidence beyond allowing it to help us see the origin, development, and confirmation of what we have identified as indeed a Talent? We must use it as a blueprint for further growth and development.

Forensic Tips for Remembering Your History

As you think through your history, keep in mind some hints that will help you remember in greater clarity. These hints and tools will help you think about different periods in your Life and make clearer judgments. They will stir your mind to easily release the good, the right, the strong, the efficient actions, and the accomplishments of your Life and history. They are simple but easily overlooked, so use them:

- Where did you live?
- Who were your neighbors?
- Where were you working?
- What school were you going to?
- Who were your favorite teachers?
- Who were your best friends?
- Who were your classmates?

- Look at old emails.
- Look at Facebook or MySpace and see old messages and friends.
- What were your favorite subjects?
- Who was your boss?
- What websites did you visit the most?
- What pets did you have?
- Who were your best friends?
- What were your favorite activities/sports/recreational pursuits?
- Where did you go on vacation?
- Look online and search Google for the years in focus.
- What did your children get for Christmas or their birthdays that year?
- What movies or TV shows did you love?
- What subjects did you get your best grades in?
- What part of your job did you love most?
- Where were you happiest?
- What clubs, associations, or groups did you belong to?

You can think up a lot more questions, so go ahead and do what is necessary to open your eyes to your history and develop your Evidence Timeline.

Another tool is to look at photographs and videos: schools, family, yearbooks, MySpace, Facebook, and so on. Read or browse through old family albums or movies. Look at old magazines. I have bought old *National Geographic* magazines for family and friends that were printed in the month and year of their birth. It is a cool way for people to remember their history. I have even bought them for my parents, who were born back in the 1930s. It is also a lot of fun to see what was popular and being advertised back then.

Finally, embrace the process. These are exercises in Life. They are meant to give Life and light to you and your Life Theory. It is like being in a darkroom and watching a roll of film being developed. The plate or film is just a dark piece of plastic. When it is placed in the developing solution and moved around, the image taken with the camera begins to appear. Shadow images are seen at the start and then, as the process and chemical reaction progresses, the full image and colors are there to see and enjoy. Start connecting the dots. Design becomes obvious when you place it in context.

Inputting Evidence into the Forensic Timeline

Remember, you have already collected a wealth of information from what you have analyzed in the previous chapters when you used the discovery tools. Each of the modules for the *Fields of Evidence* asked you to complete the Best Evidence Matrix (intellectual, physical, emotional, social, and spiritual meaning/Purpose).

The Best Evidence Matrix asked you to identify four things:

1. What was the (best) Evidence you collected? Identify the Talent.
2. When (on the Evidence Timeline) did you did you demonstrate this Talent? It also asked you to think about how many times you repeated the Talent.
3. What Evidence Tests authenticated the Talent, both Reliability Tests and other online tests?
4. Who (identify witnesses) can testify to the exceptional nature of that Talent?

Now you need to take that information and begin to plug it into the Evidence Timeline and watch the picture begin to develop!

This is an amazing process. You will begin to see themes develop and see the origins of your Design in their early stages.

In *StrengthsFinder 2.0*, Tom Rath writes,

> *Although people certainly do change over time and our personalities adapt, scientists have discovered that core personality traits are relatively stable throughout adulthood, as are our passions and interests. And more recent research suggests that the roots of our personalities might be visible at an even younger age than was originally thought. A compelling 23-year longitudinal study of 1,000 children in New Zealand revealed that a child's observed personality at age 3 shows remarkable*

similarity to his or her reported personality traits at age 26. (Tom Rath, *StrengthsFinder 2.0*, p. 18)

One proverb talks about parenting and the predictive nature of Individual Design. The proverb says, "Train up a child in *the way he should go* and when he is old he will not depart from it." I believe this says that each person, from an early age, has a unique bent or bents (physical, intellectual, emotional, social, and spiritual) that are to be understood by a parent. These bents should be encouraged; opportunities to develop them should be provided, and discipline should be required and enforced so that the child lives to his or her potential.

MYLIFESCENE.COM—CROSS NOW—MYLIFESCENE.COM
Life Scene—André

No father could ever be more proud of his son than I am of André. André is a teacher; he has always been a teacher. He is clear, thoughtful, and patient. He loves books and has a library of thousands. He loves kids, and they listen and respond to him.

I have pictures of him when he was three, pretending to read to his newborn brother, Adam. I have pictures of him when he was six reading to Adam and his baby sister, Amy. He had a classroom set up in his bedroom, and Adam and Amy were his students.

When I would play cricket I would have my three children with me. Cricket took the entire day and was played in big parks. André would be organizing games, reading to other kids, teaching them how to play together, taking them to the playground, helping them when they got hurt, and constantly connecting with them.

When he was a teen he was leading and teaching groups in his youth group. In high school he took every education class and practicum he could. Now he helps coach a Little League team, and they love him. He is wonderful with young kids. The parents of these kids love him.

I recently met a teacher in a local school district who, when she heard my last name, asked whether André was related to me. André had been in her classroom as a student teacher, and she praised his ability and told me how she wished there were more young teachers like him. She was an expert witness who had been teaching for more than twenty years, and she recognized André's Unique Design clearly.

André is and has always been a teacher. I attended André's graduation from college in June 2009. He graduated with a double major in elementary education and early childhood education and did so magna cum laude. In September 2009, he began teaching elementary school. In the summer of 2010, he spent seven weeks teaching and developing curriculum in Cape Town, South Africa. He spent this time touching the lives and minds of some of the poorest children on our planet.

André continues to live out his Design in an authentic way. He knows his Purpose and has chosen a Life path founded on his God-given Talents. My son lives who he is and has answered the question *?RU.*

MYLIFESCENE.COM—CROSS NOW—MYLIFESCENE.COM

This quote by Dr. Martin Seligman describes what André is and what André does. He has found his niche and is living his positive traits to their fullest.

> *Raising children, I know now, was far more than just fixing what was wrong with them. It was about identifying and amplifying their strengths and virtues and helping them find the niche where they can live these positive traits to the fullest.*
> —Dr. Martin Seligman,
> http://www.gulfkids.com/pdf/Elm-nafsEE.pdf, p. 2

Identifying My Place on the Life Timeline

One of the most important exercises we can each do is to calculate how many days we have lived. Part of the analysis is for us to look at Life expectancy and to see where we are in the possible span of Life. We know or should know that none of us is guaranteed any more than what we have already experienced. Life can be taken when we least expect. It is wise, though, to get a good picture as to where we might be so that we can live well and wisely.

Moses in the Old Testament said, "Teach us to number our days that we can apply our hearts to living with wisdom." What great advice.

He asks God to help him understand his mortality so that he can give all his efforts to an exceptional Life. We are told to live thoughtfully and to know we have limits. We have a Design that has an expiration date. We don't know when or how it will terminate. What we do have is a choice that today we will use our Talents to impact the world in the most positive way possible.

Calculate how many days you have already lived. The average Life expectancy in the United States is 77.6 years, or 28,340 days. How many days have you lived, and how many days do you possibly have left?

Years	Days	Years	Days
14	5,110	40	14,600
15	5,475	45	16,425
16	5,841	50	18,250
17	6,205	55	20,075
18	6,570	60	21,900
20	7,300	65	23,725
25	9,125	70	25,550
30	10,950	75	27,375
35	12,775	80	29,200

Forensic Time Use Analysis

An Evidence Timeline is not just about *what* you have done, *how* often you did it, and *where* you did it; it is also about *how* you are currently using and have used your time in the past weeks, months, and years.

So how do you use your time? It is important that you do an analysis of how you manage and apportion your time. Understanding and getting a picture of how you use your time will tell you:

1. What is it you value
2. Who it is you value
3. Whether you are living your Purpose and experiencing Passion

We give time to that which we love. Mapping how we use our time could also show that we are serious about discovering our Talents.

The following breakdown is taken from the Bureau of Labor and Statistics and reflects how Americans use their time each day. It divides Life into seven areas:

1. Working and Related Activities—8.7 hours
2. Sleeping—7.6 hours
3. Leisure and Sports—2.6 hours
4. Household Activities—1.1 hours
5. Eating and Drinking—1.1 hours
6. Caring for Others—1.2 hours
7. Other—1.7 hours

As you look at and analyze how you use your time and where you give your Life, what does it tell you?

1. What are you doing when you go to work?
2. When you "care for others," what are you doing and for whom?
3. Do you "care for others" the average 1.7 hours a day, or is it maybe more or maybe less?
4. How does your analysis of time reflect the use of your Design and Talents?

Forensic Timeline Evidence—A Formula for Future Success

There is another reason for developing your Forensic Evidence Timeline. History gives us a focus and pathway for future success. The greatest determinant for future success is the analysis of past success.

One of the greatest discoveries I have ever been involved in was while I was doing a goal-setting seminar for the Pro Sports Club. The Pro Club is a five-star facility situated in close proximity to Microsoft in Redmond, Washington. It had developed many innovative programs for health and weight management. The founder was a famous physician, Dr. Mark DeDomenico, one of the pioneers of coronary bypass surgery.

Many of Pro Club's approximately 35,000 members are Microsoft employees. Microsoft pays a large percentage of their membership and enrollment fees to encourage good health and retain great talent. This is a substantial perk.

I ran a couple of my seminars at the club in its conference rooms. Mary Walker, one of the owners, asked me to come in and do a goal-setting series to help the management staff get ready for the new year. We used *Now Discover Your Strengths* as a text for some preliminary work on team building and helping the managers focus on the strengths philosophy.

When we got to the goals part of the training, I decided to use a simple format that I used as part of a seminar series that was a precursor to the Life Scene Investigation format; I had called it, simply, "Repeat—Delete." It was a very basic concept, but since we were near Microsoft, I thought a computer analogy would translate well, and it does.

Evidence—Repeat and Delete

The concept is this: The best way to look forward and set Evidence-based goals is:

1. *REPEAT*—Perform an *AoA* (Analysis of Asset) on the past year. What is it that worked? What is it that grew, had positive results, made gains, resulted in greater Talent, and so on? Whatever it is that worked this past year needs to be identified, analyzed, and then used to build a plan. The goal should be to *repeat* these great practices. Individual goals are crafted around specific elements of the successes of the past year. Building on success seems to be a novel concept, but it is the most logical, sensible way I know.

2. *DELETE*—It is important to look at those things you failed at or consistently didn't perform well, repetitive failures: customer complaints, ineffective policies, moral issues, and so on. What is not important, you need to *delete* from your life. This applies specifically to nonmoral failures you need to jettison from your life. (Other issues also need to be addressed, as was discussed in chapters 9 and 10, the Evidence contamination chapters.)

What to Do with Weak Evidence?

What we failed at, for which we are responsible, we need to:

1. Admit to ourselves and to others who have asked us to perform at a superior level that we lack the essential ability to meet the standard of excellence required. That saves time and wasted

effort. It also allows for others who have the necessary Talents to find their Design-filled expression and engage in the process.

2. Ask for and get help from people who have a Talent in the area of our deficiency. That is sensible and honest. Trying to be someone or something we are not, nor ever will be, reflects a weakness of character. Asking for help allows others to find a place of Purpose and experience Passion. Those we include and allow to use their Talents will be grateful.

3. Delegate, if we can, to someone who has the Talent to complete the responsibility or task the way it should be done.

The questions are: what do you do first, and what should the focus of goal setting be?

Let me tell you how I approached the process. I did a forensic analysis of the Pro Club's complaint process. The head of human resources was responsible for taking care of complaints. He had started in the kitchen over ten years earlier and worked his way up to an important management position. (Another Talent of the Pro Club was its ability to employ great people.)

The complaint process consisted of regular complaint boxes that were placed around the club with cards for people to write on and state their complaints. Next, the Pro Club sent out three hundred to four hundred randomly selected emails every month, which asked members to list complaints that they had in order to assist the club in becoming a better organization. Last, they kept a list of all phone complaints. They wrote out what the problems were and kept all of them in a file.

After I collected all the data, I took it to the meeting with the managers. I asked them how many complaints they thought had been made that calendar year. We did a brief analysis of how many client visits had taken place, and our estimate was one million plus. That was based on 10 percent of the membership coming in on any given day, multiplied by 365.

I asked for numbers, and based on the million client visits, we thought that an acceptable percentage was maybe that for one in every five hundred to one thousand visits, there might be a complaint. I became a little more specific and suggested what a reasonable complaint might be, such as rudeness by a club employee, a billing problem that was not addressed after repeated attempts to resolve it, a dirty environment not cleaned up in a reasonable amount of time, equipment that was not working and then not fixed in a reasonable amount of time, and so on.

So again I asked for numbers. I got replies from one thousand to around five thousand. The reality was that the Pro Club had received fewer than one hundred substantive complaints that year. That was beyond remarkable. One complaint for every ten thousand client visits.

The lesson we learned from this forensic analysis was that the first approach to building greater success and proficiency as an individual or organization was to focus on our positive accomplishments. What those tell us is that:

1. We have the capacity to perform at an exceptional level in some areas of our lives. We need to seek out and identify what those are. Be specific.

2. What we have already done we can repeat. We have demonstrated in time, a place in history, that we have the capacity. That is not a question but a fact. We did it. So what we have done we should attempt and plan to do again!

3. What we have done we can develop to a higher level of efficiency and Performance. That is growth, the planned and responsible use of a God-given capacity. How can we take this Talent and make it an integral part of our lives?

I would encourage you to start looking at your history. If you take one of my Evidence discovery courses, you will often be required to complete a Forensic Timeline. This will allow you to see your history in context. It takes some work, but as you begin to input the information you have discovered, Life will be seen in its entirety, a mosaic of brilliant Talents!

History is never boring when you use it to look for Evidence of your Design/DNA Code and Talent. It is a history of Life that when done the LSI way results in Purpose, Passion and Performance!

> *Now pay attention! Those of you who say, today or tomorrow we are going to go to this or that city, spend a year there doing business and make money. How can you be so presumptuous, you do not even know what is going to happen tomorrow. What is your Life? You are a like a mist that appears for a little while and then vanishes into thin air.*
> —James 4:13–14

Chapter 28
The Forensic Evidence Matrix

"What does the Evidence tell me?" I call this the *essential question*. The reason we collect, identify, and test Evidence, obtain witness statements, and then complete a timeline is to interpret the Evidence. The most exciting part of the Forensic Process is the interpretation of Evidence. If you don't ask the *essential question* and come to conclusions about the Evidence, the entire process is a waste of time.

The entire Forensic Process is for the ultimate Purpose of asking, "What does the Evidence tell me?" That is the goal. It gets you thinking about a situation, an action, something good that you demonstrated, that reflected your Individual Design, your DNA Code. It is a simple question, but when you use it properly you can dissect, dig out, discover, highlight, emphasize, add color, and bring out the full height, depth, breadth, and length of your Design. The Evidence has meaning. The matrix is a tool to translate and interpret that meaning.

Evidence tells a story. That story, if it is to be interesting and filled with Life, needs descriptive words and analysis drawn from it. Using the Forensic Evidence Matrix, the most amazing picture will begin to appear—this is your Life Theory!

The Forensic Evidence Matrix shows you how to interpret Evidence in a simple but very profound and descriptive manner. What it does in answering the question "What does the Evidence tell me?" is to put flesh on the bones. You have collected Evidence of your Talents. Those Talents must be described as to what they mean, what they do, how they are demonstrated, where they are seen, and what effect they have on others.

The way the matrix is constructed is very simple. It asks you to identify a Talent and then develop what it means to possess that Talent. Analyzing the Five Fields of Evidence you focused on to discover your Evidence does that. The Life that is found when you ask the *essential question* is incredible! It simply pours out.

Do you remember looking through a microscope for the first time? Maybe you looked at a bug or a leaf. You saw a world that you never conceived of before. The leaf had a complex network of rivers to carry water and nutrients to keep it green and living. It had cells that when magnified also possessed an entire world of unique parts, with defined tasks, to ensure continued functioning. The Evidence you have collected will be magnified, and you will be amazed at the potential and power that exists within each Talent you have discovered.

Let me try and illustrate what I mean and how it works. Danelle was a teenage girl who was in our LSI discovery class. She was seventeen and attending a local high school. Danelle was a cheerleader at her high school and a very good one, from what I understand. So as part of illustrating the use of this question to the class, I used Danelle as the example. I asked Danelle about something she was good at or did really well. She obviously said cheerleading. I asked Danelle the question, "What does that tell you about yourself?" She looked at me, a little confused, and then said, "I am good at gymnastics." When pushed, she was hard pressed to describe more of her Individual Design than that. So I continued to ask questions and reveal more of her Design and DNA Code.

The following matrix I worked through with her will allow you to think through the Evidence you have collected in a logical, forensic manner, using the components of Design to guide you. Here are some of the Evidence/Design elements that we in the class were able to get out of Danelle as well as define for ourselves about what it means to be a cheerleader.

So in asking questions about a particular ability, position, action, response, demonstrated capacity, and so on, you ask yourself:

- What does this Evidence tell me about my physical, intellectual, emotional, spiritual, and social Design?
- What does the Evidence say?
- What are the logical deductions I see when I analyze this Evidence?
- What is the story the Evidence is telling me?

- If this is true, then what should follow?

These questions sound so simple. They are, but the reality is that interpreting Evidence requires common sense. Simple observations and looking for the obvious is where you have to start. It is a logical process and requires you follow it step by step and begin to put the puzzle together.

The Forensic Evidence Matrix™

Capacity	What Does It (Cheerleading) Tell Me/You about You?
PHYSICAL	<ul><li>Very fit, athletic, disciplined</li><li>Willing to maintain a healthy diet and not eat certain foods that she may like but will not allow for optimal Performance</li><li>Agile, gymnastic ability, dance, movement, etc.</li></ul>
EMOTIONAL	<ul><li>Made fans emotionally connected to their team and the game</li><li>Likes elevating people's moods by getting them involved and doing emotionally expressive actions</li><li>Has to be able to think beyond her own personal feelings when she has to perform and think about the job she has to do; she might feel down and depressed, but when she leads a cheer, she can't allow her feelings to interfere</li><li>Has to deal with tough situations when her team is losing by trying to keep the team and the fans engaged and emotionally upbeat</li></ul>

	• Handles the fear of being thrown up in the air and possibly dropped and getting hurt • Handles performing in front of large crowds
INTELLECTUAL	• Have to learn cheers, think through routines, etc. • Have to study hard enough to maintain a GPA required for extracurricular eligibility
SPIRITUAL	• Made a moral choice to agree to and sign a code of conduct that requires that cheerleaders not abuse substances, drink, etc. • Agreed to model and exemplify good character to other students
SOCIAL	• Being a cheerleader means being part of a cheer team • Being part of a team means others on that team rely on you to practice, turn up on time, work hard, keep fit, eat well, learn cheers, etc. • Have to be trustworthy to turn up at games and perform • Connects players with fans and supporters • Makes fans believe they were part of the game • Likes being onstage in front of big crowds

Take a moment to look at all the observations and Evidence that was discovered in the right-hand column. Each of those statements or Evidence observations can be rewritten and turned into a statement about Danelle. Turn each piece of Evidence into a declarative and personal "I Am . . . " statement.

- *I am* a connector.
- *I am* trustworthy.
- *I am* an individual who is strong enough to handle fear and other tough situations.
- *I am* a team player.
- *I am* disciplined.

There is a world of information to be discovered when you begin interpreting Evidence using the Forensic Evidence Matrix. Life flows from using it. People's lives begin to expand to see the reality of who they are. This is not hot air or wishful thinking but reality that is based on hard, tested and confirmed Evidence.

Think of an example or about something you recently did that was really good. Look at the Evidence you have gathered in early modules, for example, completed a major school project, finished a management certification, gave a great speech at a toastmaster event, made the cheer team, made the basketball team, wrote a brief, started a children's group, created a new real-estate listing and posted it online, made National Honor Society, won an online video game competition, received a scout award, or managed a nonprofit event.

What three demonstrations of Talent have you performed in the past week?

_____

_____

_____

Ask yourself what the Evidence tells you about yourself. Get friends involved. Ask them to work with you to brainstorm and be Life Scene Investigators, looking for and interpreting Evidence. Contact Life Scene Investigation and hire a *Life Scene Investigator Profiler*™. You need to get as much insight about the measure of your Talents and capacities as possible.

Chapter 29
My Life Theory—Final Arguments

The Forum

The forum of an ancient Roman city was the city's central meeting place, around which stood the most important public buildings. The Forum of Rome itself was considered the center of the entire Roman Empire.

The *Forum*, from which we get the term *forensics*, was the center stage of the world in Roman times. The Forum was where Life was lived. It was also a place where, if you wanted to be seen, you turned up and showed who you were.

The *Forum* was a place where arguments were decided. If you had a problem or wanted to prove a point with someone, you both brought your Evidence to the Forum and argued your case in front of the people who were there. Based on that Evidence, your case was either accepted rejected. The people voted on whether you proved your case or not.

I began this book by asking the question *?RU*. You should now be ready to answer this question in the open, out in the forum of Life. You have been taught the process of Positive Forensic discovery as it applies to the most important question of Life.

Forensic Effervescence

At the start of this book, I spoke to you about this process of *effervescence*. I told you that you would begin to experience a sense of excitement and expectation that you would not be able to stop, like bubbles in a pop bottle that force their way to the top. That process has begun, and your excitement will not stop unless you cap the bottle and walk away from the Evidence. If you do, you walk away from Life.

Much of the information you know, but now it has a context and you begin to see Life with a sense of excitement. You want to get out and do more. There is a sense of expectation that wasn't there before. You have a plan. There is a pathway to follow, and it makes sense.

I have illustrated many of the concepts in this book with "Life Scenes." I hope these have described for you what it is I hope you will be looking for, in both your Life and the lives of others. I wanted to show you how this process is not about some dry technical or "you can be anything you believe" program that doesn't deal with reality. It is not some subjective or weird "sit on a mountain and it will come to you" program, either. Life is real enough, and so is the LSI forensic way of thinking and discovering *?RU.*

CSI Effect

The *CSI* effect is a phenomenon that many lawyers have observed in trials in recent years. Many jurors expect a trial to look like an episode of *CSI*, which not only solves crimes in short order but uses fancy elements of forensic magic to entertain.

The *CSI* television program solves crimes in fifty minutes or less. Evidence is always readily discovered, processed, identified, and ultimately used to identify and convict the perpetrators. There are no tedious days searching for Evidence, frustrating witness interviews, waits for lab results that often take weeks or months, not hours, and perplexing thoughts over what the Evidence all means.

Jurors in criminal trials are expecting Evidence to have a *CSI* look to it. They want trials to move quickly and expect to see Evidence displayed in the form consistent with what they have seen on television. They forget that television is television. Your *Life Theory* can and will develop if you are patient and follow the LSI Positive Forensic Process. If you want short-term results, then you will get them from quick and incomplete forensic analysis.

Discovering your Talents and answering the question "Who are you?" is a lifelong adventure. ***Discovery*** comes first. Then you must begin to ***develop*** what you know. Then and only then you will discover more. I absolutely believe that if you fail to develop what you know about yourself today, you will stop discovering and you will stunt your growth. You have to use and develop what you have the Evidence for today.

This is a sacred endeavor. Your Life is a gift to be given to the world around you. You can move and discover more only by using what you already know, just like a baby learns to crawl, then pull itself up, then stand, and then walk. You never start walking without first standing and strengthening your legs. When you have learned to walk, you then have the ability to go faster, and ultimately you can run.

Closing Arguments

As I attempt to make my closing argument to you and challenge you to verdicts about your Talents and your DNA Code, I hope you will embrace fully *?UR*, live your Life with great *Passion*, and show the world what exceptional *Performances* you are capable of! You must be determined to live it! Verdicts must be enforced.

I want to close with arguments and illustrations from a few additional *Life Scenes*. Each of the people in these *Life Scenes* is just like you. They possess what you do, Unique Talents they are living. They have made decisions based on the Evidence they discovered. They often made courageous decisions to move away from what was "good" to embrace what they knew could be "great" if they used the new Evidence they had discovered.

Following are some questions that I want to help you answer as you set out to integrate and apply what you have discovered. They are specific to the most important areas of your quest for Purpose.

?RU—My Purpose

Trying to develop an overall Life Theory is seldom simple. I am not sure we can ever fully define a specific or single Purpose we know and live over the course of our entire lives. Who we are grows and develops as we discover more and use more of our Talents. I believe the best way to define the *?RU* is found in answering that question of Purpose; it is to have a defined *why* for our lives.

Friedrich Nietzsche penned it best when he said, "He who has a *why* to live can bear almost any *how*." Even though this specifically deals with how people can face adversity, the *why* for each of our lives must be answered; otherwise, the need to discover a Purpose or live with Purpose is irrelevant.

I began this book asking the question "What is your *raison d'être?*" or reason for being and living. Why are you here? I hope you have a clear and compelling reason for your Life and every breath you take. If you have answered the *why*, you are in a place where you can discover, knowing that what you discover has meaning and Purpose.

I believe my Purpose in Life is to help you and many others discover their God-given Design, live with Purpose; experience Passion, and demonstrate exceptional Performance. That is clear enough in my thinking. That is who I am.

So what is yours? Answer as clearly as you can. *What* is your *why?*

My Purpose is to _____

?RU—Career or Profession?

You might be in school, college, or even further along in a job, but you are still looking for direction. You know deep down that where you are is not where you should be. Your Life does not align with what you have discovered the Evidence tells you about your Unique Design and DNA.

You might have recently discovered an essential intellectual Talent, like Danielle did. Her discovery that she really had the required IQ to go to nursing school expanded her plans in a major way. Instead of looking at a one-year school and becoming a nurse's aide, she went through four years of college and became a registered nurse.

You might also have discovered something that tells you that you have new options and paths to follow that you never believed possible. The Evidence is there: reliably affirmed, witnessed to, verified by tests, historically identified, and more.

My son André's history, intellectual Talents, social Talents, emotional Talents, spiritual Talents, and everything about him said: you are a teacher! What does your history tell you? What do your grades and the subjects you excel in tell you? What does the Evidence tell you? *?RU*

Should you go to college? What about a technical school? College is not for everyone. Plumbers can make as much money as teachers. Great salespeople can make more than doctors, lawyers, and other professionals. Many salespeople have never been to college but they know people, what people want, and how to get those people to hand over their money and buy what they are selling.

One of the greatest opportunities I believe young people should look at is the military or some service organization, either through their churches or reputable nonprofits such as World Vision, Peace Corps, World Concern, Samaritan's Purse, and others. Get out of your comfort zone and be willing to be pushed. When you have to discover how to survive or help someone else survive, it is amazing what you will find. Talents will become obvious.

If you are looking to discover, go and experience Life by giving your Life and what you know now, and I promise you will discover so much more about your Talents. Giving who you are will always teach you more about yourself. Giving of yourself is not just a proven way to elevate your emotions; it is an essential discovery tool. Maybe that is a missing ingredient in your discovery quest.

You might be in a career that gives you a good paycheck but could easily be described as a "daily grind." You seldom wake up with any anticipation of a day to be embraced and enjoyed. You know you are competent, but you also know that the job will never allow you to perform at a level of sustained excellence. If you were to make the changes you now believe would bring your Life and Evidence in line with your *Life Theory*, it would demand great courage. You may have kids in college, a mortgage, and other responsibilities you feel you need to honor. I am here to tell you there is *always a way*, and most of the time it takes courage and requires a backbone.

I recently watched a great but very depressing movie, *Revolutionary Road*, with Leonardo DiCaprio and Kate Winslet. You should watch this movie if you need a push and the courage to move your Life to where you know it must be. The movie is a commentary representative of the lives of millions stuck in careers and places they know they have to move from if they are ever to experience the Passion their lives crave. It is a story of a man who refused to embrace his Purpose, for all the seemingly appropriate and right reasons, and ended with tragic results.

April (Winslet) accused Frank (DeCaprio) of not giving his full efforts to living Life and following his dreams. He basically responds by saying he does everything any good husband and father would do by working hard and supporting the family. He is so responsible that he supports them, all the while hating every moment of his job. He equates working hard while hating his job as having moral fortitude simply for not running away from his responsibilities.

Arpil ends one confrontation with a gut-wrenching response. She tells Frank he is a coward. She tells him he has no backbone because he lacks the essential courage to follow his Passion and live the Life he so desperately wants. Is that you?

What if you had to tell your parents you are going to drop out of college or change majors? You know they will fight you and possibly withdraw their financial support. They have more than likely sacrificed for many years to make it possible for you to become what they desired you to be.

1. Don't make any quick moves, and realize they probably know you best, after yourself and what you have learned through the LSI Forensic Process.
2. Have the courage to change if you know the Evidence supports your case.

There is an old legal saying that goes something like this: "If the Evidence is on your side, shout the Evidence. If the Evidence is not on your side, just shout." Being loud doesn't make your case. The Evidence does, so trust the Evidence.

MYLIFESCENE.COM—CROSS NOW—MYLIFESCENE.COM
Life Scene—Dave Barrow

Dave Barrow was one of my first coaching clients. Dave and I were in a men's study together, and he hired me to help him think through some major changes in the direction of his Life. Dave and Ellie Moore were both in the very first Talents discovery group I ever held.

Dave has been a model of grace and courage to me for many years. He has been there for me as a friend in so many substantial ways I cannot begin to tell you about. He is a man who lives his courage and integrity every day.

Dave had been a senior marketing executive in a number of software companies, and when I met Dave he was at Microsoft. He enjoyed what he did and was successful, but he knew he wasn't able to have the freedom to do what he knew he was Designed for in Life. This was a major decision for Dave.

Dave had the option to stay at Microsoft or to leave and seek a place where he knew he was using his God-given Talents to the very best of his ability. Dave was not willing to do what Bill O'Reilly's dad did and remain safe and captive in a job that slowly took his Life energy and destroyed him.

Dave had courage and left Microsoft. He soon found a great job with a Microsoft vendor, which provided a position for Dave to engage his *Purpose* more fully, to get up each day fueled with *Passion,* and his *Performance* has been one of sustained excellence for the past ten years.

Got courage? Got a backbone? When all is said and done and your career is over, what will you regret? Will you look back and only be able to wish you had taken the opportunities you were presented with to make the changes you knew you should make? Will you regret not standing up and having the courage to say you were no longer willing to do what you knew would never fully engage your Unique Design? Got courage?

MYLIFESCENE.COM—CROSS NOW—MYLIFESCENE.COM

?RU—Relationships

Who am I in relationships, and how do I function best when I use my Talents? LSI changes lives wherever it is used and applied. The Talents that define us can and must be used to discover Purpose in all our relationships. They should define whether we even have a relationship with someone or a group of someones. The Old Testament prophet Amos asked a simple question:

> *How can two walk together except they be agreed?*
> —Amos 3:3

Starting a relationship, maintaining a relationship, and building a thriving relationship that is characterized by *Purpose, Passion and Performance* is only possible based on the discovery, development, and living of our Talents.

How do we look at the world and people? Do we see it and them through glasses that focus on *Talents* and *Assets* that need to be discovered and lived, or do we see through lenses that seek to discover weaknesses and deficits and believe the way to a good Life is to avoid and fix them? Do we wish to fix the weaknesses of those who we are in relationship with, or do we wish to build their Talents? Do we look for deficits to highlight, or do we look to encourage? Do we fill with joy at their actions of demonstrated character?

The parenting relationship is the most challenging but most rewarding relationship I have experienced. I love being a parent, a father. I was not always the best father; I made enough stupid mistakes and lousy meals along the way, but I have always tried and done what I believed was best for my children. I have always tried to focus on their Talents.

I have shared with you what I believe is the essential task of parenting: *study your children to know their Talents and train them to build a Life defined by them.* That is parenting from start to finish.

If you want to see discouraged, defeated, and angry children, focus on their deficits. Find what you need to fix. Look at every report card and find the worst grades first and ask why they failed or didn't do well.

One of the best gifts I ever gave to my son André was when he turned eighteen. I walked him outside on the lawn and gave him an envelope, and that was all. Inside the envelope was something I had written him that was a reflection and a recounting of his Life and Talents. I titled it "What I Know about You."

I started by letting him know he was now a man and no longer subject to me, my rules, or my dictates for his Life. I told him he could do whatever he wanted, including joining the military, getting married, and even going to adult jail. He was a man and responsible for his Life.

I then went on to talk about his Life and the possibilities that lay ahead based on the Evidence I had seen in his Life to this point. I wrote about what I believed he could do with that Evidence and who he could become if he continued to follow it. This was not wishful thinking or just the best and deepest wishes of a father, but a logical analysis of the Evidence and what could be, if he continued to develop and live it.

I talked about his schooling, his academics, the way he treated girlfriends, his social Design, and how he went deep with his friends, how he related with his brother and sister. I spoke about his early Life as well as all the Evidence of his Talents I saw through his teen years.

I continued this "project" and when he was twenty-one years old, I wrote to him again and talked more about what I had seen in the past three years of his Life. Two years later, when André got married, I spoke to a number of his closest male friends and asked them to prepare a short "What I Know about You" and share it at a barbeque just before the wedding. I asked them to apply what they knew about André to what they believed they saw in him that would make him a great husband and potential father one day. They did, and I fought back the tears as I listened to the remarkable man my son was in the eyes of his peers and others who had been close to him in his Life.

André graduated as a teacher, which is what he has always been, as well as a man of real integrity. He started his teaching career on September 3, 2009, at Wilder Elementary School, fulfilling his *Life Theory*, which has been evident from the age of three.

For parents, I encourage you to do the same with your children. This is not simply something you wait for a significant birthday to do, but you should do it regularly. Birthdays are a great way to memorialize a document, website/page, video, or other creative communication.

Regularly ask your children when you see them do something exceptional that reflects a Unique Talent, "What does that tell you about yourself?" That builds confidence and a sense of self.

I encourage you to do it for all those significant people in your Life. Any relationship will flourish when this is applied for sincere reasons to those people whose lives you see regularly and with whom you are in significant relationships. What you say matters. Watch, see, and say what you see. That builds relationships and infuses *Passion*, and I promise it will result in better *Performances* much more effectively than pointing out obvious deficits and failures.

If you want to have a better marriage, be a better parent, get better results from your recreational team, engage your friends, fire up your sales force, have your teenager listen to you, or attract a wonderful relationship partner, see the Talents in each person and say what it is you see. That simple formula builds lives.

MYLIFESCENE.COM—CROSS NOW—MYLIFESCENE.COM
Life Scene—Krisandra Parsons

Krisandra is brilliant and beautiful, and my relationship with her has been without doubt the most positive and productive relationship I have ever experienced. I met her at Starbucks in Dallas. I was reading a novel one Friday evening, and she was in a business meeting with an employee. I waited four hours until almost 12:30 a.m., when her employee left, for my chance to talk to her. It was well worth the wait.

Having someone in your life who is close to you and sees your Talents is vital. It could be a spouse, parent, close friend, or other person. The main idea is for them to focus first on what is most important, your Talents. They should not only be able to see your Talents, they need to encourage you to develop them and live them, and they should be your biggest cheerleader. That is what Krisandra is to me.

What Krisandra has brought to my life is not a simple "rah-rah" blind sycophantic chant that simply agrees with and applauds every action or idea but a person who sees me for what I really am uniquely Designed to do in life.

What is also so amazing to me is that we give each other what is most important: the full encouragement and freedom to express or fully live our DNA. That has built and made our relationship what I have always wanted and believed a relationship could be.

The encouragement comes from texts in early morning to chat on Facebook late at night. It come in words throughout the day. It comes in smiles and winks when we are presenting. It is expressed in public and in private. It is in posts on Facebook and in phone calls to friends. It is part of everything that she does in my life and what I attempt to do in her life.

If you can find someone who will walk with you in life who is what Krisandra is to me, you will have one of the most vital ingredients necessary to not only discover your DNA Code but live it with the joy and freedom I have come to experience!

MYLIFESCENE.COM—CROSS NOW—MYLIFESCENE.COM

?RU—Positions of Influence and Power

The Gallup organization has led the way with their *strengths-based* books and *StrengthsFinder 2.0*. They write books and journals, they train those in management, and they lead the way in the integration of the strengths approach to the corporate world.

MYLIFESCENE.COM—CROSS NOW—MYLIFESCENE.COM
Life Scene—Shari

I was asked to speak at a team meeting of realtors. With the economy having taken a huge beating and the real-estate market bearing the brunt of that beating, realtors were particularly hurting. I tried to tailor my talk to address how they could deal with the downturn and adversity.

I spoke about what I normally do, focusing people on their Talents. The group was great, and I believe they were encouraged by what I said.

At the end of the meeting Shari, the team leader/CEO, got up to thank me and then did something amazing. She started to go through each individual in the room and talk about a Unique Talent she knew about them. There were at least thirty people in the group. It was remarkable. She addressed something timely and of real substance in each person's Life: no fluff, but something exceptional she knew defined them. The Life that was infused into that room, one Life at a time, was powerful!

That is what Shari does to people's lives. She sees Evidence of the Unique Talents that define who people are. She tells them what she sees and is not afraid to encourage them. She does not do it to be nice or to flatter them. She does it because that is who she is, and she is someone who is not threatened by others' Talents.

If you walked into her office, you would see exactly what I mean. I promise you would leave with a spring in your heel and with a greater confidence, knowing more about who you are. Shari is powerful because she empowers people to see what she sees, their Talents.

We can all learn from Shari. Being aware of people's Talents and openly recognizing them is not difficult when we have our eyes open. When we want to be better at what we do, we must help others be better at what they do. Some of us, such as Shari, are better than others at recognizing people's Talents. That is why Shari is a great fit in her current position. All of us, however, should say what we see when it is in front of us. Be a Shari where you are today!

MYLIFESCENE.COM—CROSS NOW—MYLIFESCENE.COM

Think through the example of the Pro Club I talked about in the chapter that explained the Forensic Timeline. Teams need to be built around Talents. Corporate goals and culture need to be designed and built using the Talents of the corporation's most valuable asset, people. The Pro Sports Club is a model for excellence because it models Talent.

Do you own or have the power to significantly influence your company? Why not determine to build a corporate culture of Talent!

That starts by knowing each employee's Talents and using your employees to do what they do best every day they show up at work.

?RU—Making Major Changes

Remember Ellie Moore, my friend who lost four hundred pounds? Ellie was for me the greatest example of a changed Life. When Ellie changed her thinking from analyzing Deficit, of which she had many, to looking at Life from a perspective of analyzing her Assets, her Life dramatically changed.

I don't know what personal challenges and deficits you face, but I know your Life can be dramatically different, just like Ellie's. Imagine for a moment what weighing six hundred pounds means. How would you look at Life?

When Ellie lived in my basement apartment, I would hear her leave the house often at midnight or later to go grocery shopping. She felt embarrassed and so she shopped when there were few people around to stare at her. That changed after a while as Ellie began to want to see and share her Life with people. I would go grocery shopping with her, and she created so many wonderful friendships at the Safeway where we shopped, she seldom if ever went shopping in the dark of night again.

Have you ever tried to find a job thinking that your physical appearance would hold you back? Ellie worked in a back office and shuffled back and forth, trying not to be noticed. That is where I first met her. She said I was one of the only people who would look her in the eye.

It didn't take much time for me to discover that Ellie was one of the most talented people I have ever known. She was exceptionally bright intellectually. She wrote beautifully. She communicated verbally with great clarity and emotion. She had deep and meaningful connections with people. She was a leader and organized groups and motivated people. She took people who had given up on Life because of their weight and made them focus on their Unique Talents, believing that if they changed their focus from weight loss to discovering their Talents and engaging in Life, the weight would take care of itself most of the time.

?RU and what mountains do you face? I don't know you, but I knew Ellie Moore. I know what she faced, and through the discovery and use of her Unique DNA and Talents she scaled unimaginable

obstacles and put aside every excuse not to give her Life to others. She discovered her DNA Code and answered the question *?RU.*

Final Challenge

Every legal case has closing arguments. Those arguments are a challenge to the jury to get them to consider the Evidence that has been presented. By the end of the case, each side, defense and prosecution, has attempted to make its case and convince the jury that its *Trial Theory*, or story about what happened, is true.

As we come to the close of *The DNA Code: The Forensics of Purpose, Passion and Performance*, I have some vital issues for you to consider. These are not just suggestions, but imperatives. Do these, and my belief is that your Life Theory will be discovered and your Purpose, Passion and Performance will receive an affirmative verdict!

1. Ask for *Design guidance*. The Designer wants you to know and experience your Design. No matter how eager or determined you are to discover, the Designer wants you to know even more. Be open to Life and what it has to show you. Each day be open to the Designer and ask for guidance to know more and to find ways to live and discover more of your Talents. Remember, the Designer promised if you seek, you will find!

2. Live today what you know today! I believe that God will often withhold showing us more of who we are until we are willing to use what we already know about ourselves today. When you use and give your Talents to others, you will always learn more. Much of the process of discovery will only open when you use what you know. Think of your children or someone you manage or coach. When someone whom we manage is not living up to their potential, why would we give them more responsibility and opportunity? When someone on a team doesn't practice, no matter how talented they are, why would we give them more time onfield in a game? Are you faithful to living what you already know about your Talents? Are you using them faithfully and with integrity?

3. What we focus on, we generally will end up getting. *As a Man Thinketh*, by William James, is a book you must read if you have not already read it. The title means if we want to grow, we don't start with what we want to get away from or avoid. We need to

have a clear Evidence-based picture of where it is we want to go and focus on that.

4. Have an open heart. Be teachable. Learn from everyone. Read books, blogs, and websites; attend seminars, go to church, take college classes; speak to the old and the young and everyone in-between; everyone can teach you when you ask them for help to grow.

5. Know your weaknesses. I touched briefly on "weakness" in the chapter explaining the Forensic Formula, and you may want to reread it. This entire book has focused on Talents. My definition of weakness can only be accomplished accurately after I have defined my Talents. You *never* start by identifying weakness. When you build a house or any structure, you start with a cornerstone from which all direction and measurements are derived. One forensic tip you need to pay attention to when seeking help with your weaknesses is this: make sure you are selective when looking for help. Seek only people who are already demonstrating Talents in that area. Do a forensic analysis on their Life and then get the Talent you need by teaming with another person who is living with Purpose, Passion and Performance.

6. Don't run from pain and tough times. Responding to adversity takes away distractions, washes away junk, and begins to reveal the Talents that come into play when they, of necessity, have to. Many people comment after they have faced, managed, and responded to situations they feared greatly or never believed they would have to confront, such things as: "I never believed I could!" "I am so thankful for what happened because I am a much stronger person for it!" Tough times also demand we use those Talents. They often bring out the very best of who we are. We either use those Talents or fall down. It is sink or swim, and when we *have to* swim we might just find out we *can*, and then we can ask what it was that enabled us to swim.

7. *Do Hard Things*, the title of the book by Alex and Brett Harris, is a great challenge. Buy it for your teen and read it yourself. If you want to discover, you need to push to discover just what you are made of. Central to the authors' message is the belief that we often find what our Purpose is in Life when we challenge ourselves. As a coach, I know how many players discover so much more when they push harder, go further,

make no excuses, and grit their teeth through the temporary pain to a place of incredible revelation of Talents they never knew they possessed. They become "pumped up" emotionally and filled with Passion!

8. Make sure you ask and allow others to help. Listen to those around you. Listen to your parents, who possibly have the best information; listen to friends, team mates, strangers, coaches, teachers, managers, work associates. Be open to listening as well as asking for their input and help.

9. Avoid contamination at all costs. Deal with contamination immediately and get whatever help you need because the consequences of ignoring, avoiding, or allowing it to be a part of your Design can be catastrophic.

10. Seek and you will find—not half-heartedly, but genuinely, earnestly. I want to know, I will discover. Life, your days are precious and not to be wasted.

11. Hire a coach or enter into a formal arrangement with someone who will help you discover *?RU*. Coaching is by my definition the discovery, development, and deployment of Individual Talents. If you find a coach who subscribes to the positive philosophy of strengths and Talents, do what you can to hire him or her. You can also find out more about the LSI coaches and coaching programs at our website, www.mylifescene.com, and if you need professional or corporate coaching at www.corp-dna.com.

When I was consulting with a company in 2000, one of the things I did daily was send out a coaching newsletter. Most days it was nothing more than a short few lines of motivation, encouragement, or thought-provoking challenge. One that I wrote evoked a response that was far more than I could ever have anticipated. It was called "Dying without Getting It." I want to share it with you in closing.

Dying without Getting It

Have you ever figured out what the bottom line is? What you are not willing to die without having, getting, experiencing, knowing, seeing, feeling, . . . ?

Today I want to continue the thoughts on *awareness* I have been looking at the past two days. We are all aware of deep, personal longings that lurk, dimly hidden in the corners of our minds and consciousness. For some, those longings will remain lurking there for a lifetime, and those people will never have the courage to discover, uncover, and bring them out into the full light of day: a place where we choose to get, to have, to experience those longings . . . or send them back to die a slow and dull death.

In terms of *awareness*, we know these longings exist. They are there! You cannot deny that they exist! For some, they reside in a place of resignation, where we believe we will never experience them.

The reasons could be many: I don't deserve to experience them; I don't have the courage to really stand up and say, "This is what I want and will not settle for anything else!"; I don't believe I have the ability to accomplish or experience_____(name it); I will never have the means to_____; why long for what you cannot have; so many of the things that I have desired and longed for just have never materialized, so why identify the deepest, strongest most Passionate longings if the more mundane are left unfulfilled! . . . and so on.

Have you ever in the quietness of early morning, the exhilaration of a sunset or sunrise on a mountaintop, the tears at the loss of a friend, spouse, child, or parent, the joy of a wedding or birth of a child, the early days of a new romance, the closing of an incredible deal, the end of a long emotional/spiritual journey, just shouted out inside, "This is what I want! This is what I long for! This is what I am not willing to die without!"

Awareness of what those longings are starts with *admitting* that those longings do exist. I am a person whose soul was Designed and built with deep personal desires, needs, and longings.

Awareness begins with the *courage* to say, "I am willing to identify what those longings are because I am not just going to browse but buy, live, attempt, whatever it is I find."

I am going to leave this here for today. These questions will not easily die except in the fearful and cowardly. For those who are not, I ask for a response. (I intend to put responses in my in *Life Design Daily* without names or identities being revealed.)

The answers to these questions are not to be feared for any reason . . . only the refusal to ask should be feared, because when the time comes for regret, with no time to do or to be . . . I don't want to be there.

Very few persons, comparatively, know how to Desire with sufficient intensity. They do not know what it is to feel and manifest that intense, eager, longing, craving, insistent, demanding, ravenous Desire which is akin to the persistent, insistent, ardent, overwhelming desire of the drowning man for a breath of air; of the shipwrecked or desert-lost man for a drink of water; of the famished man for bread and meat.
—Robert Collier

The greatest crime or, rather, tragedy of Life would be that you never answered the question *"Who Are You?"*

The greatest possible gift you can give to your Life and the Life of others is to stand up and declare, *"I AM!"*

Recommended Reading

Armstrong, Thomas. *7 (Seven) Kinds of Smart: Identifying and Developing Your Multiple Intelligences*. Updated ed. New York: Plume, 1999.

Buckingham, Marcus. *Find Your Strongest Life: What the Happiest and Most Successful Women Do Differently*. Nashville: Thomas Nelson, 2009.

Buckingham, Marcus, and Donald O. Clifton. *Now, Discover Your Strengths*. New York: Free Press, 2001.

Callahan, Theresa. *Managing for Performance: Building Accountability for Team Success*. Lake Placid: Aviva, 2012.

Csikszentmihalyi, Mihaly. *Flow: the Psychology of Optimal Experience*. New York: HarperPerennial, 1991.

Fox, Jenifer. *Your Child's Strengths: Discover Them, Develop Them, Use Them*. New York: Viking Penguin, 2008.

Frankl, Victor. *The Doctor and the Soul: From Psychotherapy to Logotherapy*. New York: Random House, 1980.

Garner, Alan. *Conversationally Speaking*. New York: McGraw-Hill, 1981.

Goleman, Daniel. *Emotional Intelligence*. New York: Bantam, 1997.

Gottman, John M. *The Marriage Clinic: A Scientifically Based Marital Therapy*. New York: Norton, 1999.

Levine, Mel. *A Mind at a Time*. New York: Simon & Schuster, 2003.

Marana, Hara Estroff. *A Nation of Wimps: The High Cost of Invasive Parenting*. New York: Crown Archetype, 2008.

O'Reilly, Bill. *A Bold Fresh Piece of Humanity*. Reprint. New York: Broadway Books, 2010.

Revich, Karen, and Andrew Shatte. *The Resilience Factor: 7 Keys to Finding Your Inner Strength and Overcoming Life's Hurdles*. New York: Three Rivers Press, 2003.

Seligman, Martin E. P. *Authentic Happiness: Using the New Positive Psychology to Realize Your Potential for Lasting Fulfillment*. New York: Free Press, 2002.

Rath, Tom. *StrengthsFinder 2.0*. New York: Gallup Press, 2007.

Rath, Tom, and Barry Conchie. *Strengths-Based Leadership*. New York: Gallup Press, 2009.

Resources

The Life Scene Investigation websites have many incredible resources for you to access.

- *Life Scene Investigation—My Life Scene (www.mylifescene.com) discovery classes and programs:*
    - *Online classes—Prima Facie Evidence*
    - *Seminars*
    - *Coaching programs*
    - *Coach and facilitator certification programs*
    - *Positive Forensic Profiler Certification*
    - *Life Scene Investigator Certification*
- *LSI Corporate Training—Corp-DNA® (www.corp-dna.com) is innovative and revolutionary in its approach to and application of Human Talent discovery and development. Our Corporate DNA programs work with corporations and organizations in these areas:*
    - *Profiling corporate success DNA*
    - *Leadership/management Talent development*
    - *Executive and management Talent coaching*
    - *Team building*
    - *Creating Talent-based Mission and Motive statements*
    - *Developing a Talent-focused corporate culture*
    - *Creating and developing Talent Innovation Labs*
    - *Developing Hiring DNA profiles*
    - *Sales, service, and team development*
    - *Corporate and executive retreats*
    - *Executive care programs*
    - *Positive Forensic Profiler—Corporate Talent Coach Certification*

- o *Please follow us on Twitter **#corpdna** for events, articles, videos and motivation*
- *LSI Education—Edu-DNA® (www.edu-dna.com) is a leader in the application of Talent discovery and development in education.. We have developed revolutionary programs using the LSI philosophy for:*
  - o *Building LSI Certified Talents Schools*
  - o *Leadership development for principals and school administrators*
  - o *Teen Discovery Curriculum for students to develop college and career plans based on their discovery of Talents*
    - ▪ *Faith-based curriculum*
    - ▪ *Generic curriculum*
  - o *Discipline responses program and curriculum for K–12 (ISS: In-School Suspension)*
  - o *OSS (Out-of-School Suspension) for serious discipline offenses*
  - o *Teacher and administration Talents training*
  - o *Anti-bullying programs*
  - o *Student leadership development*
  - o *Assemblies using forensics to motivate students*
  - o *Character development programs using the Values in Action Strengths profile*
  - o *Specialized camps for Talent discovery and development*
  - o *Individual life coaching for at-risk students in school and college*
  - o *College success coaching*
- *Study Guides for groups, book clubs, church programs, Biznik, MeetUp, professional development groups, and others. Different versions of the workbook are available for different interest groups:*
  - o *Faith Integration—Christian*
  - o *Parenting*
  - o *Leadership Development*
  - o *Professional Development*
  - o *Teens*
  - o *Women in Transition*
  - o *Leaving a Legacy (Ages 50+)*

To access and purchase these study guides, please go to www.the-dna-code.com or www.mylifescene.com:

- *Free tests*
- *Paid tests*
- *Forensic clothing with amazing designs, forensic gadgets, Life Scene tape*
- *Books*
- *Forensics Web links*

Please join our Facebook groups:

- *The DNA Code (book)—www.facebook/The-DNA-Code*
- *Life Scene Investigation (Education, Schools, Colleges, Coaching, Parenting)—www.facebook/LifeSceneInvestigation*
- *Positive Forensics (Mental Health, Education, Coaching, Relationships and Forensics)—www.facebook/Positive-Forensics*
- *Corp-DNA (Corporate, Leadership, Executive Coaching, Management, Talent Management—www.facebook./CorpDNA*

*Please follow us on Twitter **#TheDNACode** to find out about book signings, events, promotions, seminars, articles, etc.*

Speaking and media engagements: To inquire about having Mark R. Demos speak at an event, church, corporate address, keynote, conference or other event, please visit www.the-dna-code.com or email speakers@the-dna-code.com.

www.the-dna-code.com

CPSIA information can be obtained at www.ICGtesting.com
Printed in the USA
LVOW10s0215060914

402632LV00002B/2/P